Hockey Night in Canada

The Culture and Communication in Canada Series
explores culture and communication in the Canadian context, examining a wide range of contemporary cultural experience. The editors seek out works that cross disciplinary boundaries, offering fresh perpectives and stimulating debate. In this way, the series will act as a foundation for future research in the area in Canada and abroad.

Series editors: Richard S. Gruneau and Martin Laba, Department of Communication, Simon Fraser University

OUT OF THE GARDEN: TV AND CHILDREN'S CULTURE IN THE AGE OF MARKETING
Stephen Kline

HOCKEY NIGHT IN CANADA: SPORT, IDENTITIES, AND CULTURAL POLITICS
Richard Gruneau and David Whitson

Forthcoming
HITS AND MISSES: THE PLEASURES OF POPULAR MUSIC
Martin Laba

SUSTAINING DEMOCRACY? JOURNALISM AND OBJECTIVITY
Robert Hackett and Zhao Yuezhi

For details of other titles in the series, please contact the publisher.

Richard Gruneau and David Whitson

Hockey Night in Canada
Sport, Identities, and Cultural Politics

Culture and Communication in Canada Series

Garamond Press
Toronto

Printed and bound in Canada
Cover designed by Karo Design Resources, Calgary

The cover illustration is from an original intaglio entitled *HOCKEY NIGHT IN CANADA* by K. Gwen Frank.

A publication of Garamond Press

Garamond Press
77 Mowat Ave., Ste. 403
Toronto, Ont.,
M6K 3E3

Canadian Cataloguing in Publication Data

Gruneau, Richard S., 1948-
  Hockey night in Canada

(Culture and communication in Canada)
Includes bibliographical references and index.
ISBN 0-920059-05-8 (pbk.)   ISBN 0-920059-39-2 (bound)

1. Hockey - Canada.   2. Hockey - Social aspects - Canada.   I. Whitson, David, 1945-   .   II. Title.
III. Series.

GV848.4.C3G78 1992   796.962'0971   C92-093872-8

The Publishers acknowledge the financial support of the Canadian Studies and Special Projects Directorate of the Department of the Secretary of State, Government of Canada.

Contents

Acknowledgements

So many people have helped us with this book that it will be impossible to thank them all. We've drawn heavily from numerous interviews with people in Canada's sporting community over the last two decades, as well as from documentary and secondary materials collected while researching earlier books and projects. We've also benefited from interviews with current and former hockey players, officials, and hockey historians conducted in conjunction with an educational television series on Canadian hockey produced by Simon Fraser University and Spectra Communications for British Columbia's Knowledge Network. One of us was heavily involved in the planning of this series and in the subsequent creation of a course on hockey and Canadian popular culture in the Canadian Studies Program at Simon Fraser. Both the television series and the course were co-originated, co-designed, and co-taught with Martin Laba of the Simon Fraser Department of Communication, and a number of Martin's ideas have found their way into this book. We also want to acknowledge the support of Rowly Lorimer, former Director of the Simon Fraser Canadian Studies Program. Rowly arranged the funding that allowed us to research and write this book through the SFU Canadian Studies Program, the Department of

Continuing Studies, and the Canadian Studies Program of the federal Department of Secretary of State.

We were fortunate to work with two outstanding research assistants, and each of them left his mark on the project. Mike Gasher contributed research materials and insights into the business and subculture of hockey developed during his many years as a sports journalist. We also benefited from Mitchell Peacock's research skills and his ability to draw on his former playing experience and contacts in junior hockey. In addition we owe a debt to Martin Laba, Stephen Hardy, David Skinner, Steve Kline, Ken Dryden, Kim Sanderson, and Denise Bukowski, all of whom offered comments on various sections or chapters, although they are not in any way responsible for the uses we've made of their suggestions. Thanks also go to Peter Saunders at Garamond Press for his unwaivering support of this project and his infinite patience, Robert Clarke for editorial advice and copy-editing, Marie Leiren and Linda Callan for secretarial assistance, Lucie Menkveld for help with administrative details, Rebecca Bates for babysitting beyond the call of duty, and Barb Bentley for briefly taking over the Gruneau/Bentley household so that the last bit of this book could be written.

Finally, we want to thank the two people who have by far contributed the most to the book. Shelley Bentley and Cathie McDougall offered love, support, and advice throughout a project that went on far too long. We know there were many times when they felt "that damn hockey book" would *never* be finished. But at long last, we are now able to put this project to bed.

Rick Gruneau
David Whitson
West Vancouver and Edmonton

Introduction

Like many Canadian men of our generation, we have vivid memories of the seemingly endless pick-up hockey games that made winter fun in our youth. As we moved into organized hockey, there was the cool air of the indoor rink, the dank smell of the concrete dressing room with its battered wooden benches, the friendships and anxieties of team life, the coach with the station wagon and the faded team jacket. We also have vivid recollections of youthful fandom and hero worship, of hanging around Maple Leaf Gardens for the Jr. A double-header on Sunday afternoons, of pleading with our parents to allow us to stay up to watch *Hockey Night in Canada*, of flipping hockey cards in the schoolyard, and of arguing about which was the better team, the Leafs or the Canadiens. These memories of sights, sounds, and feelings are the stuff of nostalgia. But they are also the stuff of identity — part of the attachments that both of us have to the places, times, and social influences that shaped our developing conceptions of self.

This is not to say that hockey has been the most important element in the making of our personal identities. Neither of us went on to play the game at a high level. We both chose to pursue other sports, and we followed career paths that have taken us a long way from the game we loved in our boyhoods. Yet, like an old song whose melody keeps running through your head, hockey's influences are something that we can't forget. Hockey was the one thing in our youth that virtually all boys seemed to have in common — the stuff of everyday conversation, the regularly shared experience of after-school and weekend play. Perhaps the strongest of all our feelings of commonality came when we watched *Hockey Night in Canada* on Saturday nights. Even at an early age the TV program made us feel like part of a national community.

It was only years later that both of us realized how much the commonality of these experiences, places, and feelings had been influenced by our own geographical, historical, and social locations in Canadian society. We were both Torontonians, we grew up in the 1950s and early 1960s, and our families were what most Canadians would describe as "middle class." The social world we knew then was far more ethnically and racially homogeneous than the Toronto, or the Canada, of the present day. And, of course, in retrospect it is glaringly evident that many other people's experiences and feelings about hockey were markedly different from our own. In those days, only a few girls or women played hockey, and while some were clearly fans, the association of girls and women with the game tended to be defined only through the participation of the men in their lives. Furthermore, there were always boys in our communities who seemed generally uninterested in hockey or, more importantly, never seemed comfortable with it. There were also boys whose economic circumstances demanded that they work during the times when the rest of us were playing, or whose families and communities encouraged other activities that they saw as more truly connected to their religious or cultural heritages.

Today these differences in experience and feeling still exist. In many instances they've become more pronounced. Equipment costs more, outdoor rinks are a fading part of many municipal budgets, and the time commitment for parents and players in organized hockey is greater than ever before. As a result the game is often further out of reach for people in marginal economic circumstances. Moreover, in an increasingly multicultural Canada, hockey no longer commands the automatic cultural allegiance it enjoyed in past decades. Multiculturalism, in turn, is only one part of a much broader fragmentation of audiences for commercial entertainments in contemporary Canadian society. Hockey now competes with a host of other popular pastimes, products, and symbols that provide sources of individual and collective identification for Canadians: everything from skateboarding, baseball, basketball, and soccer, to rap music, hip-hop, grunge rock, dance clubs, Doc Martens, Madonna, and thrash metal. Yet, despite this cultural diversity, hockey continues to have a powerful grip on the imaginations and collective memories of Canadians.

Hockey does this because of its apparent naturalness, its sheer ubiquity, and its history. For many Canadians hockey has come to feel like a natural extension of seasonal rhythms. In their book *Home Game*, Ken Dryden and Roy MacGregor aptly refer to it as one of "winter's expectations." In addition Dryden and MacGregor argue that while participation in hockey is far from universal, it continues to be remarkably broad ranging. Millions of Canadians play hockey in one form or another — young and old, boys and girls, urban and rural, French and English, East and West, able and disabled. Millions more follow the game passionately, and even people who dislike hockey have difficulty escaping its reach, its omnipresence in the media and in the everyday conversations that occur at the office, the playground, and the school. Added to this is a history that has allowed the game to represent something quintessentially Canadian. For better or worse, ice hockey is something "we" invented; it is "our" game.

So it is hardly surprising that of all the sports played in Canada hockey has long been celebrated as something unique. Writing in the 1960s, Al Purdy called hockey "the Canadian specific"; Dryden and MacGregor call it "our common passion"; Scott Young refers to it as "the language that pervades Canada"; Peter Gzowski exalts it as "the game of our lives." These are just a handful of examples from a long list of claims about the game's importance in Canadian culture. But in our view there has not been enough analysis of either the substance behind these claims or the reasons why Canadians have felt such a powerful need to make them. Canadian libraries are brimming with team histories and statistics, engaging tales of great players and events, biographies and picture books. There are also innumerable fragments of social analysis about the game in novels, short stories, magazine articles, occasional scholarly essays, and government reports. The problem is that none of this adds up to a comprehensive analysis of the nature of hockey and its role in Canadian culture.

You'd think there'd be no shortage of sustained intellectual commentary on hockey in Canada given the large number of writers, artists, and scholars who have alluded to the game's significance. But only a few Canadian intellectuals have been willing to take hockey seriously as something suitable for social and cultural analysis. This has been especially true for academics. It might be acceptable to be passionate about the Canadiens, the Canucks, or the Oilers —or perhaps even be so masochistic as to care about the Senators — but one's work should be about more "important" things: the constitution, the fur trade, social inequality, poststructuralism, the Canadian novel. Conduct a quick overview of the scholarly disciplines of Canadian history, sociology, literary theory — even of cultural criticism in general — and one quickly realizes that hockey has largely fallen beneath the higher earnestness of Canadian intellectual practice.

This book is written partly out of frustration with the ambivalence of Canadian academics towards hockey. It is also motivated by more pragmatic concerns. Both of us frequently discuss hockey in courses on media, popular culture, sport, and leisure that we teach at our respective universities. At Simon Fraser there is a whole course now in the Canadian Studies program on the social and cultural analysis of hockey. But it is hard to find enough background reading that situates hockey in a broad social and cultural context. With this in mind we undertook this project hoping to make our own work in the classroom a little easier. Our idea was to write a book about hockey that could be assigned in university classes on popular culture or Canadian society, as well as in courses focused directly on the social analysis of sport and leisure. Yet at the same time we also wanted to produce a book of interest to anyone with a curiosity about hockey and its changing place in Canadian culture. Our overall goal was to examine the changing character of hockey in Canada as one small part of the making of modern sports, of commercial entertainment, and, indeed, of modern experience itself.

The approach we've taken in the book stands at the crossroads between history, sociology, and a comparatively new field known as contemporary cultural studies. Over the last twenty years, growing numbers of intellectuals in Western societies have awakened to the social significance of popular culture and commercialized leisure. As a result, the analysis of popular culture and commercialized leisure has recently achieved unprecedented intellectual legitimacy. Part of the mission of cultural studies today is to question the distinctions that earlier cultural critics, trained in traditional Western aesthetics and literary theory, had erected between high culture (for example, the arts) and commercial mass culture (for example, soap operas, sports, videos). For these critics art is something that always privileges intellectual abstraction over familiarity of experience. The quality of art is said to lie in its ability to speak a language of universal aesthetic truths — truths that defy the limitations of specific cultures and enrich the human spirit. Art is art, the argument runs, no matter whether the objects in question were produced in Greece thousands of years ago, in the South Pacific hundreds of years ago, or in Moose Jaw last week. Commercial mass culture, on the other hand, has long been said to lack these positive universal qualities. Its appeal has depended simply upon an ability to engage people in familiar pleasures and practices. For these reasons, Western cultural critics have consistently differentiated art from mass culture, even to the point of attributing a wide variety of social and psychic ills to the latter.

In recent years this automatic elevation of one kind of culture over another has been called into question. For one thing, the apparent line between art and mass culture has become increasingly blurred since the 1960s. Art galleries now conduct exhibitions on comic art, Mozart appears on sweatshirts, doctoral dissertations are written on Marilyn Monroe, the Doors, and Pee Wee Herman. Moreover, a generation of intellectuals who grew up listening to, say, the Rolling Stones, tends to have a rather different view of mass culture than did intellectuals in the past. In contemporary cultural studies today, the first order of business is no longer to evaluate various aspects of cultural life as necessarily high or low, good or bad, educative or diversionary. Rather, the primary goal is to explore complex relationships between culture and society, history and meaning, image and context. At issue are important questions about the role of *all* contemporary cultural forms and practices (such as the ballet, rock music, theme parks) in the general formation of social life. What forces have influenced the development, availability, and popularity of different cultural forms and practices? What pleasures and meanings do various groups derive from these cultural forms and practices? What kind of relationship is there between cultural production, pleasure, meaning, and inequalities in power? How have the structures, meanings, and uses of different cultural forms and practices changed over time, and what significance, if any, can be attributed to these changes? These questions do not exhaust the range of topics relevant to contemporary cultural studies, but they provide a brief glimpse of some of the issues that have come to define contemporary cultural studies as a field of study.

There are a small number of sociologists in Canada and the United States who have attempted to understand sport with these questions in mind. Similarly, throughout the 1970s and 1980s sport began to figure prominently in the work of social historians increasingly attentive to the growth of commercialized leisure in North America. Sport also began to draw a measure of attention in British cultural studies. However, sport has been a marginal area of interest for Canadians and Americans who define themselves as cultural theorists and critics, and it remains on the periphery of work in North American cultural studies. Popular music, television news and drama, movies, rock videos, pulp fiction, advertising, melodrama, theme parks, malls, and museums are among the favoured topics of the day, with sport typically receiving only passing mention despite its manifest presence in popular culture. Exceptions occur when cultural theorists have directed their attention to representations of the body in media, or to the politics of spectacle. But even in these instances there has been more interest in activities like professional wrestling or body building than in such seemingly mundane pastimes as football, basketball, baseball, or hockey.

In our view, any approach to contemporary cultural studies that ignores these immensely popular pastimes has its priorities wrong. So in this book we begin with the premise that hockey deserves a prominent place in Canadian cultural studies. Building on this premise, our analysis focuses upon the related themes of identities and cultural politics. We argue that the centrality of hockey in Canadian cultural life has never been inevitable or predetermined. Hockey is not, as some commentators have implied, the result of a cultural manifest destiny rooted in Canadians' struggle for survival in the vast spaces of a rugged northern country. Rather, the sport we call hockey has emerged out of a series of clashes of cultures and traditions that have occurred against the backdrop of Canada's development as an industrial and consumer society.

Hockey's relationships to various identities, and its position in Canadian cultural politics, have always been defined by these clashes and social changes. Our discussion begins by exploring the clash between different interpretations of sport and culture in general, and hockey and Canadian culture in particular. This leads to an examination of the history of struggles surrounding hockey's transformation from a diverse and loose collection of folk games to the intensely organized sport we know today. We then shift the focus of our analysis to the pressures, limits, and struggles that have influenced Canadian hockey from the 1950s to the present day. We look inside the hockey subculture, explore current debates, and examine how the game is changing. For it is clear that hockey is not the same game now that it was even twenty years ago. It has a different feel, a different economy, a different set of relations to the way Canadians live. Like many other areas of Canadian culture, hockey today has been influenced by current movements for multiculturalism, human rights, fair play, and community-centred adult recreation on the one hand, and forces of deregulation, market segmentation, free trade, rural depopulation, and globalization on the other. At the same time, the subculture of hockey has retained its own unique adaptations and forms of resistance to these movements and forces.

Canadians' sense of what hockey is, and what it means, is also being challenged by the political and cultural debates now raging throughout the country. At the very moment that Canada itself is in question, and new voices are clamouring to have their identities recognized, many of hockey's deeply rooted meanings, traditions, and associated identities need to be reassessed. Hockey has a capacity to induce the recollection of familiar experiences and to subtly connect this recollection to a seemingly less complicated image of Canadian society. In a time of uncertainty, and in a Canada increasingly characterized by difference, this comfortable familiarity and ability to convey an older sense of Canadian identity have an engaging and enduring appeal. They help sustain our ability to imagine a national community.

However, this older sense of Canadian identity is rooted in an image of a common culture that has often papered over some of the most deeply rooted inequalities and conflicts in the society. The image is also quaintly at odds with Canada's ongoing political and cultural tensions. In this time of national soul-searching, hockey's association with representations of comfortable familiarity may well be important as a point of connection for Canadians. But this association can also promote nostalgia and illusion rather than interpretation and understanding. At the very least, hockey's enduring link to the idea of "Canadianness" is something to be analysed rather than romanticized. And, in this analysis, the game's associations with other cultural identities — identities associated with locality, consumerism, ethnicity, class, race, and gender — need to be brought more directly into the account.

PART I

HOCKEY, CULTURE, AND SOCIAL DEVELOPMENT

Chapter One

Hockey and the Politics of Culture

Shortly after the 1972 Canada-Soviet hockey series, the Russian writer Yevgeny Yevtushenko suggested that Phil Esposito was Canada's greatest poet. It was a remark guaranteed to get wide circulation in the Canadian press — something to be repeated reverently in reference to Esposito's legendary scoring ability, but also newsworthy for its apparent irony. The very idea of casting the hulking Esposito in the role of poet — a man of "culture" — seemed wonderfully paradoxical; for the world of North American professional hockey has typically been a hyper-masculine world centred upon physical prowess, controlled aggression, and often boyish off-ice fun. Indeed, one observer of the '72 series noted how the players on Team Canada were generally "like teenagers in their enthusiasms and interests: simple men of instinct, not highly rational. Lusty, capricious, fun-loving and proud, quick to anger, always ready to belly-laugh and clown."[1] There is little room in this world of instincts, physical performance, and masculine comradeship for self-conscious theories of art. On the contrary, in hockey's world of old-fashioned masculinity, poetry has a vaguely effeminate character

— the activity of effete and physically inept artists and intellectuals. Imagine the ribbing Esposito must have taken about his sudden elevation to the heights of Canadian artistic achievement.

But if professional hockey players have often been uncomfortable with the highbrow world of art and culture, the reverse has arguably been just as true. Canadians with highbrow sensibilities may occasionally watch and enjoy hockey, but the game doesn't seem to have undergone the kind of cultural gentrification that we sometimes find, for example, associated with baseball. On the contrary, hockey has long been subjected to considerable intellectual snobbery. It is a game whose sheer physicality and potential for seemingly random violence have been at odds with an intellectual sensibility that has valued control of the emotions and the cultivation of taste for "finer" things. In this sense there has always been some resistance to the idea of discussing hockey as a form of "culture," a word usually reserved for serious art, not popular sport. It might be conceded that hockey has inspired a variety of works that have the status of culture: a painting by William Kurelek or Ken Danby; a poem by Al Purdy; a short story by Hugh Hood, Mordecai Richler, Hugh MacLennan, or Roch Carrier. But this isn't the same as suggesting that the game is culture in and of itself, or that the players are bona fide cultural producers or artists.

Indeed, the very idea of viewing sport of any kind as "culture" has always raised problems for Canadian intellectuals. To accept this idea, the old argument runs, is to accept an absurdly populist understanding of the meaning of culture. George Woodcock typifies this view when he suggests that if one includes *everything* in the definition of culture, the word becomes devalued. The arts, in particular, become submerged in activities "that are in no way artistic" and this development "obscures the special role and special claims of artists."[2] When this occurs it becomes difficult to discriminate between activities that contribute to the development of civilization and those that merely amuse. From the viewpoint of many intellectuals, sports fall squarely into the sphere of mere amusement.

This implicit rejection of the artistic merits and cultural significance of sports has never been universally accepted. A significant minority of Western intellectuals have long argued that sports can be just as civilizing, and can invoke universal aesthetic possibilities that are just as enriching, as other artistic practices. In his now classic book *Homo Ludens*, the Dutch historian Johan Huizinga asserts that the play element in culture is the foundation for everything that is civilizing in Western life. According to Huizinga, play creates culture; when sports are pursued playfully — that is, for their own sake — there is no reason why they should be any less civilizing than other forms of autonomous cultural expression.[3] Over forty years later the U.S. philosopher Michael Novak extended this argument to lofty heights in his book *The Joy of Sports*. For Novak, sports embody "universal truths" no less than many other forms of artistic expression; indeed, Novak argues, sports should be understood as a metaphorical statement about ultimate human possibilities.[4]

Arguments of this type have usually been offered in an effort to make the case that playful sport can be a legitimate part of a civilizing culture. If we accept that sport is rooted in the playful essence of the human spirit, it is a short step to the argument that sporting pastimes necessarily share in the free creativity that animates the arts. Once this point is won, it follows that sport can be removed from the category of "mere" amusement. Sport can be seen to be every bit as deserving of respect as any other form of culture. Armed with this kind of argument, intellectuals fascinated by sports have been able to indulge their personal interests without sacrificing their highbrow credentials. Proponents of this view still tend to adopt a discriminating view of culture, but they want to broaden the definition of culture to include elements such as the goal-scoring poetry of an Esposito or the play-making artistry of a Wayne Gretzky. Implicit in this broadened view is the idea that the essential artistry of sport, like that of all art, can be corrupted or trivialized. In this regard, there has been no shortage of cries from Western intellectuals about the loss of artistry in modern sports or the apparent corruption of sports by commercialism and the win-at-all costs ethos of modern Western societies.[5]

Finally, there is a more open-ended, less judgemental, way of understanding the relationships between sport and culture. Culture can be viewed more broadly as the complex web of meanings, beliefs, and ways of living that characterize any society. This is the definition most often in use when people note the important role that hockey plays in Canadian culture. From this perspective, the game can be understood simply as part of the way Canadians live and make sense of their lives. Hockey's rhythms, meanings, structures, and contradictions can all be understood as a constitutive part of everyday Canadian experience. They are also an important part of the Canadian collective memory. Hockey acts both as myth and allegory in Canadian culture. The game has become one of this country's most significant collective representations — a story that Canadians tell themselves about what it means to be Canadian.

One of the biggest problems in discussions of sport and culture is that different meanings of the word culture tend to be used interchangeably, so that they blur together in confusing ways. There is more to be wary of here than simple linguistic confusion, because the use of different meanings of culture in discussions of sport has rarely been politically innocent. We can't just pick the meaning we like best — for instance, that sport is mass entertainment rather than "culture," that sport is art, or that sport is part of a whole way of life — without also accepting a host of background assumptions. For that reason it is important to ask what these background assumptions are and why such seemingly different perspectives have become referenced by the same word. What implications stem from adopting different definitions of culture in the study of sport? Which definition provides the best frame of reference for a critical analysis of hockey, and why? To answer these questions we need to probe more deeply into the history of the concept of culture itself.

Culture, Sport, and the Civilized Ideal

The concept of culture has a complex and contested history.[6] Early uses were generally limited to the idea of cultivation — initially, that of crops and animals. The word "culture" was employed as it is in biology to refer to physical growth or development. Gradually this use of culture as a noun of process was extended metaphorically to the cultivation of human intelligence and sensibilities. As this metaphor became more common it came to refer generally to the disciplines and practices through which human minds could be cultivated and society thereby improved — the arts and literature, for instance. By the eighteenth century there was considerable discussion of these practices, now seen collectively as a context or medium through which people might be educated to realize their human or divinely inspired capacities.

It wasn't long before a rather different understanding of culture also began to emerge in Western societies. This was culture seen as a pattern of human development: the sum total of practices, objects, and meanings that define a whole way of life. In this formulation the concept of culture took on a more anthropological character as a noun of configuration. Yet this use was often mixed with the earlier sense of culture as a *process* of development, including the practices of cultivation and the objects produced by these practices. Viewed in this combined way, the idea of cultural development could be extended to include the general concept of human progress. Culture came to be seen as a synonym for civilization.

The more anthropological conception of culture also facilitated the possibility of intercultural and even intracultural comparison. It became possible to speak of *different* cultures rather than one universal process of cultural development or civilization. Such comparisons opened up a space for the radical notion that culture was something made by human beings, rather than a realization of abstract ideals. If culture could be viewed simply as a human construction, a varying historical expression of the way of life of different human groups, on what basis could the quality of different cultures be evaluated? Different cultures — different ways of living — might all be seen as valid. In the eighteenth and nineteenth centuries this problem of cultural relativism was partially solved for European intellectuals through a widespread commitment to the ideas of civilization and human progress, combined with a celebration of selected civilized practices and objects from antiquity (such as Greek theatre, art, and philosophy). In many instances, the culture of the European upper classes was seen as the modern expression — perhaps even the pinnacle — of a complex civilizing process that had begun in classical Greece.

Accomplishments of law and statecraft, built on a concern for reason and social justice, were typically seen as key elements in the development of civilized Western culture. It was also widely agreed that the roots of civilization lay in the less utilitarian practices through which ideas and sensitivities were developed. Specifically, they lay in those contemplative and artistic practices whose manifest purpose was to stimulate the expression of truth, beauty, and human development (for example, philosophy, art, literature). The idea of a civilizing "culture" rooted in these contemplative and artistic practices became a means to differentiate the institutions and achievements of Western societies from those of "primitive" societies, whose members were preoccupied with subsistence.

All of these beliefs provided a framework for bringing together the ideas of culture as cultivation, and as a whole way of life, in a hierarchical and exclusionary manner. To be "cultured" — indeed, to be civilized — meant being knowledgeable about a particular kind of culture, one specific way of living, a way of living that was European, economically privileged, and, in most instances, masculine. In its most general usage, the word "culture" came to refer primarily to those practices of thinking, speaking, and aesthetic appreciation characteristic of men who had a nineteenth-century upper-class education. The cultured person was someone knowledgeable and discriminating about philosophy, literature, painting, music, and drama — what we now refer to as the arts.

The corollary of this understanding of culture was that the great mass of people were uncultured, that entire groups and societies somehow stood outside culture. This assumption posed no great difficulty for those to whom class, culture, and civilization were virtually synonymous. Culture, or at least knowledge of particular cultural forms and practices, had become a marker of social class, gender, and racial differences. However, the democratizing and popularizing forces at work throughout the nineteenth and twentieth centuries increasingly called this interpretation into question. Not only did the high arts begin to receive greater exposure throughout the populations of Western societies, but also other more popular pastimes, languages, and ways of living became more visible and struggled for legitimacy.

The economic successes of nineteenth- and twentieth-century industrial capitalism expanded disposable incomes and created new demands for consumption and entertainment. In addition, new communication technologies rapidly opened up possibilities for a much broader dissemination of cultural products. Inexpensive books and newspapers, then records and radio, cinema, and television became the vehicles for transmitting a new and readily affordable mass culture. Not coincidentally, both the increased wages and shorter working hours that together contributed to a more democratized access to leisure were conditions that working people had fought for. These struggles in turn were very much bound up with more directly political struggles, such as extension of the franchise to non-property owners and women, the establishment of trade union and other legal protections for workers, and the creation of political parties not bound by the vested interests of the dominant classes.

Campaigns to improve the lot of disenfranchised or marginalized people frequently included demands for increased access to education (including adult education, as well as formal schooling for children) and entertainment. The push for greater access to entertainment, in particular, was connected to the workers' struggles to gain more free time — time that could be invested in family and community activities, as well as in commercial recreations. The establishment of regular weekends away from work in the late nineteenth century helped to create the audiences that made these entertainments profitable. At the same time, there were growing pressures for public facilities (museums and libraries, as well as parks and skating rinks) that could bring recreation and "culture" within the reach of those who couldn't afford private education and private clubs. The accessibility to recreation and to "improving activities" was seen to be desirable because then working people could lead fuller lives (more full than possible with a sixty-hour work week), participate in the arts and literature, and take what they saw as their rightful place in "the great project of modern development."

Such demands evoked a variety of responses among privileged intellectuals and political leaders — responses that demonstrated considerable disagreement over the meaning of culture as well as the legitimacy of particular cultural forms or practices. On the one hand, there were campaigns designed either *to repress* or *to regulate* popular entertainments, especially those associated with drink, gambling, and spectacle. On the other hand, concern over undesirable recreations inspired numerous attempts at *reform*. Considerable support developed for initiating the apparently uncivilized masses of people into the world of higher culture, but only on terms set by dominant groups. The concert hall, library, even the playing field came to be seen as potential sites for education and class conciliation — sites for the construction of a common culture that would reaffirm the civilizing value of the cultural accomplishments of the privileged classes. Aspects of traditional or popular cultures that seemed unrespectable and uncivilized were accorded legitimacy *only* when they had been picked up by dominant groups and remade in accordance with those groups' preferred values.

All of this was part of the cultural context within which different sports began to develop as distinctive areas of modern social life in the nineteenth century. The formative influences of such cultural struggles are evident in the history of Western sport through the transformation of unorganized and often rough sporting recreations into organized and supposedly more civilized amateur athletics. Amateurism, in Canada and around the world, began largely as a set of practices that both presupposed and promoted masculine and class identities. The amateur code celebrated the ethos of the gentleman while systematically excluding non-Europeans, women, and the working classes from sport. However, it wasn't long before amateur sport was conceived of more broadly as a force for social improvement in modern life. Amateur sport became more widely understood as something that promoted the "civilizing" values of hygiene, fairness, emotional control, and respectability.

In some quarters it was even suggested that amateur sport could aspire to the status of high culture. Pierre de Coubertin's self-conscious use of imagery from classical Greece in his promotion of the modern Olympics in the 1890s — and his belief that the Olympics should be both an athletic and artistic festival — set the stage for later claims that amateur sport and art were two sides of the same cultural coin. Both sport and art, it was argued, could trace a line of continuity from the heights of civilization in classical antiquity to the age of modern societies. By this standard, civilizing sport had every right to join high art in the pantheon of modern "cultural" activities. Subsequent attempts to justify sport as a legitimate component of culture in the twentieth century have received much of their impetus from these late-nineteenth-century arguments.

The Critique of Mass Culture

The most serious opposition to nineteenth- and twentieth-century movements for cultural democratization has come from a minority of self-appointed guardians of culture who have believed that the majority of people are incapable of achieving the intellectual and aesthetic discrimination required by serious literature, art, and music. The British critic and educator Matthew Arnold is an example of such a self-appointed cultural guardian in the nineteenth century, and in this century the poet T.S. Eliot has played a roughly similar role.[7] More recently, the U.S. philosopher and classicist Allan Bloom kept elements of this tradition alive with his controversial book *The Closing of the American Mind*.[8] In their different ways all of these critics have sought to defend the integrity and presumed civilizing qualities of a privileged European minority culture against the extension of higher education to mass audiences and against the mass production of literature, art, and music that speaks to popular tastes. They suggest that the apparent triumph of mass taste and majority thinking in modern societies, particularly in higher education, has eroded the standards of cultural excellence upon which a truly humane and civilized common culture might be created. This erosion of standards supposedly threatens the very foundation of Western civilization.

Such arguments have given strong support to hierarchical distinctions between elite minority culture and mass culture and, in many instances, between Western and non-Western ideas. The origins of such distinctions go back to classical antiquity, but their modern form developed in the face of growing movements for social, economic, and political equality in the eighteenth and nineteenth centuries. Arguments about the decline of culture and civilization gave voice to the perceived threat that "the masses" posed to paternalistic class or colonial rule.[9] In this context, the relationship between high culture and mass culture came to be defined as a tension between those cultural forms deemed part of the great tradition of Western intellectual and aesthetic accomplishment, and those produced by or for people unschooled in the appreciation of the finer aspects of human civilization. As part of this argument, it was sometimes suggested that the great civilizing tradition of Western culture and the popular traditions of European folk cultures were once organically connected expressions of an older way of life. But this organic relationship is said to have been effectively destroyed by the technological, economic, and political forces at work in modern life.[10]

The phrase "mass culture" quickly became a derogatory label for describing virtually all mass-produced versions of serious art forms (such as pop music and the romance novel). In the twentieth century the mass-culture label was also applied to emerging art forms such as photography and the cinema and to a variety of entertainments ranging from hobbies to commercial spectator sports. Many of these activities had their own well-established traditions, but it was argued that they usually lacked the intellectual and aesthetic content of high culture. Or else it was suggested that new technologies and the growing market for commercial entertainment and diversion threatened to undermine the authenticity and civilizing function of traditional cultures in favour of a modern mass culture used only for amusement or diversion. Indeed, much of the criticism of mass culture assumed an inherent tension: on the one hand there was *culture* (seen as aesthetic or educational activities leading to self-improvement and overall human development or, less often, as an authentic expression of traditional folkways); and on the other hand, *entertainment* (seen as mindless diversion, mere amusement, or barbaric spectacle). Implicit in this tension was the idea that if activities appealed to the emotions rather than to reason, stressed fun rather than disciplined cultivation, or were produced primarily for commercial purposes, they were likely to be culturally trivial at best. At worst, the argument continued, the retreat from self-improvement and free creativity evident in modern commercially produced entertainment was potentially barbarous.

Most criticisms of mass culture have been profoundly conservative. They have variously mixed anti-democratic sentiments with a romantic longing for an older time when everyone knew their place and didn't complain much about it. This has been especially true in the case of critics who have doubted the abilities of "the masses" to ever become properly "cultured," but it has also been true for reformers who have believed that the widespread promotion of civilizing culture is the best defence against the levelling tendencies of modern mass society. The problem is that this promotion of culture has often included a rigid and sometimes puritanical aesthetic and moral sensibility. From the nineteenth century to the present day, the most vocal critics of mass culture have usually viewed themselves as defenders of tradition, judgement, taste, and morality in the face of the democratizing and secular tendencies of modernity.

One significant aspect of this sensibility is that it has often been characterized by a one-dimensional, almost paranoid view of science, technology, and the mass media. Conservative mass-culture theorists have usually emphasized the negative side of these features of modern life — their role in the destabilization of the old order, the frightening power they potentially give to the masses, their capacity to run amok and become things unto themselves outside of any regulatory system of morality. The contributions of science and technology to the control of disease, to increasing the availability of food and other socially necessary goods, and the contributions of mass media to human learning have been downplayed to the point of invisibility. It is not that conservative culture critics have never been optimistic about the potential of new technologies; some were initially optimistic about television, for example. However, such optimism has usually turned to despair when the technology has become implicated in the dissemination of mass culture.

Variations of these criticisms of mass culture have been expressed on the political left as well. The left-wing version of mass-culture criticism received its classical expression in an influential strand of German critical thought that first developed in Frankfurt in the 1920s and 1930s and later became popularized in other parts of Europe and North America in conjunction with the new left of the 1960s. The touchstone authors in what is now sometimes called the Frankfurt school tradition of social criticism include Theodor Adorno, Max Horkheimer, and Herbert Marcuse.[11] One of the central ideas articulated by writers associated with the Frankfurt school was that modern mass culture was a powerful agency of mystification and diversion. Whatever potential the working classes in capitalist countries may have once had as a source of emancipation and human liberation was undercut by the coalescence of capitalist and administrative power with the new technologies of mechanical reproduction and mass marketing being developed in the twentieth century. Popular music and pulp literature, the cinema, mass circulation newspapers, and large-scale sporting spectacles had all become part of a culture industry whose standardized products had deadened the radical consciousness of the working classes. These industrially produced entertainments promised happiness, but failed to offer liberation. The apparent democracy of the market, and the pleasures offered by the culture industry, masked the inequality, violence, and exploitation of modern capitalism so completely that people literally spent their way through life believing themselves to be free individuals rather than victims.

Although different writers in this tradition have inflected this argument in various ways, they all shared a view of the culture industries as successful purveyors of mindless diversion and false consciousness. Writers in this tradition have also typically juxtaposed the artifice, standardization, and commercialism of mass entertainment to the creativity and authenticity supposedly expressed through autonomous or self-generated cultural practices. The basic argument, however, is that in the heavily administered world of modern capitalism, autonomy, creativity, and authenticity have been almost completely extinguished. For that reason, neither art nor critical theory can ever pretend to be disengaged. The task of these disciplines is to explore the "negative," to provide a critique of what exists and to reaffirm the idea of utopia.

The Limits of Mass-Culture Criticism

We have already noted that many cultural studies researchers and theorists have become highly critical of the distinction between high culture and mass culture. Conservative theories of mass culture have been subject to particularly intense criticism for their logical inconsistencies and factual inaccuracies, their connection to class and masculine privilege, their one-dimensional approach to technology, and the implicit contempt for the cultural tastes of ordinary people that runs throughout the perspective. Yet theories of mass culture identified with the political left often share in some of these problems. For example, radical mass-culture criticism also tends towards a one-sided view of technology. This view allows for the romanticization of what can be produced by hand or through one's own direct participation in contrast to mass-produced cultural goods and the apparent passivity of spectatorship. It also underplays the importance of technological innovations for education and the democratization of cultural activities of various types (for instance, through the printing press, radio, and television) and for opening up new forms of creative possibilities and pleasures (for example, the artistic and political possibilities opened up by cheap cameras, computers, or VCR technology).

Ironically, radical mass-culture theories can also harbour a negative view of the masses, albeit in a markedly different form than their conservative counterparts. Writers in this tradition tend to believe passionately that people living in so-called mass cultures have the capacity, indeed the duty, to become more than they are. But in their desire to help people break out of the bonds of delusion and false consciousness, critics have sometimes slipped into an implicitly patronizing view of the very people they want to liberate. The audiences who consume mass-culture products are portrayed as singularly gullible and naive because of their failure to recognize that popular music, television, romance fiction, and sports, among other things, are little more than narcotizing and ideologically conformist commercial spectacles.

We believe that these criticisms from the left have value insofar as they have explored the inequalities and biases of the commercial organization of modern mass culture and the widespread effects of new technologies on cultural production and reception. Radical mass-culture theories have also been important in drawing attention to patterns of ownership and distribution in the entertainment industries and to the significance of advertising in defining new market-led priorities. All of these elements are interconnected, and they have undoubtedly changed the context in which cultural performers, whether athletes or actors, produce. Such changes have greatly restructured the cultural choices available to different audiences — including sports fans — and have emphasized *some* values in the culture (and some audiences) at the expense of others.

Nonetheless, the blanket dismissal of commercial mass culture as crass, diversionary, and conformist — as nothing more than an aspect of "bread and circuses" — is highly problematic. Whether the critique comes from left or right, there has not been a sufficient willingness to recognize the craft and expressive creativity that can be present in the mass-produced cultural products of modern times. For instance, the demands of commercial cinema clearly influence directors and actors, just as the demands of commercial sport have an impact on high-performance athletes. But this isn't the same as saying that there is no creativity in the performances or that what is being produced lacks cultural authenticity. It is even more important to be critical of the tendency of mass-culture theories to see audiences as monolithic, passive, and, in the case of left-leaning critiques, manipulated by ideology. For example, the active engagement of the audience with performance that is often assumed in the case of certain types of theatre or concertgoers is not credited to the sports fan or the country music fan. Performers and audiences alike are viewed as creative, or at least thoughtful, in one set of activities, yet passive and vulnerable to manipulation in another.

A great deal of evidence can be marshalled to show that audiences for commercial mass entertainments are much more creative, more active, and less open to political or ideological conformity than these critiques suggest. For instance, sports fans sometimes reveal a surprisingly active side: as players themselves, chronic letter-writers to editors or callers to phone-in radio programs, lobbyists for recreational land use, collectors, coaches, volunteers, consumers of volumes of secondary background materials, and oral historians. Furthermore, the precise political or ideological fit between sport as a mass-culture product and the values of sports fans can't necessarily be *assumed* in the way these theories suggest. There is no reason why it is not possible to be both a radical trade unionist and a follower of the Montreal Canadiens. Nor is it impossible to be a Canadian nationalist and harbour an affection for the Los Angeles Kings or the Boston Bruins. This isn't to say that sports audiences are never manipulated, or that sports don't act conservatively in certain ways, in certain contexts. Indeed, the subcultural world of hockey in Canada has often been profoundly paternalistic and conservative. The point is that the ideological meanings and effects associated with different cultural forms and practices can never be automatically guaranteed.

Hockey and Canadian Cultural Criticism

Canadian intellectuals have articulated their own variations both of conservative and radical mass-culture theories. In common with mass-culture theories more generally, the major villain has often been technology. For example, writing in 1956, Gérard Pelletier worried about how television would disarm viewers, make them open to suggestion, and render them passive. Later, both Pelletier and a fellow Quebec journalist, André Laurendeau, would express their concern over television's ability to act as an "instrument of modernity that challenged the very fundamentals of Quebec society."[12] In contrast, anglo-Canadian critics from as early as the turn of the century have tended to link this suspicion of technology to a broader fear of the United States as a source of cultural degradation.

Humanist cultural conservatives, in particular, worried that a commercially driven and technologically dominated American mass culture threatened Canada's allegedly civilizing European traditions. This fear was a significant factor in arguments expressed during the 1920s and late 1940s about the need to promote a distinctive national culture in Canada to stave off the effects of American commercial mass culture. Commenting on the early postwar period, Canadian historian Paul Rutherford notes how anglo-Canadian intellectuals feared "the swelling amount of available trash, be that comic books, Mickey Spillane novels, soap operas, Hollywood movies or pop music: such material could well drive out taste and quality, defeat Culture, and debase the public mind."[13] The answer to this assault by American mass culture was provided by the Massey Commission in 1951: a "made-in-Canada" culture was necessary to protect Canadians against the perils of vulgarization. It goes without saying that this is a qualitatively different kind of conservatism than that offered by the Progressive Conservative Party of the 1980s and 1990s. For the most part, today's Tories are economic neoliberals more inclined to ignore or even embrace commercial American mass culture than to reject it. By contrast the older conservative tradition — which includes George Grant and Harold Innis — expresses a continuing worry about Canadian cultural decline in the face of American individualism, technology, and the homogenizing pressures of commercialism.[14]

Some of the flavour of this critique has also been evident in more left-wing versions of anglo-Canadian cultural criticism. The assumption that mass culture can be written off simply as bread and circuses has been so deeply rooted that few left-wing Canadian intellectuals have felt the need to study it in any detail. In those rare instances when mass culture has been discussed at all from a left perspective, the line of argument has often been roughly similar to the position outlined above. The emphasis has been on the colonization of an apparently indigenous Canadian popular culture by a commercial mass culture centred south of the 49th parallel. In this regard it is notable that one of the few book-length radical critiques of mass culture produced in Canada over the past two decades focuses upon hockey.

In *The Death of Hockey*, written during the early 1970s, Bruce Kidd and John Macfarlane documented what they saw as the gradual takeover of Canadian hockey by U.S. business interests.[15] The result was the ascendance of a single U.S.-dominated professional league and the decline of senior amateur hockey in communities across the country. Kidd and Macfarlane concluded that Canadians should take back their own game through a new system of community-owned teams. *The Death of Hockey* was not the first book to point to the power of hockey to dramatize Canadian hopes and aspirations. But it certainly was the first to link this argument to a critique of unfettered commerce, U.S. ownership, and the homogenizing ideological forces of U.S. mass entertainment. Although they didn't make the point directly, Kidd and Macfarlane suggested implicitly that the recovery of hockey from U.S. capital could be viewed as one small step towards a broader "left-nationalist" project. That project was to link political emancipation in Canada to the recovery of a wide range of threatened cultural practices — in art, literature, and popular culture — that defined Canada's cultural identity.

It is undoubtedly important to think about what is distinctive and worth protecting in the values and traditions that have taken root in Canada. It is also important to understand how the marketing imperatives of commercially produced mass culture, including those originating in the United States, set limits and exert powerful pressures upon all aspects of the production and consumption of culture in this country. In this regard, both conservative and left-wing nationalist writing on Canadian culture has furthered our understanding of the Canadian condition. Yet, having said this, we also need to recognize how Canadian critical traditions have drawn on the theories of elite minority culture and mass culture and have shared their theoretical and conceptual limitations.

At the risk of immense simplification, there are four distinct tendencies in Canadian cultural criticism that are pertinent to the analysis of Canadian hockey. The first and most obvious is the continuing tendency of many Canadian intellectuals to adopt a restrictive view of culture that overly privileges the arts and devalues the significance of mass culture or the study of popular entertainments. The unwillingness of many Canadian intellectuals to take hockey seriously stems from the prevalence of this position. Secondly, in cases where critics have identified hockey as a valued and distinctively Canadian cultural practice, they have tended to romanticize the game as it existed in the past and compare this idealized past with the apparent corruption of the present. A third, related problem is a tendency to view hockey as if it represents an organic connection with the Canadian landscape or national psyche — an essence that exists outside of the influences of social structure and history. Finally, a good deal of writing on hockey has tended to condemn the game's commercial character without adequately considering either the many contradictions of commercial hockey or its capacity to be interpreted in different ways by different audiences.

For instance, in three quite different and engaging discussions of hockey — Kidd and Macfarlane's *The Death of Hockey*, Peter Gzowski's *The Game of Our Lives*, and Doug Beardsley's *Country on Ice* — hockey is depicted as an authentic and (ideally) autonomous expression of Canadian culture. Nonetheless, the writers argue that both the game's artistry and its capacity to dramatize the Canadian collective spirit have become increasingly threatened by "outside" forces in the society. Doug Beardsley, for example, notes how the "game that for over a century has highlighted the best of the Canadian spirit has fallen victim to forces that have distorted our entire culture: high finance, big business, television and meaningless violence. These have done their dirty work on the game of hockey, one of our greatest national — even natural — resources."[16]

Peter Gzowski makes a similar argument and adds a subtle anti-American twist when he suggests that NHL hockey "began to sour" in the 1970s because of all the new U.S. markets it was trying to tap. To do this the NHL diluted the quality of its play and marketed goon hockey as roller derby on ice to U.S. audiences unfamiliar with the game's dual traditions of aggression *and* artistry. As a result — and with the additional impetus of Canadian losses to Soviet teams — the game plummeted to unprecedented depths before Canadians began a "counter-revolution" in the 1980s. Gzowski is careful to hedge his argument by acknowledging that although the NHL had been dominated by U.S. teams for years, in the old six-team league the players were almost all Canadian, and in "cities that at least had snow in the winter, the Rangers, Bruins, Red Wings, and Black Hawks seemed part of the Canadian game, part of the tradition."[17] The sour period of the 1970s in hockey is represented as a time when the game drifted from its inherent "Canadianness" while promoters pursued the Yankee dollar. There are obvious echoes here of longstanding Canadian fears about the negative consequences of selling "our" natural resources to the United States. Kidd and Macfarlane sum up the fears succinctly: "As with so many of our resources, the sellout of hockey was the inevitable consequence of our proximity to the United States and our cheap faith in free enterprise."[18]

These arguments are provocative; but in our view it is wrong to base the discussion on an idealized, organic conception of hockey as a natural Canadian cultural resource, something that developed almost magically out of an exposure to ice, snow, and open spaces. Doug Beardsley argues, for example: "Ice binds us together, shapes and defines both our style and our substance. It informs us, connects us rink by rink to ourselves. In the Canadian psyche, the motion we create on our national icescape is the nearest we come to permanence."[19] In this kind of argument "the Canadian psyche," if such a thing can be said to exist, is defined almost exclusively by an association with the landscape. Hockey is then held up as one of the most potent expressions of Canadians' connections to this landscape. Yet surely this leaves too much out of account and glosses over too many differences in Canadians' experiences — differences rooted in racial, ethnic, class, and gender relations. There is something to be said for the argument that hockey draws on and dramatizes the Canadian experience with long winters, the cold, and large open spaces. The problem arises when Canadians' appreciation for hockey is mistaken for "nature" rather than something that is socially and culturally produced.

The organic conception of hockey as Canadian culture provides a ready contrast with a game that has supposedly been removed from that culture by virtue of excessive commercialization or Americanization. By this logic, pick-up games and non-commercial amateur hockey are ostensibly closer to the game's essence than professional hockey. Kidd and Macfarlane's suggestion that by the early 1970s hockey had become "just a business" — a game "used for something for which it was never intended" — is an example of such an implicit contrast. Kidd and Macfarlane note that commercial spectacle has also been one of hockey's intended uses, both for bourgeois entrepreneurs and working-class fans, from at least the 1880s. But they imply that "community hockey ... built on love of the game particularly, love of sport generally, and community loyalty" lies closer to the true meaning of the game.[20]

It is difficult to determine the foundation for the argument that there is any one single legitimate "intended use" for hockey. Hockey has always had a range of different meanings and intended uses for various groups in Canada. The game has variously been a form of backyard play, a type of "civilizing" amateur sport, an opportunity to drink and gamble, a source of profit, and a community symbol. Moreover, these different uses of hockey have often blended together in complex ways. For example, it was hockey's ability to dramatize community loyalty that provided much of the foundation for the commercialization of the game. So it seems arbitrary to separate out the tradition of "community hockey" from traditions of commercial spectacle. It is even more arbitrary to imply that the dominance of the commercial tradition in hockey has been due to excessive Americanization. Like it or not, profiting from the game has been as Canadian as the beaver.

The real issues of importance here are the unique struggles and compromises surrounding the relationships between professional hockey and other ways of playing the game. In large measure, it is precisely these relationships that Kidd and Macfarlane want to explore. But these struggles and compromises are best understood without any necessary contrast to an allegedly more authentic, civilizing, or inherently Canadian game. Rather than search for idealized cultural forms and practices as a basis for criticism, we find it more fruitful to focus upon the close relationship that has *always* existed between culture and power. It is only then that we can usefully go on to evaluate changing connections between culture, values, and identities.

Sport, Power, and Popular Cultures

What gets defined as "culture" in Western societies, and how it is defined, have always been matters of negotiation and struggle between powerful and less powerful social groups, often with differing ways of life. The privileged place of elite minority cultures does not develop "naturally"; rather, the hierarchy of cultural distinctions in modern societies has typically come about because some groups have been able to establish their own preferred visions of civilization and cultural quality as more legitimate and more prestigious than those of others. The point here is not so much that, say, jazz and cinema have become widely accepted as art forms while commercial hockey and country music have not. Rather, we need to understand how differences in power — for example, between social classes, men and women, and various ethnic and racial groups — are an inevitable part of the creation and legitimation of such cultural classifications.[21] It is also necessary to pay attention to the variety of public and private organizations (such as schools, grant-giving agencies, the media) through which *some* skills, practices, and identities are established as being more worthy of serious attention than others.

In recent years social scientists and historians have begun to pay much more attention to the complex social processes in Western societies that have led some beliefs and practices to be viewed as "culture" while others are ignored or reviled. Along the way they have made popular culture into a serious object of study by demonstrating its fundamental interconnectedness with other areas of social life such as work, social unrest, and the changing nature of family life. We now know that it was primarily the nineteenth-century leisure classes that maintained a view of culture as a separate and autonomous activity. By contrast, popular cultures — traditions of mutual help; of story-telling and work songs; of domestic artistry; and of physical tricks, games, and amusements — were precisely the means through which working people honoured their own histories and brought moments of pleasure into ways of life that were routinely very hard. Popular cultures encompass all the various modes of expression, pleasure-seeking, and entertainment through which people negotiate their relationships with one another, with an imagined past and future, and with the institutions and prescriptions of a dominant culture. Today this meaning of "the popular" can't simply be limited to the folk arts and traditions of the past; it extends to include a large part of mass culture as well. In this way the concept of "popular cultures" builds on the idea of culture as a noun of configuration — different ways of living — rather than on the more restrictive definition of culture as a type of cultivation, either of self or human refinement. In our view this approach provides the most useful starting point for a social and cultural analysis of the nature and role of hockey in Canadian life.

But what about the argument that sport at its best has the capacity to be an element of "civilizing culture"? Isn't it useful in the social or cultural analysis of sport to retain some of the evaluative criteria implicit in a view of culture as a type of self-refinement or human refinement?

In this way one might still use the civilizing ideals of high culture as a standard against which to evaluate the current state of sport. There is certainly no doubt that sport has a history of creative expression and achievement that makes such comparisons attractive. This is particularly obvious in those individual sports where timed or measured performances show dramatic advancement, or where experimentation with and mastery of new forms (dives, jumps in figure skating, manoeuvres in gymnastics) take these sports into new territories of aesthetic achievement. Moreover, there is an undeniable artistry associated with the mastery of physical skill that is demonstrated by the greatest athletes in virtually every sport. In these ways, modern sports provide contexts in which people can be introduced to important traditions of human achievement and can learn to appreciate the pursuit of excellence in other endeavours.

But even if we were inclined to believe that sport at its best counts as a form of civilizing culture — as a few people in the Olympic movement continue to insist — some important problems remain. For one thing, the great leaps in achievement that have occurred in many sports have required levels of discipline, physical danger, bodily and ethical abuse (with the Ben Johnson scandal as a case in point) that have arguably been far more dehumanizing than civilizing. Sport also has deeply rooted and enduring traditions that are at odds with a definition of culture as intellectual and aesthetic refinement. The folk ancestry of modern sport lies variously in a wide range of religious rituals, festival amusements, tests of strength, and games of chance. Many of these various rituals and game-contests were extremely violent, oriented to spectacle, casual hedonism, and excess. Similarly, modern sport has ties to a romantic tradition of martial prowess and masculine adventurism that has often fetishized the value of robust physicality over the development of intellect. At its worst, this emphasis on virility, adventurism, and prowess has devolved into a reactionary bodily narcissism.[22] The problem is that these diverse cultural legacies threaten to remain as much a part of sport as playful creativity, disciplinary mastery, and the pursuit of human excellence. Proponents of the civilizing character of modern sport have made frequent references to the role of sport in the high culture of classical Greece, but they have always been haunted by the spectre of the Roman coliseum.

A more subtle problem is the difficulty that occurs in postulating as an evaluative basis for judgement some kind of universal aesthetic or moral standard as the basis of "culture." Too often in the past the identification of such universal standards has been constrained by the value positions and vested interests of Western cultural elites. Sectional interests and values have been misrepresented as universal standards of cultural excellence, often with prejudicial consequences. For example, in sport a variety of primarily modern, European, male, and middle-class ideas have provided the foundation for arguments about why sport of a certain type ought to qualify as a form of civilizing culture. This is not to say that all universalized discussions of sport, culture, and values are without merit. It is only that such discussions have typically been insufficiently attuned to the socially constituted character of their own foundational assumptions.

In any case there is no need to justify the value of studying sport by claiming that sport ought to be viewed as art or high culture. Modern sport is significant as a central dimension of popular experience and collective memory; nothing more, nothing less. Understanding this significance hinges on our ability to uncover, analyse, and evaluate the nature of the role that sport plays in the broader constitution of social and cultural life. Sport is a long way from being the most important cultural practice in the making of any given society. But, for Canadians, one sport — hockey — has been very important indeed.

Chapter Two

Origins of the Modern Game

One of the many indicators of hockey's growing importance in Canadian popular culture during the twentieth century is the liveliness of debate over the game's origins. An assertion that Kingston, Ontario, was the true "birthplace of hockey" in Canada was made as early as 1903 by Captain James Sutherland, one of the game's pioneers in eastern Ontario. Sutherland later went on to become President of the Canadian Amateur Hockey Association (CAHA), and his reputation helped him to successfully champion the Kingston claim for over forty years.[1] In 1942 the CAHA published a report, *The Origin of Hockey in Canada*, which supported Kingston's claim. In the wake of that report a Kingston delegation invited the CAHA to establish a Hockey Hall of Fame in the city. When the CAHA and the National Hockey League accepted Kingston's proposal, hockey organizers and civic boosters in Halifax and Montreal were incensed, and the result was a lengthy and spirited debate. However, since the 1970s most historians have come to agree that the early success of Kingston's drive to be recognized as the birthplace of hockey owed more to successful lobbying than to historical evidence. Much of the city's claim was based on a handful of references to "shinny" on Kingston Harbour found in the diary of a single Kingstonian from the 1850s.[2]

More recently, references to "the manly game of shinty" have been found in the *Kingston Chronicle and Gazette* as early as the late 1830s and early 1840s.[3] But these references still do not necessarily validate Kingston's longstanding claim to be the birthplace of hockey in Canada. For it is clear that the case of Kingston is far from exceptional. There are numerous accounts of ball and stick games of various types being played on ice in North America as far back as the eighteenth century. Indigenous people may well have played such games even earlier. There is evidence that both the New York Dutch and the New Englanders were playing a game called hockey in the colonial period, and hurley — an Irish game played with broad sticks — was played in Nova Scotia in the early nineteenth century.[4] By the mid-nineteenth century a number of different ball and stick games played on ice were well established in the Halifax-Dartmouth area, including shinny, a game called ricket, and various adaptations of field hockey. Folk games like these were played about the same time on the ice at Kingston Harbour.

None of these folk games had much in common with the sport of hockey as we know it today, beyond the fact that they were recreational physical contests being played with a stick on ice. The folk games mentioned in most early histories of hockey were informal pick-up games with unwritten rules, widespread local variations, and little, if any, organization. People participated in them as a form of popular amusement when time and weather allowed. The size of the playing area would depend on the amount of good ice available; the games would last as long as the players wanted to keep going; the equipment could be anything handy.

Today the legacy of these distant folk games is kept alive in activities ranging from road hockey to spontaneous pick-up games in backyards or on city streets, outdoor rinks, and frozen ponds, lakes, and rivers. But hockey is now much more than a popular tradition. The game has been transformed into a highly organized modern sport played with similar rules and equipment not just throughout Canada but around the world. Furthermore, hockey has become geared to national and international spectacle, to commerce and entertainment, and to selling everything from beer to national identity. If we want to understand the origins of hockey it is necessary to differentiate clearly between the folk games and sporting recreations of the past and the modern sport of our current time. Of course, by implication the very phrase "modern hockey" presupposes a time when hockey can somehow be said to be not modern. But where do we draw the historical line between modern and seemingly premodern sports? When did the folk games of the past give way to more modern sports, and why? So far there have been few attempts to answer these questions in the case of hockey. But there are a number of more general explanations of the modernization of sport that provide a useful starting point.

Sport and the Emergence of the Modern World

Historians and sociologists have often argued that the development of modern sport was simply part of the broader emergence of urban industrial societies. For example, the advent of new industrial technologies in Western societies, and the accompanying growth of large industrial cities, lent themselves to a reorganization of work, leisure, and family life around timed industrial production. Older popular recreations that had been governed by the natural rhythms of the days and seasons didn't adapt well to a modern urban world governed by the clock and factory whistle. At the same time, an increasingly urban and industrial society contained new classes of professionals and entrepreneurs with the resources, management skills, and inclinations to create standardized rules and formal sports organizations. In addition, industrialization brought a host of necessary technological innovations. The telegraph, mass circulation newspapers, trains, and trams, as well as technological innovations in equipment and facilities were all necessary factors in the emergence of distinctively modern sport.[5]

Some writers have made an even broader argument. For example, in his widely influential book *From Ritual to Record: The Nature of Modern Sports* Allen Guttmann suggests that the development of modern organized sport was primarily a response to the growth of a secular and scientific worldview in Western societies over several hundred years. From this standpoint, urbanization and industrialization virtually take on the status of secondary effects. Whatever causal role they may have played in the social development of sport can only be understood in the context of a much deeper cultural transformation that fundamentally altered how people thought about themselves, their relationships to the natural world, and to one another.

According to Guttmann, "primitive, ancient, and medieval societies" were largely dominated by tradition, superstition, and religious ritual. Family and community, labour, leisure, and religion were highly interconnected features of cultural expression in such traditional societies, and it was difficult to draw clear-cut boundaries between them. Furthermore, work and leisure and private and public life all took place within a clearly delineated social hierarchy. With few exceptions the dominant values in social life emphasized collective duties and obligations rather than individual rights, and the existing order tended to be seen as a natural expression of how human beings should live. In this context, traditional sporting recreations were necessarily defined by the influences of religion as well as the inequalities of existing social class, race, and gender relations. As a result, sports lacked their own independent systems of regulation and organization and were primarily oriented to ritualistic and *qualitative* meanings.

The emergence of new forms of rationality in Western societies — typified by growing acceptance of the scientific method and the inherent scepticism associated with it — was instrumental in a widespread process of secularization that gradually encompassed sport. In combination with the associated development of industrial economies and bureaucracies, sport gradually became transformed into a more rationalized activity, subject to bureaucratic regulation and increasingly oriented to record-setting and *quantitative* assessments of the meaning of the sporting experience — culminating in today's fetish for statistics and record-keeping. As this occurred, sport began to take on more of the cultural characteristics of modern industrial societies: that is, it became governed by notions of individual achievement, equality of opportunity, and maximum performance.[6]

It is sometimes suggested that there is a necessary connection between the modernist rationalism that Guttmann describes and the process that sociologists refer to as "institutionalization." In everyday language, the word "institution" is typically used to refer to prominent community organizations such as schools, banks, and hospitals. On occasion the meaning is extended to include sports teams. For example, the Montreal Canadiens are sometimes referred to — with considerable justification — as an institution in the city of Montreal. But in the language of contemporary sociology "institution" has a slightly different meaning. Sociologists use the word to refer to distinctive patterns and rules of conduct that: (1) persist in recognizably similar form across long spans of time and space; and (2) represent well-recognized and widely accepted ways of doing things in society.[7] However venerable the Montreal Canadiens may be, it is arguable whether they qualify as an institution in the sociological sense of the term. The notable institution, in this case, is hockey itself — an institution that in turn is part of the larger institution of modern sport.

The distinction is somewhat subtle, but it helps to think of institutions more as tendencies, processes, and prescriptive procedures — as ways of doing things — than as specific social organizations or symbolic objects. From this standpoint, the institutionalization of modern sport can be understood as the process whereby one dominant set of patterns, rules, and ways of playing has emerged to define and regulate our contemporary sense of *what* sport is and *how* it should be played. More precisely, *a* way of playing has come to be seen as *the* way of playing.[8] This has involved certain necessary conditions, such as written rules and the creation of formal organizations capable of establishing and regulating preferred conditions and standards of play for the modern era.

The concept of institutionalization figures notably in an impressive study of the modernization of sport in New York City between 1820 and 1870 conducted by the U.S. historian Melvin Adelman.[9] Like Guttmann, Adelman begins by highlighting the periodic, localized, and minimally structured character of folk games and sporting recreations in Western societies prior to the early nineteenth century. The great variations in rules and game-forms from community to community made it difficult for any kind of sport to develop beyond its local manifestations. The problem was more than just a question of poor communications and transportation in pre-industrial times. It was also a function both of the strength of community loyalty to different games and types of play and of the absence of any great sense of *need* for formal written rules or a standardized approach to playing games. The minimally organized and periodic character of local sporting recreations was simply a taken-for-granted part of cultures that had yet to modernize. As part of the process of modernization sport began to develop as a distinctive, more standardized, and universal institutional form.

Many aspects of the sports that Adelman describes as "premodern" in early nineteenth-century New York were also characteristic of the sporting pastimes in Canadian communities around the same time. Consider, for example, the different stick and ice games that thrived in the Halifax region in the early years of the nineteenth century. Hurley, ricket, shinny, and an ice version of field hockey all featured slightly different rules and appealed to different social groups within the area. Ricket in the 1840s was a game in which players skated, carrying hurley sticks in pursuit of a cricket ball. Two "rickets" or stones were placed at each end of the ice surface about four feet apart, and the objective was to put the ball through the opposing team's ricket some ten, fifteen, or twenty times, as agreed before the match. The game simply continued until one side or the other reached the agreed number of goals. More notably, ricket was a game that could have as many participants as the ice could hold.[10]

By contrast, games of (field) hockey on ice had more fully developed rules that specified limits and playing positions. An 1867 report in the *Halifax Reporter* records an instance where the two games of ricket and (field) hockey were being played simultaneously on the same ice surface at Oathill Lake. At one end, amidst about fifteen hundred skaters, a group of young men "took up hurleys and followed the ball" in a game of ricket. At the other end, officers of the British garrison and fleet played (field) "hockey." The writer of the report went on to note how "A ricket ball on ice ... is like an old hat on the road, to be hit by everybody." When "the aristocratic hockey ball" encroached upon neighbouring games the "plebian hurleys" would pass it around before giving it back. The words "aristocratic" and "plebian" were being used somewhat loosely here to compare the army and navy officers (who had become acquainted with field hockey in their private-school days) with the more heterogeneous group of civilians who were ricket enthusiasts.[11] Ricket remained a popular game in the Halifax region until well into the 1870s and co-existed with a variety of other ice games that attracted people through their various cultures of class and ethnicity.

While Haligonians were still playing minimally organized local games in the 1860s and 1870s, sport in New York had already begun to develop a more coherent and institutionalized character. Adelman concludes that in the period between 1820 and 1870 premodern ways of playing in the city were increasingly broken out of their anchorage in more traditional cultures as the city embarked on the path of modernization. For example, New York's ascendancy as an economic and communications centre required a new organization of space based on economic utility and value. People interested in using land recreationally began to compete economically with other potential users for access. The competition for space and the capital requirements necessary for building facilities demanded the creation of formal organizations. At the same time, growing concerns about urban anonymity in an increasingly large and heterogeneous population created opportunities for sport to be promoted as a new form of civic identification and belonging. Local politicians, businessmen, and professionals all began to have a stake in the promotion of sport both as a new form of urban entertainment and as healthy recreation. The modernization and institutional development of sport followed in the wake of these pressures and opportunities.

The Early Institutionalization of Hockey

Studies in sport history often suggest that traditional sporting recreations and modern sports are qualitatively different forms of cultural life. There may well be certain transhistorical *continuities* between the games of the distant past and the modern sports that developed in the nineteenth century — for example, the common demonstration of bodily energy and movement, the joys and satisfactions of physical mastery, and the capacity for sporting competitions to represent, or symbolize, elements of life beyond the game — but it is the *discontinuities* between traditional sports and modern sports that are given the greatest analytic significance. The key point is that there isn't necessarily any direct evolutionary line between the folk traditions of various sports in the past and the institutional origins of the sports we play and watch today.

By this reasoning there is little point in engaging in debate about which folk game, played where, or when, is the true precursor to the modern game of hockey. The real origins of the game as we know it are synonymous with the beginning of hockey's institutional development. Once this is acknowledged there is no mystery about the birthplace of modern hockey in Canada. Sport historians are virtually unanimous in their recognition that hockey's organizational roots, early written rules, and formally regulated codes of conduct first took hold in Montreal during the 1870s. Indeed, the first recorded indoor exhibition of ice hockey in Canada took place at Montreal's Victoria Skating Rink in March 1875. The game itself wasn't appreciably different from many of the outdoor stick and ball games being played across the country at the time, but the context and rationale for the game were unique and pointed to the many changes that were to follow.

For one thing, play on an indoor rink meant subordinating the open, wide-ranging nature of outdoor shinny, ricket, or field hockey on ice to the 200-by-85-foot boundaries of the Victoria Rink. More importantly, the game was a formally scheduled entertainment event organized to take place during the evening, when potential spectators were finished with the working day. Furthermore, certain features of play were modified as concessions to the requirements of spectators and to the limitations of the indoor ice surface. The substitution of a flat block of wood for the ball typically used in related outdoor games was particularly notable. The idea was to find something that would slide along the ice rather than rise up, bounce, and possibly injure spectators or break the windows of the rink.[12]

Coverage of the 1875 game in the *Montreal Gazette* described how a "very large audience gathered to witness a novel contest on the ice."

The *Gazette* went on to suggest: "That the game is like lacrosse in one sense — the block having to move through flags placed about 8 feet apart in the same manner as the rubber ball — but in the main the old country game of shinty gives the best idea of hockey."[13] The *Gazette*'s commentator, while acknowledging similarities to lacrosse and to the Scottish folk game of shinty, nonetheless chose to highlight the apparent novelty of the game. Of course, one game is by no means a sufficient basis upon which to make a claim that something new was emerging in Montreal, but we know that a number of attempts to publish and refine hockey's rules and to create formally organized clubs and associations all occurred in Montreal within a very short time after this first indoor exhibition.

There is fragmentary evidence beyond the *Gazette*'s description of the 1875 game to suggest that the models for hockey games played in Montreal in the late 1870s drew variously on a combination of rules and equipment from Haligonian shinny, rugby, and lacrosse. McGill students and members of the Montreal Football Club made up some of the earliest teams, and it was a former Haligonian and future McGill student, J.G.A. Creighton, who is widely regarded as the inspiration for the first indoor exhibition of this "novel" game. By 1877 there were at least three formally organized hockey clubs in Montreal, and a set of rules borrowed from English field hockey had been published in the *Montreal Gazette*. Within another couple of years these field-hockey rules had been modified further in an effort to standardize play in the city. The Montreal version of hockey borrowed heavily from rugby's traditions of physical contact, and it maintained the rugby tradition of being an "on-side" game with no forward passing. A tournament featuring the Montreal version of hockey became an important part of the first Montreal Winter Carnival in 1883 and offered competition between the best clubs in the area: McGill, the Victoria Hockey Club, and the Québec Hockey Club. The tournament provided a great deal of public exposure for the Montreal game, and as a result clubs adopting variations of the Montreal rules soon developed in Ottawa, Quebec City, Kingston, and Halifax.[14]

By the fall of 1886 interest in hockey on ice had reached the point where organizers of some of Montreal's prominent clubs accepted a proposal to hold a tournament to determine a formal championship for the city. The very idea of such a tournament prompted sportswriters at the *Gazette* to up the ante and call for a "Dominion Championship" to be played as well. The *Gazette* also called for the creation of a "Dominion Hockey Association" to develop hockey as a "national pastime" and to give it "a higher standard of excellence, both as a game and in the eyes of the public."[15] The sentiments expressed in the *Gazette* articulated a growing sense that the organized ice hockey that had developed in Montreal might well find a broader audience. Accordingly, in 1886 a number of Montreal clubs invited representatives from Ottawa and Quebec City to form the Amateur Hockey Association of Canada (AHAC). The resulting association largely adopted the newly established rules on team size, equipment, and modes of play used by Montreal's leading hockey clubs in the mid-1880s. This included seven-man teams, bully-style face-offs (as in lacrosse and rugby), the on-side rule, and the mandatory use of a puck that had to be "one inch thick and three inches in diameter, and of vulcanized rubber."[16]

The title "Amateur Hockey Association of Canada" was undoubtedly grandiose for what was essentially a local organization.[17] And there was considerable resistance in some communities to the perceived arrogance of a supposedly national association dominated by Montrealers — resistance that frustrated the AHAC from ever realizing its national ambitions. Nonetheless, the AHAC was the first formally constituted organization that set itself up with a view to defining the nature of hockey for a broad constituency, popularizing the new game, and regulating the state of play. By 1886, then, we have evidence of the early institutionalization of hockey in Canada. The first organization had been created with a mandate, in theory at least, to make *a* particular way of playing hockey into *the* way of playing.

Shifting Cultural Meanings, Uses, and Identities

Montreal's foundational role in the institutional development of hockey shouldn't be surprising. Montreal had long been the financial and trading centre of the Canadian colonies, and by the 1860s it had become an industrial centre as well. In addition the city's longstanding role in the development of communications in pre-Confederation Canada was strengthened with the opening of the Montreal Telegraph Company in 1847 and the establishment of a rail link with Toronto in 1856.[18] The market-driven urban society that developed in conjunction with these changes promoted a separation of work and leisure linked to the emerging routines of commerce and industrial production. It also featured the expansion of a local middle class of professionals and businessmen with the skills, resources, and inclination to create sporting recreations that organized leisure in new ways.

Hockey was only one part of this much broader organization of sporting recreations. The Montreal Curling Club, founded in 1807, was the first club to promote a form of organized sport in Canada.[19] In addition Montreal was the home of the first cricket and hunt clubs in the 1820s; of the first formal "demonstration" of lacrosse in 1834; of the first specialized sporting facilities in the 1840s and 1850s; of the first lacrosse club in 1856; and the first so-called "national" sporting association, the National Lacrosse Association (NLA), in 1867. The NLA was of particular importance for the later development of organized hockey because its constitution provided the model used later in the creation of the AHAC.

But more important than the simple fact of organization was the subtle way in which the cultural meanings and uses of sport in Montreal changed during the nineteenth century. The earliest clubs were constituted to provide social outings for the anglophone elite in the community rather than the opportunity to demonstrate physical skills in a competitive situation.[20] When more competitive game-contests were held in the years before the 1840s they tended to be limited to holidays and special occasions. Although many of these early game-contests brought together people from different classes, races, or ethnic groups — for example, whites and Indians, professionals and manual workers, British colonials and native-born Canadians — their cultural meanings were defined through the class, ethnic, gender, and racial prejudices of the time. This was evident, for example, in practices such as the awarding of trophies for "gentlemen" and the offer of cash prizes for everyone else.

By the late 1850s it is possible to detect the beginnings of a more achievement-driven emphasis to sport emerging within the city. A growing class of anglophone businessmen and professionals — with many of the members now native-born rather than transplanted from England — began to modify the older paternalistic traditions. The culture of business and professional life began to place a greater emphasis on organization, regulation, competition, and the values of self-improvement. Prominent businessmen and professionals would struggle to apply these values to create new forms of sporting recreation in the image of their own cultural ambitions. As this occurred, exhibitions and tournaments increasingly became organized in a more regular fashion, and there was a proliferation of clubs and organizations that recruited their members from more diverse segments of the Montreal community. The older anglophone elite gradually withdrew to ever more exclusive social clubs, and an approach to sport more geared to competitive achievement emerged within the dominant class.

It has been argued that the development of organized lacrosse in Montreal was the most important harbinger of an emergent Canadian sporting culture in the late nineteenth century.[21] There was a major influx of English, Scottish, and Irish immigrants to Canada between the 1820s and 1850s, and many of Canada's earliest sporting traditions were constituted at a time when British influences were at their strongest. It was more than just an array of popular sports that were imported from England, Scotland, or Ireland — sports like hurley, shinny, English field hockey, rugby, and cricket, as well as cockfighting, horse racing, and boxing. Also imported were the traditions and identities variously associated with the people who participated in these sports. In Canada these traditions and identities were mediated by a new social, cultural, and geographical context, but their influences remained a significant part of the collective memories of different groups. Particularly notable was the powerful British public-school sensibility that stressed the role of "manly games" as necessary training for the young gentlemen of an emergent gentry class.

The young native-born Canadian men responsible for organizing lacrosse in Montreal during the 1850s — and later, those who developed organized hockey in the 1870s and 1880s — adopted much of this British public-school sensibility. At the same time, while many of these men went on to the highest echelons of power and influence in Canadian society, they were certainly not members of any landed aristocracy or gentry class; rather, they were upward-striving businessmen and professionals committed to the values of individual achievement through commerce and public service. Moreover, in the years leading up to and immediately following Confederation, they were beginning to express a clear sense of their own Canadianness. For example, George Beers, a leading force in the organization of lacrosse, repeatedly drew attention to the differences between British and Canadian games and argued for the promotion of lacrosse rather than cricket.[22] Ironically, it was baseball, a U.S. game, that had pushed cricket to the cultural periphery in Canadian communities across the country by the 1870s. But hockey had no visible competitors and was well placed to become the winter game of choice for young anglophone professionals and businessmen with an emergent sense of national belonging.

The national culture imagined by many Canadian professionals and businessmen wasn't always consciously articulated. The economic and political self-interest that resulted in the formation of the new Canadian state was not accompanied initially by any significant impulse to imagine a distinctive national culture.[23] Indeed, for much of the late nineteenth and early twentieth centuries the desire to build national political structures and economic policies took precedence over the perceived need to define a distinctive national culture. Privileged English Canadians often viewed a national culture as something that would simply follow in the wake of the creation of a modern nation-state with a stable dominant class — a class whose intellectual leaders embraced the Victorian ideals of "culture" and self-improvement. The prevailing view was that culture was something that educated amateurs took on at their leisure, by choice and by training.[24] The versatility and civilized sensibilities of these educated elites would supposedly leave their stamp on the national culture as a whole.

This rather patrician view of culture co-existed with the idea that most Canadians were either unlikely to have the resources to choose self-improving practices in their leisure or simply weren't interested in them. A civilizing national culture might then require that educated elites use their resources to create institutions and cultural programs that were socially beneficial and morally uplifting. In the case of sport, this goal raised significant problems: many of the traditions of popular sporting recreations from the past seemed to be so uncultured, so uncivilized. Popular sporting traditions were part of a culture of entertainments centred upon gambling and the tavern and sometimes involving violent, and exceedingly cruel, activities — examples include blood sports like cockfighting or dogfighting. These popular entertainments dramatized older forms of public spectacle, and they typically aspired to little more than the provision of pleasures and opportunities for sociability and for winning money.

Many of these activities had been subjected to significant campaigns of regulation and reform from as early as the 1820s.[25] But the rationale for these campaigns shifted subtly throughout the nineteenth century. Much of the initial impulse to regulate drink and popular spectacle in the Canadian colonies stemmed from a combination of Methodist moral sentiment and Tory fears that public immorality would lead to political sedition. However, by the end of the nineteenth century the spirit of regulation was also being driven by a more widespread public anxiety about the perceived threats, uncertainties, and dislocations of a society developing a modern urban and industrial culture: social unrest, psychic disorders, disease, vice, and cultural decline. In this context the regulation of leisure and popular culture became heavily influenced by an evangelistic spirit of moral entrepreneurship.

Movements for moral reform had struggled to make recreation increasingly rational in most Western societies throughout much of the second half of the nineteenth century. In many instances this activity meant denying public legitimacy to popular sporting traditions and game-contests in favour of more socially improving "cultural" activities like literature, art, or music. Yet the old idea that sports promoted manliness continued to be attractive to a great many people, especially in a society where men in positions of power were increasingly involved in business and professional activities far removed from more traditional markers of masculine competence such as martial prowess, hunting ability, or physical strength. If sports could promote manliness in addition to good health, there seemed good reason to find ways of reclaiming them as socially useful activities.

The most obvious way to do this was to link the idea of play to conceptions of personal health and moral utility. Games were seen to be of questionable value if they were simply idle recreations or opportunities for (potentially vice-filled or politicized) social gatherings. However, if they could be properly organized, regulated, and controlled — made more "rational" — there might be a legitimate use for them as an arena for healthy activity and moral training. Games could then serve to introduce habits of discipline, hygiene, and self-improvement not only to young gentlemen, as suggested by the British schoolboy code, but also to every young man. In order for this to happen, modern games would have to be organized and promoted on a more universalistic basis than had the games of the past. Both Allen Guttmann and Melvin Adelman are clearly correct to suggest that the idea of a universalistic form of achievement-driven, healthy, and morally useful sport — ideally separate from politics and society — was a uniquely modern vision.

Modernization, Institutionalization, and Power
The rapid spread of this self-conscious cultural modernism in sport can easily lead to an overstatement of the extent of change that actually occurred in the nineteenth century. The early social development of modern forms of sport in North America was highly uneven. Older ways of playing and older meanings attached to sporting activity were not simply extinguished by the emergence of modern sports; rather, these older ways and meanings often remained as influential residues of a variety of social class, ethnic, and regional cultures. These residual cultural fragments usually existed in a precarious tension with the more institutionalized forms of sporting practice being promoted by professionals and businessmen in large cities, and they occasionally provided a basis for negotiating compromises in institutional rules and styles of play.

Differences in power played a major role in shaping the outcomes of these negotiations, but the role of power is frequently downplayed when people discuss the institutionalization of modern sport. Institutional development is often viewed as a response to a more abstract set of social "needs" or pressures. Melvin Adelman's discussion of the modernization of sport in New York provides an example of this. In addition to viewing New York as a setting and stimulant for modernization, Adelman also points to the importance of "the institutional needs" of various sports to establish their own order. By this he means that the modernization of sport was more than just a passive reaction to the broader modernization of society; rather, it was also a response to a set of unique internal requirements for growth, organization, and competition that varied from sport to sport and influenced the "degree to which modern sports structures evolved in each one."[26] He is certainly right to say that the various organizational structures, rules, and procedures in different sports are not *directly* explainable by such broad social determinants as the emergence of scientific rationality, industrialization, urbanization, or technology. But a problem arises whenever anyone uses language implying that the institutions that define modern sports are social things rather than analytical categories meant to direct our attention to sets of commonly accepted practices and processes that exist across generations. The institutions of modern sports can't have "needs" the way people can, and we should pay close attention to whose needs are really being identified when such claims are made. The implication that abstract institutional needs play a role in the process of modernizing any sport too easily confuses the needs and interests of specific groups of people — for example, the needs and interests of men, or of a particular social class — with those of sporting institutions as a whole.

It is only a short step from the reification implicit in such language to the self-serving arguments so often made by sports organizers and promoters about the "needs" of the sport, or the "good of the game." These arguments have a distinctive social origin. They only became possible with the institutionalization of self-consciously modern sports, because such sports required that players form an allegiance to an institutional authority (for instance, a sport governing body) beyond their individual interests or those of their teams. As part of the process of institutionalization, by the early twentieth century sports organizers began to argue that sport, like civilized society itself, involved an implicit social contract. The universal gains to be made through the institutionalization of self-consciously modern sports were thought to be so great that they overrode any one set of individual or community interests.

Yet these claims to universality conveniently ignored the inequalities in power that typically underlay early attempts to organize sports as "self-governing" cultural practices and institutions. The very definitions of what practices were "sporting," what sport should ideally mean, and how sport should be played and governed were rarely constructed democratically or by the mutual consent of the participants. Most often, these definitions were negotiated by a narrow circle of men from the dominant classes in the major economic and political centres of Western industrial societies in the late nineteenth century. More notably, these groups often struggled to articulate their own interests and values as if they were completely synonymous with universal interests and values.

The case of organized hockey in its earliest years in Canada illustrates this tendency clearly. By the early 1890s, hockey teams were being formed in cities and towns across the country, although they were not always playing by the same rules. In addition, new associations were being formed to organize and regulate the game. The Ontario Hockey Association (OHA), formed in 1890, included a number of teams in Eastern Ontario. West of Toronto the Southern Ontario Hockey Association "linked eight towns around Brantford, Hamilton, and Niagara Falls into two leagues."[27] By the mid-1890s most of the larger towns in Canada had developed intra-town and inter-city leagues.

One of Canada's leading sport historians, Alan Metcalfe, has argued that the sponsors and organizers of these associations, teams, and leagues were the "privileged segments" of Canadian communities: "amateur athletic associations, universities, garrisons, banks, collegiate institutes, and in Winnipeg, several mercantile firms."[28] This is not to say that less privileged groups didn't form teams from time to time or play occasional challenge matches of hockey-like games. On the contrary, organized club and league play only encompassed a small portion of the teams playing hockey-like games in Canadian communities. Among the examples Metcalfe cites in this regard are a team of plumber's helpers in Ottawa; two teams of workers from Canadian General Electric in Peterborough; and two teams that played for the "Coloured Championship of Halifax and Dartmouth."[29] However, only the championships of the highly organized hockey teams were recognized, and it was these teams that lasted. Likewise, only the members of the middle-class hockey associations in the major cities had the resources, time, and managerial skills — as well as the inclination to promote and defend a particular way of playing — to define the rules of play and the game's dominant cultural meanings.

The fate of "Halifax rules" in hockey reveals how differences in social resources and opportunities influenced the institutional development of the game. During the 1880s, the hockey being played in Halifax had developed out of the earlier tradition of ricket played in the area. Ricket was a fast-paced, wide-open game, similar to lacrosse in its emphasis on forward passing. By contrast, the Montreal rules governing play in Quebec, and promoted by the AHAC, only allowed the puck to be advanced by stickhandling. The Montreal game was slower, more deliberate, and more physical. The two styles of hockey developed somewhat independently until teams from Dartmouth and Halifax ventured out to play Montreal teams in the late 1880s.[30] In the wake of this contact, hockey in the Halifax area eventually adopted rules inclined towards the AHAC game. The AHAC rules already existed in written form whereas the Halifax game had no published regulations. Furthermore, sponsoring athletic associations were stronger and better established in Montreal. The executive members there had greater resources at their disposal and were better positioned geographically to promote their game over any others.

The waning of the Halifax rules had little to do, then, with the appeal of the game on the ice, let alone any internal institutional need for a standardized way of playing or a universal authority. Nor can we look to such abstract imperatives to explain the complex culture of moral entrepreneurship that would shape the institutional foundations of hockey from the 1880s to the early twentieth century. In this case the preference was not for any one set of technical rules over any other; rather it was for the underlying moral rules that would constitute the game as a civilizing cultural practice.[31] A key aspect of the institutionalization of hockey in the late nineteenth century was the struggle to win universal consent for a set of moral rules that originated in a specifically male and privileged understanding of the meaning and possibilities of sport.

A vision of amateurism based on imported traditions of the British public-school code quickly became the touchstone of middle-class moral entrepreneurship throughout Canadian sport in the late nineteenth century. From the outset, however, this vision of amateurism contained a notable tension between social discrimination and the ideal of class conciliation, between the narrow defence of class exclusivity and the urge to universally promote healthy and morally utilitarian games. It was often said that amateur sport promised to bring people from different social classes and racial and ethnic groups together to share in healthy and manly competition. But this sharing was only to occur on terms set by the business and professional classes. Moreover, in their earliest and most reactionary stage of development these terms specified not only that certain types of behaviours were ungentlemanly and uncivilized, but that some people, by definition, were incapable of engaging in sport as a higher form of culture at all. Thus, in 1873 the Montreal Pedestrian Club defined an amateur as:"One who has never competed in any open competition or for public money, or for admission money, or with professionals for a prize, public money or admission money, nor has ever, at any period of his life taught or assisted in the pursuit of Athletic exercises as a means of livelihood, or is a laborer or an Indian."[32] The explicit exclusion of labourers and Indians from this definition of amateurism was not simply a result of their perceived inferiority. It also derived from the often superior skill of aboriginal and, to a lesser extent, working-class athletes, in lacrosse, snowshoe racing, and foot races.[33]

The skills of these athletes had increasingly become a problem as a result of the changes and stresses of the time. The 1870s were an important period of transition in Canadian economic and cultural life. National political structures were still new and future policy directions unclear. In addition, the Canadian and U.S. societies were both engaged in struggles to subjugate their aboriginal populations and experiencing hard times economically. The severe recession that characterized much of the 1870s hit home at the very moment that the dominant classes in both countries were working to consolidate the broad-scale industrial reorganization of work. All of this opened up new forms of political unrest, racial insecurity, cultural uncertainty, and labour militancy. Working-class organizations grew throughout the 1870s and pressed their demands for increased wages, reduction of work hours, and improved work conditions.[34] In this context of uncertainty and increased working-class militancy, older traditions of class paternalism were under attack, sometimes violently. As a result the privileged position of the dominant classes in Canada seemed less secure than in the immediate past, and not surprisingly some members of the dominant class became less receptive to the idea of losing in sports to people they defined as their social inferiors.[35] In keeping with this view, the earliest expressions of amateurism in Canada paradoxically combined racism and an overt defence of class exclusivity with the developing ethos of rational organization, moral utility, and universality.

Later definitions of amateurism in the 1880s retained the central argument that playing for money was morally problematic. Gradually, however, more universalistic moral ambitions in sport began to rival racist and overtly class-prejudiced definitions of amateurism. Indeed, many Canadians were simply uncomfortable with an older British model of amateurism that saw civilizing sport as something only for leisured "gentlemen." Metcalfe, for instance, cites a correspondent for the Montreal Lacrosse Club in 1878 who argued, "As Canadians, it does seem peculiar that the honest young mechanic who spends his leisure time in healthy recreation, should be classed as a professional and excluded from amateur competition."[36] Not wanting to convey the wrong idea, Metcalfe goes on to emphasize that the "honest" working man referred to in this endorsement was someone who accepted the values of the dominant classes — someone who, while not a gentleman by pedigree, had at least learned to act like one. In 1884 an Amateur Athletic Association of Canada (AAAC) was formed, largely to regulate the issue of amateurism, and by the 1890s the AAAC had become an evangelist for the "encouragement of exercise" and the "advancement and improvement of athletic sports among amateurs."[37] During this time organized hockey, particularly the OHA, enshrined amateurism as a hallowed principle. Anyone wanting to play in sanctioned competition was expected to toe the ideological line.

Many people still weren't even in the game. For example, organized amateur sport in Canada simply wasn't created with women in mind, and the obsession with manliness that underpinned the culture of gentlemanly amateurism effectively kept women, and especially working-class women, on the sidelines. Nonetheless, by the turn of the century the values of rational recreation and moral entrepreneurship were being gradually extended to include sports for women. In the "Gay Nineties" there was a growing concern about women's perceived inactivity as well as a general phobia about the unfettering of women's sexuality. Canadian moral entrepreneurs began a campaign to produce physically healthy and morally strong mothers of the next generation. If sporting discipline was "a means of refrigerating the passions and creating spartan habits" among boys, it could surely be valuable for girls too.[38] That meant promoting exercise and discipline for girls and women, but only in a way compatible with prevailing conceptions of femininity and "proper" levels of physical effort.

There is evidence that women began to play hockey in substantial numbers in the 1890s. For example, in Ottawa, Isobel Stanley, the daughter of the Governor General, reportedly played for a Government House team in a victory over Rideau Ladies Hockey Team.[39] There are many press reports of women's games throughout Ontario and Quebec during the 1890s. Quebec, in particular, was home to a number of strong women's clubs after the turn of the century. Yet, based on scanty evidence, it appears that most women's teams in the period of 1890 to 1910 remained informal. They were socially, rather than competitively, oriented. Women's teams received little organizational support, and while some spectators were drawn to the novelty of women playing a competitive physical game, women's involvement in the kind of hockey played by men was largely frowned upon and discouraged. Moreover, women were simply absent from the administration of the major hockey clubs and amateur organizations of the time. From the outset, organized hockey developed as a male preserve.

Sport, Modernity, and Cultural Struggle

It is difficult to imagine the class or gender relations in Canadian sport at the end of the nineteenth century as an evolutionary adaptation to broader social changes. This raises an additional limitation of most theories of the modernization of sport. To an extent, an evolutionary tone is implicit in the very use of the word "modern." That is why some sport historians try to avoid the word in favour of the seemingly less value-laden term "organized sport."[40]

Yet the problem of evolutionary thinking doesn't necessarily lie with the concept of modernity itself; rather, it lies with the tendency for many theories of modernization to imply that modernity is a more developed, or higher, form of social and cultural life. The most highly rationalized sports tend to be viewed as the most historically and culturally mature forms of sporting expression. These are also sports, not coincidentally, that are found in the most highly rationalized and technologically developed societies. For this reason the idea of modernization can be easily confused with westernization, complete with an implicit contrast between the "developed" or "mature" sports of the West and the premodern folk sports and traditional recreations found in the "undeveloped" societies of the Third World.

It is by no means necessary to understand the link between sport and modernity in such an implicitly positive way. On the contrary, critics of Western mass culture have often been less than enthusiastic about modernity. The emergence of mass spectator sport in the late nineteenth and early twentieth centuries has often been viewed as a symptom of cultural decline, even barbarism. By contrast, generally positive evaluations of modernity tend to be deeply sedimented in the very categories and ways of thinking employed by many of the writers whose theories we've discussed so far. These categories and ways of thinking have themselves been influenced by a cluster of ideas and assumptions in Western social thought that the British sociologist Anthony Giddens refers to as the "theory of industrial society."[41]

Throughout the late eighteenth and nineteenth centuries a growing number of writers suggested how technical know-how, linked to new forms of secular rationality, individualism, and the values of technology, were decisive factors in the formation of the modern industrial world. The emergence of a rational, achievement-driven industrial society was thus inextricably linked to the very idea of modernity. But, even more importantly, it was generally argued that this transition was socially progressive. According to these thinkers, modern industrial society undoubtedly had its growing pains and problems, but it was preferable to the society of ignorance, inequality, and poverty that preceded it. Selected aspects of the theory of industrial society thus became an important element of the liberal intellectual tradition in Western life. That tradition provided a consistent alternative to reactionary views on culture and society — views that defended class privilege and a simpler, less technologically driven way of life as the benchmarks of "culture" and civilization.

It is also important to remember that urban industrial (and even postindustrial) societies in the West are also likely to be *capitalist* societies. The organization and culture of capitalist production have been every bit as important to defining the tenor and tone of life in these societies as the urban industrial character of their productive systems. Industrialism and capitalism in the West emerged together in the nineteenth century, and the best modernization theorists have not been blind to the importance of economic imperatives in the making of modern sport. Nonetheless, in discussions of the making of modern sport there has been a significant tendency to underplay the distinctive contribution of capitalist social relations and processes, such as the necessity for economic growth, the division of classes into buyers and sellers of human labour power, and the centrality of the value of exchange in commodity production. In addition, not enough attention has been paid to the many *irrational* tendencies associated with the emergence of industrial capitalism: for instance, the normalization of unemployment, the constant pressures to revolutionize production, and the fluctuations of the business cycle.

By contrast, we argue that the very meaning of modernity in Western societies has been indistinguishable from a vision of human possibilities intimately connected to the expansion and successes of Western capitalism. This is a vision of possibilities caught up in the perceived necessity of constant growth and a continual revolutionizing of economic production and cultural practice. To begin to think of oneself as modern in nineteenth-century Europe or North America meant coming to terms with a world in which the market was developing an unprecedented cultural prominence. The radical expansion of market freedoms in the nineteenth century, the growing pressures of market competition, and the emerging idea that self-development could be achieved through economic development all contributed to a bourgeois world where everything was in flux — a world in which constant innovation, uncertainty, and agitation were becoming the norm.[42]

At one level, the impulse to organize human life "rationally" in such circumstances was simply linked to desires for competitive advantage in the marketplace and for more efficient systems of political organization. But more broadly, that impulse was also linked to a desire to control contingencies, to regulate uncertainty, and to create a degree of stability in an uncertain modern world. The problem was that attempts to employ human reason creatively to regulate nature, social, or cultural life involved a necessary destruction of traditional forms of life — and this was as terrifying and destabilizing as it was comforting. An inherent tension between the quest for control, stability, and permanence on the one hand and the unstable and contingent nature of life on the other became a central feature in a uniquely contradictory culture of capitalist modernity. The modernization of sport in Western societies — including the making of modern hockey in Canada — cannot be understood adequately without reference to this contradictory capitalist culture.

Here we will note only one key set of distinctively capitalist tendencies and struggles that tends to be downplayed in conventional explanations of the modernization of sport: the struggle over labour discipline in the making of the new industrial order. Throughout the second half of the nineteenth century, growing industrialization in Canada's fast-changing capitalist economy meant subjecting workers to new forms of work organization in the factory and the office, to the technical requirements of machinery, and to the competitive pressures of a system geared to extracting maximum productivity from human labour power. Wage work in the nineteenth century increasingly became a matter of routine and repetition, inflexible in its use of time and space. People had to come to work at specified times, work specified hours, and stay in specified places in order to accomplish their designated tasks in workshops and factories. All of this required powerful new forms of work discipline and surveillance so that owners could get maximum returns on their investments in labour. These forms of labour discipline weren't simply limited to the workplace itself. Sociologists and labour historians have noted how the implementation of rational work discipline in capitalist societies could only be developed "in conjunction with an equally rational leisure discipline: the traditional patterns of release and riot had to be subordinated to the timed needs of the industrial labour process. By the end of the century leisure was no longer an occasional event (a fair or carnival or harvest festival), but the routine experience of non-work."[43]

The developing culture of rational recreation and moral entrepreneurship in nineteenth-century Canada was significantly shaped, then, by growing demands for a workforce whose leisure posed no threat to the orderly workings of commerce, factories, and mills. With the eventual filling in of the frontier and the expansion of cities as specialized sites for commerce and industrial production, the growing concern over irrational leisure linked a fear of moral disorder with economic and political expediency. The drinking, merrymaking, and sometimes disorderly recreations popular among the emergent urban working class came to be seen as activities that disrupted the daily routine of business by encouraging absenteeism, debt, and insubordination. As a result, governments made play in the streets illegal, heavily regulated tavern locations and hours, and controlled alcohol consumption at public events. They banned certain types of sporting activity likely to encourage "irrational" violence, such as cockfighting, and promoted more rational forms of recreation in their stead.

Still, despite these pressures to institutionalize new forms of labour and leisure discipline, a popular culture of commercial entertainments flourished in many Canadian cities throughout the late nineteenth century. In Montreal, for example, the daily recreational activities of working-class men were often centred in locations like Joe Beef's Canteen, a well-known waterfront warehouse tavern whose entertainments included minstrels, newspaper readings, performing bears, and a menagerie of monkeys, parrots, and, on occasion, wild cats. Because most wage workers put in a six-day work week, their only day clear for recreation was Sunday, when sporting activities and drinking were officially prohibited. Yet Montreal developed a thriving illegal Sunday entertainment industry, which catered primarily to working-class men.[44] By contrast, middle-class Montrealers were far more likely to participate in more self-consciously rational forms of recreation, such as amateur sports. However, even the middle classes were significant consumers of commercially supplied recreation from the time of Confederation to the end of the nineteenth century. And by the early twentieth century the perceived rationality of recreation in Canada was becoming increasingly defined for all Canadians through the purchase and consumption of commodities. It was only in the context of an emerging capitalist consumer culture that professional hockey developed enough popularity and legitimacy to challenge the hold of amateurism over the emerging culture and institutional structures of the modern game.

Conventional histories of sport often give the impression that the sporting remnants of traditional life have been voluntarily abandoned for better, more rational ways of doing things. Or else they imply that traditional sporting practices simply fell into disuse from neglect and lack of interest as urbanization, industrialization, new technologies, and values opened up the possibilities for more modern initiatives. Yet this impression obscures two factors: a great many traditional sporting practices were actively pushed to the cultural periphery; and the differing powers of individuals and groups were key to this push. The British cultural theorist Stuart Hall makes this point clearly with reference to the study of cultural change as a whole: "'Cultural change' is a polite euphemism for the process by which some cultural forms and practices are driven out of the centre of popular life, actively marginalized. Rather than simply 'falling into disuse' through the Long March to modernisation, things are actively pushed aside, so that something else can take their place."[45]

We take our cue from Hall's argument. The history of sport is better understood as a history of cultural negotiation, compromise, and struggle rather than as a "long march to modernization" — a quasi-evolutionary movement between the sport played in "traditional" and "modern" times and societies. It is a history in which some practices, like the Halifax rules in hockey or much of the simple hedonism and communal character of an older popular culture, have been driven out of the centre of popular life so that something else can take their place. Undoubtedly, such struggles have often been, and continue to be, partly about "tradition" versus differing conceptions of "modernity." But these struggles have also always been about power and privilege; about whose values count and whose do not; about who gains advantage from certain changes in technology, values, or patterns of social organization, and who is disadvantaged. What was at stake in nineteenth-century struggles around the emerging institutional world of modern sport in Canada was nothing less than the capacity to define the dominant meaning of sporting practice, the scope of socially acceptable forms and ways of playing, and the legitimate uses of time and the human body.

Chapter Three

The Making of
Early Professional Hockey

During the mid-1890s organized hockey was still largely focused in eastern Canada, particularly in the larger towns and cities, but within a decade the sport had spread across the country. Most Canadian communities contained at least one commercially operated ice arena where games were played throughout the winter months. Moreover, the increase in new teams and leagues was breathtaking in its pace and scope. By 1905, according to Alan Metcalfe, there were "bank leagues in Saint John, Winnipeg, Ottawa, and Toronto, and leagues involving manufacturing, mercantile, and hardware companies in Ottawa, Winnipeg, Toronto, and Montreal."[1] There were also growing numbers of inter-school leagues, leagues featuring age divisions, and teams sponsored by ethnic societies, churches, and other religious organizations.

Even more notable than the numbers and geographic distribution of new teams, divisions, and leagues was the degree to which the game continued to be heavily influenced by anglophone businessmen and professionals who championed the values of moral propriety and self-improvement. By the turn of the century a clear distinction between the rational use of leisure time and seemingly irrational amusement had become fully institutionalized in Canada. Rational recreation was promoted in amateur sports organizations, schools, municipal parks, and libraries. Irrational leisure — typically associated with drinking, gambling, and "rough" sport — was patrolled by the police. Amateur hockey was championed as a form of rational recreation, and its emerging rules and organizational structures were largely in the grip of the moral entrepreneurs. Yet by the end of the first decade of the twentieth century the early structures and culture of hockey had begun to change. Increasingly it became the economic rather than the moral entrepreneurs who most effectively defined the nature, uses, and meanings of the game. As a result, the hockey that most Canadians came to see as their own throughout much of the twentieth century was strikingly different than the hockey that had developed initially as part of Canada's emergent culture of modernity.

Why did this happen? Why were the moral entrepreneurs who were committed to hockey as a purely amateur game unable to maintain control? What factors allowed professional hockey to develop first as a powerful rival to the amateur game and then as something that eclipsed it? To answer these questions we need to examine the inherent contradictions of anticommercial moral entrepreneurship in a society increasingly dominated by the marketplace, new forms of social differentiation, and the values of an emerging consumer culture.

Commercialism and Contradiction in Nineteenth-Century Sport and Leisure

The pleasures of sporting recreations in nineteenth-century Canada included the simple enjoyment of play, the thrill of physical mastery, the warmth of sociability, and the sense of well-being brought about by healthy exercise. But sporting pleasures were also expressed through the excitement, uncertainties, and symbolic identifications associated with spectacle. Any sporting competition that ended with a clear-cut winner and loser, whether human or animal, provided opportunities for spectators to participate vicariously in the drama of competitive struggle. People could invest their emotions in the contest to a point where they could worry about the threat of loss and anticipate the joys of victory. A high level of emotional investment in the contest provided a subtle dimension of risk, as spectators could, quite literally, gamble with their feelings. A financial wager on the outcome elevated the risk and the excitement to an even higher level.

So it is hardly surprising that the sporting wager was a key element in the expanding world of popular Canadian recreations well before Confederation. By the 1870s gambling had injected a significant element of commerce to activities as diverse as horse and foot races, quoits, cockfights, bare-knuckle boxing, handball, baseball, rowing, bicycling, and billiards. Money also figured prominently in nineteenth-century sports and games through formal stakes offered by patrons and sponsors to the victors of specific contests and through roughly calculated gate receipts. Horse racing was one of the earliest Canadian sports to charge spectators at the gate, and sometimes the stakes were extraordinarily high. Although the stakes were typically smaller, there were even more instances of challenges in quoits and billiards, cockfights, boxing, rowing, bicycle racing, and foot racing. A great deal of this gaming behaviour was sponsored by tavern owners wanting to promote activities geared towards entertaining a largely male clientele. The links between money, alcohol, male culture, sports, and the tavern were formed very early in Canada's sporting history.

In the second half of the nineteenth century money became indispensable for virtually every kind of sporting pastime, from casual recreation to commercially oriented spectacle. The central reason for this development lay in the dynamics of market exchange, which were changing life across the country. Land, for example, had become drawn more fully into the realm of monetary exchange in Canada throughout the nineteenth century, changing from something controlled by the Crown, the church, and a small landed elite to a more widely available commodity. The resulting commodification of urban space, and the beginning of inflation in land values, immediately began to exert powerful pressures on recreational land use. Sporting facilities in mid-to-late nineteenth-century Montreal were often initially constructed by affluent groups for their own exclusive use; Montreal's Victoria Skating Rink was an example of just such a facility. However, increased taxes, operating costs, and competing pressures on space forced some sporting clubs "to abandon their grounds to developers while others were forced to look for ways of generating income to meet rising costs."[2] Charging the public for the use of facilities, taking money at the gate for demonstrations and challenge matches, or renting facilities to other clubs or groups became a matter of economic necessity. For that reason, even the most devoutly amateur sports clubs were pressured into considering the bottom line in addition to moral propriety.

A second dynamic of the marketplace that influenced the commercial character of nineteenth-century sport lay in new pressures on work, leisure, and family life — pressures that arose both as a result of the growing commodification of human labour power in Canada after the 1840s and the increased demand for consumer goods of various types. A more competitive commercial and industrial system induced employers to determine the monetary value of human labour power more precisely than ever before. The system also required a labour force of wage workers located in close proximity to the factory, the workshop, and the office. As the Canadian economy became more diversified beyond resource extraction and agriculture, urban growth was fuelled by the demand for this kind of workforce. In turn, a growing urban population of wage earners created new markets for products and services that had hitherto been provided in non-market form through more traditional family and community relations. For example, tools, home furnishings, or clothing that had once been produced in the home, or bartered for, became mass produced and could be purchased with a portion of a worker's wages or a farmer's income. It was only a matter of time before a similar process would occur in the areas of leisure and entertainment.

By the 1870s many traditional forms of popular entertainment once centred in the home or local community — for example, dancing and song as well as games and sports — were becoming more widely available as commercial entertainment commodities. The clear delineation of work and leisure created a situation in which large groups of people were available for the consumption of entertainment at regular and predictable times. The emergence of wage labour and mass production thus created the conditions necessary for the development of mass audiences; these audiences in turn began to take on an exchange value of their own. Audience attention also became something that could be marketed to advertisers through the growing world of newspapers, specialist magazines, and trade publications. The 1890s were the forward edge of a new age of consumer advertising in Canada. A new style of advertising tended to emphasize product performance over product character, thereby stimulating the desire to consume rather than merely informing the public about what wares were available and how much they cost.[3] This self-conscious promotion of consumption flew in the face of established middle-class and Protestant values of thrift and self-restraint.

The increasing transformation of more and more areas of human experience into relationships governed by economic exchange was one of the most striking features of Canadian life after the mid-nineteenth century. As a result the moral regulation of leisure was awash in contradictions. The first problem for moral entrepreneurs was that the very idea of rational or civilizing leisure was an apparent paradox.

Almost by definition, the popular understanding of leisure was that it was something done after, and indeed in contrast to, work, duty, and routine. Most people understood leisure as the setting for deeply personal experiences of sociability and pleasure and as a sphere of their lives where they could indulge personal whims and choices. The challenge for the dominant class and its middle-class allies was how to encourage habits of discipline and self-improvement in leisure while still acknowledging popular rights to the "free" use of leisure time.[4]

This challenge turned on a key tension that lay at the core of the relations between work, leisure, and culture in late nineteenth-century Canada. Religious, cultural, and business leaders were committed on the one hand to the control of leisure and yet, on the other, to a grudging acceptance of the ideological importance of free time as a reward for work and membership in a liberal and democratic society. The attempted resolution of this tension was manifest in the dual process of banning or regulating activities deemed to be irrational, immoral, and uncivilized while promoting more suitable, and more rational, forms of recreation. In English Canada people were supposed to learn that pleasure was something that always had to be balanced against the higher earnestness of the Protestant work ethic. For French-speaking Canadians, pleasure was something to be mediated through the institutions and rituals of the Catholic Church. However, it was the Protestant vision that most infused the early institutional development of Canadian sport. In English Canada the hope was that if given the opportunity through schools, religious organizations, parks, libraries, and amateur sports teams, Canadians would voluntarily choose "improving activities" over "wasteful hedonism." Yet, the moment the ideal of truly "free" time was accepted, the possibility existed that people might stubbornly elect to use that time in wasteful or irrational ways, no matter how hard civic and religious leaders worked to prevent it. In that case, all one could hope for was to regulate wasteful or irrational leisure activities and restrict their spread to specified areas.

By the 1880s the pace of the commodification of culture in Canada, and conflicting views about the nature of popular rights, provided additional complications to these tensions. If the majority of business owners and managers sought to extend the working day, and defined workers' needs only as simple physical survival, there were nonetheless some who believed that happy workers were more efficient; and these bosses were prepared to offer tacit support for workers' attempts to carve out more leisure from the work week. With this came the growing realization that workers were consumers too, that they provided a valuable market for new entertainment commodities. These commodities were sold with little reference to the concerns of moral entrepreneurs. For every moral entrepreneur selling rational recreation in Canada in the late nineteenth century there was also an economic entrepreneur ready to market anything that was potentially profitable — drink, sex, or spectacle — whatever its alleged effects on morality. The competitive drive for profit that lay at the core of Canada's burgeoning capitalist economy was becoming more *dependent* upon the stimulation of collective needs and capacities to consume. Ironically, many Canadian businesses began to have a vested interest in cultivating excess and intemperance, in feeding imaginary appetites to the point where ideas about what constituted individual needs became more fuelled by consumptive fantasies.[5]

Attendant to this, more and more leisure choices, opportunities, forms of personal satisfaction, and identity also began to depend on the market. Market transactions have acted as a concentrated field of personal satisfaction in Western societies since at least the sixteenth century.[6] However, in the nineteenth century — when the Western market system combined with industrialization, technological innovation, and wage labour — the goods and consumption styles made available by mass production began to exercise a new kind of authority. In English Canada in particular, the new forms of wage labour and industrial work put additional pressures on older patterns of family and community life with their tradition-bound forms of satisfaction and identity and their accompanying spaces, times, and opportunities for leisure. As these older patterns of family and community life became reconfigured, there was a parallel weakening of the distinctive and relatively stable forms of satisfaction and identity created by traditional cultures. In this context, the marketplace itself began to "assume the tasks of instructing individuals how to match their needs and wants with the available stock of consumption styles."[7]

This general tendency had considerable significance for the popularization of commercial recreations in late nineteenth- and early twentieth-century Canada. Immigrants who had left their home countries behind, or people who had moved to the city from the countryside in search of work, often struggled to retain their traditional forms of personal identification and community. Others sought to build ties to new communities and to develop new sources of satisfaction. Both objectives could be achieved by participating in voluntary associations such as hobby clubs, workingmen's associations, religious and ethnic societies, sports teams, and arts and civic organizations. However, increasingly — and especially for people whose work or life circumstances made formal voluntary participation difficult — satisfaction and identity

became something to be pursued through the consumption of commercial goods. In a world of strangers the consumer marketplace became
a powerful new common denominator. Not only did it provide a common source of consumer durables for private consumption and self-
expression, but it also created new opportunities for public consumption
and the expression of collective identity through shared patronage of
commercial entertainment. A sense of community identification with
particular teams or entertainers could suddenly be purchased with a
portion of one's wages. This possibility further strengthened the appeal
of commercial entertainments, and it increased the likelihood that
sporting competitions would soon become even more widely available
leisure commodities.

In addition, the emergence and popularization of new sports, and
the push to standardize all forms of "modern" sporting competition,
created an unprecedented demand for mass-produced sporting equipment. Research by the U.S. sport historian Stephen Hardy suggests
that in the United States a network of manufacturers, distributors, and
retailers of baseball equipment had meshed as early as the 1860s. At
this early stage the production of sporting equipment initially operated at little more than an artisan level of trade. By the 1880s more
entrepreneurs had begun to realize the scale of the market emerging
for sporting goods in North America, and the result was the emergence
of "a mass of capitalists on the make" in the sporting goods field.[8]

Two fundamental concerns drove this mass of capitalists on the
make. The first was the problem of securing a significant market share
in a fledgling industry that was highly competitive. As part of the struggle for brand recognition, manufacturers often published guidebooks
to the rules of various sports in the hope of creating customers.
Manufacturers also sought to promote brand recognition by negotiating rights to supply major sporting associations, leagues, and top clubs
with "official" equipment. For example, Stephen Hardy writes that
when the U.S. sporting goods firm Peck & Snyder introduced its new
tennis ball in 1886: "The firm happily announced that it had been
'adopted by the United States National Lawn Tennis Association and
by the Intercollegiate Association, as the Regulation Ball to be used in
all match games.' There was a similar message on lacrosse balls; since
there was no American governing body in lacrosse, however, it could
only state that Peck & Snyder published the rules of the Montreal
Lacrosse Club and that this ball had been 'adopted by all the leading
clubs.'"[9] Hardy notes that the influential Spalding Sporting Goods
Company pursued such sanctions "seemingly from every sporting club
in existence." Spalding even went so far as to sponsor whole leagues

in various sports in selected markets throughout North America. In hockey, for example, Spalding set up its own leagues in Montreal before the First World War with a view to carving out a premier role in the growing Canadian market for hockey sticks, skates, and protective equipment.[10]

The second concern that drove entrepreneurs in the sporting goods business was the problem of stimulating demand. Sporting goods manufacturers and retailers had a vested interest in avoiding any differentiation between commercial and amateur sports. Their goal was the promotion of sport as a whole. Retailers, especially, became instructors not only of sporting technique but also of the apparent benefits of healthy exercise and sporting competition. To do this they appropriated the language of moral entrepreneurship in very general terms. As one U.S. sporting goods dealer wrote in the early twentieth century, "If you don't do something to encourage sports, the nickelodeons are going to win hands down."[11] The point was to make the public case that any one of the increasingly popular organized sports — whether commercial or amateur — was preferable to less healthy and less rational forms of leisure.

The twin ideas of a unified world of sport and the universal values of healthy athleticism soon found their way into the broader iconography of early twentieth-century advertising in both the United States and Canada. The celebration of youthful male exuberance, health, and athleticism became increasingly evident in advertising codes that equated athleticized bodily imagery and the expenditure of energy through sport with happiness and success in a modern market-driven society. The popularization of this imagery correlated with a growing revulsion in American and Canadian popular culture towards body odour, stained teeth, bad breath, and other alleged manifestations of ill health. Such views, typically created by affluent male advertising executives, were a harbinger of the impact that upward-striving middle-class values would have over the emerging culture of consumption.[12]

Early twentieth-century advertising was just beginning to exploit desires to "fit in" that had become palpable in a more mobile, more individualistic, and rapidly changing modern industrial society. For both men and women, bodily propriety emerged as one of the key dimensions of appropriate conformity. Longstanding middle-class concerns about the importance of health and self-improvement became connected to a deepening anxiety about appearance and status. This connection promoted widespread uneasiness about the body in its natural state, thereby creating markets for a legion of health, beauty, fitness, and self-improvement products. Advertisers promised popularity and success, but only if the purchasers mediated the natural body with the right consumer choices. Young men, in particular, were instructed that commodities pertaining to sport and exercise were particularly appropriate consumer choices. Whether the items consumed pertained to amateur or professional sports became increasingly irrelevant.

Popular Culture and Early Canadian Professional Sport

Like the sporting goods industry, the beginning of organized professional sport in Canada emerged in response to a recognition of potential markets. Professional sport first took hold in Canada when businessmen came to believe that they could make money by staging challenge contests of various types on tours aimed at the larger urban areas. By the 1870s a number of semi-professional athletes had begun to tour "the various picnics, fairs and Caledonian Games held annually in central Canada."[13] Indeed, in the two decades following Confederation runners, walkers, bicyclists, and rowers all staged frequent competitions of various types for cash prizes. In the smaller centres these competitions often amounted to little more than an itinerant semi-professional arriving in an area with a view to challenging a local athlete. But in the larger centres the competition quickly became more systematic. Notably, Toronto and Montreal soon became regular stops on a developing North American circuit for touring male and female professionals in a variety of individual sports.

Circuit professionalism lent itself to the formation of whole groups of travelling athletes who competed among themselves from city to city. It also established the foundation for an additional network of entrepreneurs, facility owners, and promoters in Montreal, Toronto, and major cities in the northern and eastern United States. Hockey was drawn into this network almost immediately because of the commercial character of so many of the ice rinks upon which the game depended. For example, by 1880 there were nine commercial rinks in Montreal, and the number of rinks increased significantly in the ensuing years before reaching a high point in the early 1890s.[14] At many of the rinks, as Alan Metcalfe points out, "Bands were in nightly attendance, carnivals and masquerades were held, and skating races were run to attract participants and spectators. The rivalry between the proprietors was fierce, with several owners resorting to unethical methods to increase their share of the profits. On several occasions the ice was hacked to pieces during the night."[15]

The covered Crystal Rink, operated by Samuel Robertson, was one of the most successful of these business enterprises. From the summer of 1879 the rink was used for a wide variety of amateur and professional sports and commercial entertainments, including masquerades, dances, social skating, professional "go-as-you please" races, hockey, and boxing. Robertson was a key figure in the attempt to organize an official series of games to determine the "Hockey Championship of Montreal" in 1886, and the Crystal Rink became home to one of the founding teams in the Amateur Hockey Association of Canada.[16] The rink's atmosphere was a long way from manifesting the genteel culture typically associated with the idea of amateur sport. For example, a boxing exhibition in September 1879 ended in riot "when the crowd broke into the ring and fought until the ring collapsed."[17] Robertson was apparently more interested in making money than in selling moral propriety and the virtues of self-improvement.

Robertson's concern for profit was typical of the entrepreneurs who became part of the growing Canadian-U.S. network of promoters, sponsors, facility owners, and sporting goods salesmen in the late nineteenth century. The cross-border character of this network had considerable significance. To a great extent, the culture of moral entrepreneurship adopted by dominant groups in Canada took much of its character from British ideals and models that could be adapted to the Canadian context. The upward-striving professionals, clerks, and businessmen most responsible for the early institutional development of sport in Canada may have been conscious of their Canadian identities, but they tended to value British culture as an exemplary model of disciplined creativity, civility, and propriety. By contrast there were aspects of American culture that were seen to be considerably less than admirable. One might well do business with Americans, even compete against them in the friendly spirit of manly games, but that did not necessarily mean accepting the libertarian sensibilities, unrestrained individualism, and commercialism that seemed to define so much of American culture.

Yet, from as early as the 1840s many Canadians often found a welcome alternative in American popular culture to the didactic tendencies and strait-laced morality that dominated anglo-Canadian institutional and cultural life. According to Paul Rutherford, the absence of an indigenous tradition of popular literature in early nineteenth-century Canada led to "a parasitical dependence upon the dreams, the romances, the adventures, the tragedies, the plays, the epics, all the stuff of fancy and fantasy manufactured by outsiders."[18] Imported British publications undoubtedly defined many of these dreams and fantasies, but American books and periodicals — and American images, stories, and fantasies — were also readily available and competing successfully with British materials in the sphere of popular culture. The strengthening of communication links between Canada and the United States as a result of telegraphy and new train lines after mid-century, and growing levels of literacy among the working classes in the following decades, further increased Canada's cultural ties with the United States.

The strengthening connections between American and Canadian cultures went far beyond the world of the popular magazine and the book. Indeed, working-class Canadians, many of whom were only marginally literate, were particularly amenable to the greater openness to commercial entertainments and the pleasures of spectacle that appeared to exist south of the border. This is not to say that there was no interest in "improving activities" among the many different people — the labourers, artisans, tradespersons, clerks, domestics, and shopworkers — who made up the Canadian working class. On the contrary, many working-class organizations in the late nineteenth century were committed to the struggle for increased access to literacy, libraries, parks, and museums. These struggles were not only about gaining more time away from work, but also about bringing recreational facilities and programs to working-class communities. Often this meant struggling *against* the commercial provision of recreation and entertainment in favour of activities subsidized by companies, unions, or local governments. Yet, at the same time, most working-class Canadians also embraced an inclusive, innovative, urban popular culture that welcomed into its ambit a vast repository of commercial and semi-commercial entertainments. This culture was imbued with a tolerance for commercial spectacle, and a sense of popular rights to pleasure, that resonated more closely with the rapidly expanding world of American popular entertainment than the dour world of propriety and seriousness promoted by cultural leaders within the dominant classes in Canada.

In the case of sport, this is why many working-class Canadians were likely to be attracted to U.S. commercial entertainments, whereas the more privileged classes were drawn primarily towards the model of British "gentlemanly" amateurism.[19] Nowhere was the attraction to commercialism more evident than in the remarkable growth of baseball in Canada as a semi-professional and professional sport. Men from the pre-industrial working class in Ontario formed organized baseball teams as early as the late 1830s. By the 1860s baseball-like games had gained popularity among working-class men in the Hamilton area, and by the 1880s baseball clubs and leagues had been formed throughout

Ontario, and in parts of Quebec, the Maritimes, the Prairies, and British Columbia.

From the outset commercialism never seemed to be a problem for the organizers, players, and fans of baseball in Canada. As Metcalfe notes, "Payment for services, payment for lost time, prizes and gate receipts permeated all levels of the game."[20] This tolerance for casual commercialism not only had a foundation in baseball's class origins, but was also tied to the popularity of the game in rural areas. Rural baseball teams sometimes found it difficult to compete on an equal footing with urban teams without some kind of commercial sponsorship or financial inducements to skilled players. However, the commercial character of Canadian baseball escalated during the 1870s when the Canadian game became more closely intertwined with its commercially established U.S. counterpart. Throughout the 1870s and 1880s Canadian teams from Victoria to the Maritimes played regular challenge matches against U.S. teams, and in some instances they began to hire U.S. professionals. Widespread acceptance in 1876 of rules created in New York opened the door to the formation of a number of short-lived professional leagues in Canada during the following decades, and many of these leagues aggressively recruited skilled U.S. players. By the time Toronto and Hamilton placed franchises in the U.S.-centred International League in 1886, baseball was already an established North American professional spectator sport.[21]

In addition to its close ties to rural and working-class life, baseball attracted men and women from a broad range of occupations, communities, and racial and ethnic groups. It was also ideologically heterogeneous. For example, while baseball was in the main unapologetically commercial, there were often considerable disagreements — particularly in the time between the 1850s and 1880s — about how teams should be organized, who should have control, and who should reap the profits.[22] For example, player-organized teams provided a different model for commercial baseball than teams in which an individual or company "owned" the contracts of players. At the same time baseball was also being increasingly appropriated as an "improving activity" by middle-class reformers and moral entrepreneurs. Because of this organizational and ideological heterogeneity, baseball was promoted throughout the final decades of the century by widely varied organizations, including unions and factories, banks, local businessmen, fast-buck artists, schools, sporting goods companies, and temperance societies.[23]

By the turn of the twentieth century hockey was the only other sport in Canada that had comparably broad patterns of recruitment or was being promoted by such diverse organizations. But hockey's institutional foundations were significantly different than baseball's. The folk origins of Canadian baseball lay in the cultures of rural and working-class life in Canada, but its institutional form only became solidified through a connection with established baseball organizations in the United States — organizations controlled by economic entrepreneurs interested in making a profit through their promotion of America's "national game." By the time hockey had developed any significant degree of institutional form in Montreal in the mid-1880s, baseball was already effectively commodified. Baseball thus provided an early model for the possibility and legitimacy of professional team sport in Canada. Given the immense popularity of professional and semi-professional baseball in Canadian communities in the summers of the late nineteenth century, the odds were not good that the proponents of amateurism would gain full control over hockey.

Representation, Identities, and Creeping Professionalism

Perhaps the greatest threat to amateur control lay in the degree to which the organized sports that emerged in Canada during the last thirty years of the nineteenth century — even the most self-consciously "amateur" sports — had become powerful vehicles for expressing community aspirations, spirit, and pride. Initially these connections were grounded in the close personal identifications that many community members maintained with the players. Cheering for the home team in the early years of organized baseball, hockey, or lacrosse meant cheering for teams that were likely to be composed of family, friends, or at least acquaintances. It could be credibly claimed that the quality of a team's performance actually said something about the community that produced it — not only about the skill levels of its players, but also about the character of its people. When local athletes or community teams began to represent their communities, the significance of winning or losing increased dramatically. Throughout the late nineteenth century the representative character of sporting spectacles provided a new way of speaking metaphorically about relationships between identities, status, and power in Canadian life.

The most encompassing, and most traditional, of these identities was the obsessive concern for manliness in sporting competition. Sociologists and social historians have noted that masculine identity and honour have been a crucial aspect of the stakes of sporting spectacles throughout much of the history of Western societies.[24] In the face of this deeply sedimented tradition, losing has often carried the possible connotation of effeminacy, especially in combative sports where the winner prevails through sheer physical domination. By the same token, the ideals of fighting hard, not quitting, and never backing down or admitting defeat have been minimum conditions for symbolically maintaining the integrity of masculine identity in a losing cause. It is only in this way that *both* winner and loser have been able to emerge with their masculine pride fully intact.

Obviously, the stakes associated with spectator identification in sporting spectacles have not been restricted to masculinity alone. In the history of Canadian sport the display of masculine competence and the affirmation of masculine identities have always existed alongside — or have been subtly layered into — the dramatization of class, racial, ethnic, regional, and national identities and rivalries. In the late nineteenth and early twentieth centuries there were two distinct levels of social and individual identification with the contestants in sporting spectacles. First, the growing towns and cities in Canada included a host of subcommunities within which many people maintained the majority of their social contacts: for instance, neighbourhoods, frequently defined in terms of class, race, or ethnicity; and broader ethnic or occupational communities. In the larger urban areas of Toronto or Montreal, or later in Western centres like Winnipeg or Edmonton, many people's primary sense of membership was to these subcommunities rather than to the city as a whole. To further promote such identifications, the churches, unions, and occupational and ethnic associations sponsored a wide variety of recreational activities, including organized sport. The major organizations that defined the rules and conditions of sporting activities in the late nineteenth and early twentieth centuries may well have been dominated by the urban anglo middle and upper classes, but leaders in a variety of local ethnic and religious communities were quick to see that sponsorship of sports teams might encourage a sense of attachment and commitment.[25]

These attachments could not be disentangled from what were often vigorous ethnic rivalries and barely concealed class animosities. Conclusions about the superiority of one competitor over another could readily be extended to broader social groups with whom that competitor could be identified. So when a team of Irish or French-speaking Catholics triumphed over a team of English Protestants, or a team from a working-class neighbourhood beat a team from an affluent community, the people involved felt that the result truly mattered. It brought them a sense of pleasure, pride, and satisfaction.

Despite these internal rivalries, sport was also beginning to lend itself well to broader forms of civic identification, to a shared sense of belonging to a particular town or city as a whole. When a local favourite went forward to challenge an individual or team in another town or city, and especially if that town or city was perceived as an economic or political rival, the contest was inevitably followed with great interest. Indeed, the threat of a symbolic loss of superiority, or the chance to advance community prestige, meant that some communities began to dedicate considerable energy and resources into supporting their teams and ensuring that they were competitive with the best. In the face of such high stakes players came under heavy pressure to uphold community pride, to perform well, and, ideally, to win. Moreover, in situations where the home or favoured team was faring badly, or lost a contest, spectators were often willing to protest violently — the fans wanted to make a point about *their* own competence and worth as men, as members of a particular social group, or as residents of a proud community. The momentary sense of superiority or inferiority experienced when a "representative" player or team won or lost became especially significant to people who didn't have much power in other areas of social or cultural life.

Thus, moral sanctions against commercialism — and even against illegal and violent acts on the playing field, ice rink, or the stands — were rivalled from the outset by the strength of popular attachments to teams as expressions of individual and community pride and competence. Nineteenth-century custodians of amateurism feared that commercialism in sport would put an overly great premium on spectacle rather than play, that it would lead to inflamed passion and violence rather than moral discipline and self-improvement, and that it would deflect people from participating in sport fairly and "for its own sake." But they failed to see that commercialism was not the whole problem. The idea of participating in sport simply for its own sake was challenged the moment teams began to act in a representative way for specific communities. A longstanding taste for spectacle in popular culture, a desire for competitive teams in communities that lacked the populations and resources of the major cities, the articulation of individual and collective identities in sporting competition, and the impulse towards civic boosterism in a competitive market society: all of these elements combined to create markets for professional hockey. Not only was there a growing potential market for the game as a commercial product, but there was also a growing labour market for "travelling" semi-professional players.

Morris Mott, a Canadian historian and former pro hockey player, provides an example of some of these tendencies and pressures towards professionalism in a useful discussion of debates about hockey in Manitoba in the period between 1904 and 1911.[26] Because of the costs of playing facilities, equipment, time away from work, and travel for intercommunity competition, many amateur hockey clubs in Manitoba were under a great deal of economic pressure. Rural teams in particular wanted more liberal rules to govern amateur hockey in Manitoba because they felt disadvantaged in their competitions with teams from Winnipeg. As the largest city in the province, Winnipeg was more likely than towns such as Souris, Neepawa, Portage la Prairie, or Brandon to attract athletes who were travelling across the country in search of work or business opportunities. The promoters of hockey in the smaller centres were by no means unconcerned about violence or cheating in sport; they simply wanted to be able to put competitive teams on the ice and offer their citizens the highest calibre of hockey possible. But this was going to be difficult without increased freedom to generate revenues and to compensate players financially.

Rural Manitobans were not alone in wanting more liberal rules to govern the play of amateur hockey in the first decade of the new century. Much of the remarkable expansion of organized hockey teams and leagues that occurred in Canada during the late 1880s and 1890s may have developed under the auspices of amateur associations, but an uncompromising commitment to amateur goals and principles was the exception rather than the rule. New teams and clubs across the country sought the sponsorship of the existing amateur associations because they wanted recognition, access to rules and know-how, and quality competition. But these teams weren't always interested in the ideological baggage that accompanied such sponsorship, especially if they thought that "pure" amateurism gave an unfair advantage to affluent clubs or to teams located in big cities.

Even if hockey teams were committed in principle to the amateur philosophy, the cost of travel, accommodation, and time away from work associated with higher levels of inter-community competition provided an insurmountable financial burden for all but the most affluent clubs. The only solution was to actively seek sponsorship — from the town or city, or from private benefactors — and to encourage fan support either through a series of travelling exhibition matches or a regular program of home games. It became necessary, in short, to sell the team as a product. With this in mind, barnstorming hockey teams played to large crowds throughout Canada and the northern United States throughout the late 1880s and 1890s, demonstrating the game's potential commercial appeal. But regular programs of games in the growing cities of Quebec and Ontario quickly became an even more lucrative source of revenues for hockey.

By the end of the century, key games involving prominent amateur clubs in the cities could count on thousands of paying spectators.[27] The irony is that these were the teams most likely to be affiliated closely with the organizations that had taken responsibility for championing the values of amateurism. Even the most self-righteous proponents of the amateur game were not above charging spectators a fee in order to make money for their teams and associations. However, for many people, both within and outside the amateur associations, this simply dramatized the arbitrary and hypocritical character of existing regulations defining the limits of amateurism and professionalism. More and more organizers, players, and fans began to wonder why some commercial practices, like taking money at the gate, were acceptable within the definition of amateur sport, while others, like lost-time payments for players or honorariums for referees, were not.

With the development of regular league play, and the active solicitation of fan support, there was the beginnings of a subtle shift in the relationships between hockey teams and their audiences. In certain instances, the relationship between fans and teams began to change from a sense of direct membership in a community to which players and club management also belonged, to a relationship more like that of a loyal customer, with the mutual obligations between merchant and customer that this relationship once implied.[28] Indeed, many teams and clubs involved in league play found it necessary to broaden their constituencies and find new customers among the emergent urban mass audiences. Not only could teams and clubs offer regularly scheduled, exciting hockey games, but they could also market the prospect of belonging to the community of team supporters — there were plenty of people eager to jump at the prospect of belonging to such sporting communities, even if "community" here took on a meaning more akin to shared brand allegiance. It was a very short step from the idea of marketing teams for the purpose of expanding gate receipts in amateur hockey to the formation of teams that included professionals — specialists whose livelihoods depended upon fulfilling customers' expectations for skilled play and winning performances.

A growing appreciation for the importance of specialists and experts in other areas of life helped to justify this creeping professionalism. Increasing complexity in the Canadian division of labour, in government, and in the processes of production and marketing were producing new specializations throughout the society. Early Victorian culture had placed a significant emphasis on the values of versatility and fair play in the upbringing of the respectable middle classes. But a capitalist industrial culture that was at once becoming more individualistic, more bureaucratized, and more diversified placed a greater value on specialization and technical expertise.

This concern with technical proficiency could be found within the developing culture of amateur sport in Canada as early as the 1880s. Many of the self-consciously modern promoters of amateur sport noted the example of science in the formation of rules, the design of training, and the mastery of various sporting disciplines. Before too long the idea of "scientific play" rivalled amateurism's traditional emphasis on fairness and on playing the game for its own sake.[29] Teams or individuals that played "scientifically" were said to be exercising human reason in the quest for self-improvement and higher performance. This contrasted to individuals or teams who were said to be stubbornly bound by tradition or, worse, who lost themselves in passion and emotion in their play. Yet the value placed on scientific play within the amateur tradition in Canada implicitly dissolved some of the distinctions between amateur and professional sporting activities by attaching great importance to the rationalization of technique. Whether pursued as an end in itself, or as a means to an end, the emphasis on technique essentially had only one logical consequence: improved performance.

It followed inevitably that the best technique, and the best performances, would be demonstrated by specialists. Professional athletes could then be represented as rational experts rather than amoral cheaters or prostitutes. Morris Mott cites a correspondent to the *Winnipeg Saturday Post* who suggested in 1908 that an athlete becomes a professional "because he is good," while those who remain amateur "can't play well enough to get money."[30] Indeed, professionals were *expected* to be good, to apply their technical expertise to help their teams win, and to give spectators value for money. It began not to matter if the home team was made up of players from outside the community or city. What mattered was that the team be successful, and that the whole community was able to identify with that success. Professional and semiprofessional sport quickly came to be about the buying of talent and the selling of winning. Players who didn't produce were booed by the crowds, while home teams that lost regularly couldn't count on loyal support. The fan-as-customer was promised results, and came to expect them.

Open Professionalism and Amateur Retrenchment
The debate about amateurism and professionalism in hockey became especially intense during the first decade of the twentieth century, when amateur teams regularly began to draw large crowds for league play and major challenge contests. The remarkable expansion of hockey

teams and leagues in the 1890s had created a great deal of confusion about the quality of play in different communities and regions. A variety of associations, teams, and clubs were competing for several different championship trophies. The Senior Amateur Trophy, the prize of the Montreal-based Amateur Hockey Association of Canada, was arguably the most prestigious of these trophies. In Ontario, senior teams affiliated with the newly formed Ontario Hockey Association competed for their own championship trophy, the Cosby Cup, emblematic of the provincial championship.[31] Not surprisingly, there was considerable interest in inter-provincial challenges between senior OHA teams and teams in the AHAC. Calls for a "Dominion Championship" had been made in the Montreal press for years, and the establishment of a strong hockey association in Ontario quickly led to a considerable degree of interassociation and interprovincial rivalry.

In 1891 the Ottawa Hockey Club won the Cosby Cup and also advanced to the championship game in the AHAC for the senior amateur trophy. Although there was no formal means to recognize a dominion championship, the 1891 AHAC final between Ottawa and the Montreal Amateur Athletic Association (MAAA) was touted as a match between Canada's best two teams. In March of the following year, Canada's Governor General, Lord Stanley, donated a cup both to formally acknowledge the dominion championship and to emphasize "the importance of having the games fairly played under generally recognized rules."[32] It was significant that Lord Stanley's new trophy was not to be controlled by any one association; rather, it was to be a permanent challenge cup awarded by an independent committee of trustees.

Ottawa lost the AHAC title once more to the MAAA in 1893, establishing the Montreal team as the first widely recognized hockey champion of Canada. However, for our purposes the actual winners of this first Stanley Cup, and of subsequent cups, are less important than the fact that the cup created a truly national hockey championship for the first time. The existence of the cup fuelled interleague and interprovincial rivalries and generated unprecedented press coverage and spectator support. According to the *Montreal Star*, five thousand people witnessed the 1894 Stanley Cup final between Ottawa and the MAAA. Spectator response was so enthusiastic that the *Star* noted, "Tin horns, strong lungs and general rabble predominated."[33] Faced with such enthusiasm, the Stanley Cup's trustees decided very quickly that amateur competition didn't preclude the idea of making money. By 1897, when the Montreal Victorias defended a challenge from the Ottawa Capitals of the newly formed Central Canadian Hockey Association, the cup trustees decided upon a best-of-three challenge series to take better advantage of lucrative gate receipts. Six years later, nearly eighteen thousand fans attended a four-game Stanley Cup series at Westmount Arena in Montreal.[34] The Stanley Cup was on the way to becoming a major commercial spectacle.

With all of this activity came frequent allegations that many of the top amateur teams were actively recruiting players from outside the community and paying them under the table. By the turn of the century there was a well-established stock of skilled players travelling between different teams, divisions, and leagues on a seasonal basis in search of cash payments and employment. Amateur players were signing flimsy agreements with no next-year option clauses and were easily enticed by teams that made them a better offer.[35] However, even though accusations of professionalism were rampant, most of the well-established teams and associations — especially those seeking the Stanley Cup — were able to avoid disqualification or suspension. Amateur hockey had developed an organizational culture based on an endless round of finger-pointing, evasion, and collusion.[36] Still, all the while virtually everyone paid lip service to the high ideals of amateurism.

There was considerably less antiprofessional rhetoric in the United States, and a significant number of Canadian players migrated to Michigan and Pennsylvania hoping to make a living from the hockey skills they had developed playing for "amateur" teams in Ontario and Quebec. Pittsburgh was an especially popular stop for Canadian players, because local teams there provided jobs in addition to salaries of $15 to $20 a week.[37] Players who had been expelled from Canadian amateur leagues as "professionals," or those simply wanting to play hockey for money in a more open environment, provided a foundation for a strong semi-professional league in western Pennsylvania in 1902-03. During the same time, a former star for the Berlin (later Kitchener) senior team, John Liddell Macdonald Gibson, organized a semi-professional team in Houghton, Michigan, to play in an Upper Peninsula League. Gibson had gone to Detroit to study dentistry, and after graduation he set up a practice in Houghton and began to play exhibition hockey. An arrangement with a local entrepreneur led to the formation of the famous Portage Lakes — a team committed to bringing winning hockey to the community. The Lakers began with a string of victories over teams from St. Paul, St. Louis, Detroit, Duluth, Pittsburgh, Montreal, and the University of Toronto. They went on to play the Pittsburgh Bankers for the unofficial championship of the United States and then issued a challenge to the Ottawa Silver Sevens, the reigning Stanley Cup champions. Ottawa couldn't be enticed into the competition, but the Lakers were able to play, and defeat, the

Federal Amateur Hockey League champions, the Montreal Wanderers. In the wake of the victory they posed for a team picture that carried the title "World's Champions."[38]

The remarkable success of the Lakers, and of games involving Houghton, other Michigan teams, Pittsburgh, and Sault St. Marie, led to calls for more regular league play. In the fall of 1904 the managers of the hockey arenas used by these teams formed the first openly professional hockey league, the International Hockey League.[39] Some of the best "amateur" players in Canada immediately jumped to play in the new league, which became stocked almost exclusively by Canadian players — prompting concerns about the drain of hockey talent to the United States. In the wake of the formation of the International League, the two major Canadian senior leagues, the Federal Hockey League and Eastern Canadian Amateur Hockey Association (ECAHA) became increasingly (but not openly) professional. Meanwhile, in 1905 a group of wealthy mine owners and industrialists in the booming mine towns of northern Ontario formed the Temiskaming Hockey League, with teams in Renfrew, Haileybury, and Cobalt. At first these teams weren't openly professional; but the owners were committed to buying as much skilled talent as possible in order to secure the Stanley Cup for their communities, and their teams quickly became synonymous with the highest calibre of hockey played in Canada. By 1908 professional hockey in Canada was almost fully out in the open. The Temiskaming League had turned openly professional, and a fully professional league, the Ontario Professional Hockey League, had taken root in western Ontario. In the same year the ECAHA's Montreal Wanderers won the Stanley Cup and subsequently declared their status as a professional team.[40]

The emergence of open professionalism in Canadian hockey contributed to a growing sense of desperation on the part of the game's moral entrepreneurs. From the mid-1890s there had been ongoing controversies in hockey over an emphasis on winning at the expense of fair play and good sportsmanship. Much of the controversy centred upon the widespread use of "ringers" or "travelling players" on amateur teams and on the practice of under-the-table payments. There was even greater concern over the lengths players would go to in order to win, as well as over the violent behaviour of spectators. Commentators frowned on repeated incidents of hacking, tripping, and excessive roughness, but their ire was particularly raised by the more overt brutality evident in open fighting on the ice and in mob scenes involving fans and players. There are stories of four deaths on the ice in eastern Canada in 1904.[41] In addition, in 1905 a young francophone player was killed by a blow from a stick in an emotionally charged game between teams from the largely francophone, Catholic community of Alexandria and the anglophone, Protestant community of Maxville. Two years later another player was killed in a Federal Hockey League game between Cornwall and the Ottawa Victorias.[42]

All of this prompted a militant reassertion of the values of pure amateurism from certain individuals and amateur associations. In Ontario, OHA president John Ross Robertson (a Member of Parliament and owner of the *Toronto Telegram*) drew attention to coal-throwing by fans in Lindsay, "bottle tossing in Peterborough, and the inadequacy of police protection in smaller towns."[43] Hockey seemed to be out of control and, in a remarkable oversimplification of the problem, Robertson targeted professionalism as the culprit. The OHA stepped up its vigilance and struggled to tighten its authority over the game in Ontario. It threatened expulsion and blacklisting for anyone accused of professionalism or anyone who knowingly competed against professionals. The burden of proof was to fall on the accused. In a kind of sporting McCarthyism, individuals were assumed guilty and had to prove their innocence. More importantly, in 1904, with the advent of open professionalism in hockey, the OHA adopted John Ross Robertson's proposal that indictments of professionalism should carry a lifetime ban on participation in any sanctioned amateur competition in any sport. The basic principle was, "Once a professional always a professional."[44]

Yet there was still no clear-cut *national* authority in hockey to enforce such a rule. Nor was there an effective national body with sufficient strength to act as a moral regulator of amateur sport in general. The Montreal-based Amateur Athletic Association of Canada was arguably the closest thing. It began as an organization aimed primarily at overseeing and regulating track and field, but it soon expanded to other sports and sought to broaden its mandate, first as a regulatory agency and secondly as a promoter of healthy, civilizing sport. The AAAC spent much of the 1890s struggling to consolidate its position as the dominant amateur sports organization in Canada. It became fixated on investigations of professionalism in all its various guises: job-placements, sponsorship, performance bonuses, outright payment for playing or refereeing, and participation on teams with, or in challenges against, known professionals.[45] In 1898 the AAAC tried to strengthen its legitimacy by forming an alliance with the American Amateur Athletic Union, and the association's name was accordingly changed to the Canadian Amateur Athletic Union (CAAU).

The old AAAC had long claimed jurisdiction over amateur hockey and was closely connected to the AHAC and a number of its teams. Indeed, the AAAC and CAAU were largely controlled by the powerful

Montreal Athletic Association (MAAA), whose teams were regular contenders for the Stanley Cup. The CAAU also owed much of its authority to the affiliation of major lacrosse associations in Quebec and Ontario. Lacrosse and hockey were both highly professionalized "amateur" sports, and a number of organizers in both sports wanted to liberalize the definition of amateurism. One of their major concerns was the longstanding rule prohibiting amateurs and professionals from playing on the same team. In the case of hockey, the early successes of AHAC teams in Stanley Cup play, and the large amounts of money that Montreal teams made by selling hockey as a commercial spectacle, meant that the Quebec-based amateur hockey leagues of the day had a vested interest in adopting a liberal approach to professionalism.

Yet the forces for reform within the AAAC/CAAU encountered stiff resistance from conservative purists. In 1904 the MAAA proposed amendments to the CAAU constitution designed to liberalize the amateur code, but its initiatives were met with indignation and hostility from more traditional moral entrepreneurs, especially in Toronto. Tensions ran so high that the MAAA severed relations with the CAAU three years later and formed a short-lived rival association. However, by 1909 the defenders of pure amateurism had consolidated control and were able to create a strong new national organization, the Amateur Athletic Union of Canada (AAUC). The highly restrictive and punitive conception of amateurism adopted earlier by the OHA was endorsed by the majority of amateur associations that became affiliates of the AAUC after 1909.[46] Within a few years there was a growing lobby, particularly from western Canada, to create a truly national association affiliated with the AAUC to promote and regulate amateur hockey in Canada. In response the Canadian Amateur Hockey Association (CAHA) was formed in 1914. With the formation of the CAHA, the organizational and philosophical separation of amateur and professional hockey in Canada was complete.

Chapter Four

Media, Audiences,
and the NHL Monopoly

Between the late 1890s and 1913 a series of investment and export
booms drew over two million immigrants to central Canadian cities
and the industrial frontiers of the north and west. At the same time
new technological achievements accelerated the dissolution of the pre-
industrial experience of time and distance promoted by the trains,
telegraphs, steamships, and photographs of previous decades. The completion of a national rail link in 1892, matched with coast-to-coast wire
services, greatly enhanced the abilities of Canadians to imagine themselves as a national community. Over the next three decades, tele-
phones, phonographs, automobiles, movies, and radio would intensify
the experience of dissolving time and space. There was also an optimism at the turn of the century about economic prospects for "the
common man" and the nation as a whole — editorialists of the era
trumpeted the advent of "Canada's century." Meanwhile the Canadian
city was becoming a symbolic monument to technology and progress.
Civic leaders across the country promoted their towns and cities

through projects that celebrated visions of industrial growth, economic prosperity, and a "modernizing" culture.

The proliferation of hockey teams from the mid-1880s to the end of the first decade of the twentieth century — and the changing meanings and uses of the sport — formed an integral part of these economic, demographic, cultural, and technical developments. The popularity of intercommunity challenges in amateur hockey and the emergence of openly professional hockey teams both reflected and dramatized the optimism and aspirations of the new civic boosters who were championing the twin ideals of progress and prosperity. The newly built commercial and municipal hockey rinks that had become the "homes" of prominent senior amateur and professional teams also became important landmarks in the modern Canadian city. Hockey was emerging as a notable element in a fast-changing world of urban commercial entertainment, a world more and more influenced by mass media, advertising, and mass consumption.

Culture, Media, and the Popularization of Pro Hockey

One notable indicator of the sweeping changes in Canadian culture was the growing prominence of a new generation of industrialists and lumber, mining, and banking tycoons who were making their fortunes in the wide-open entrepreneurial atmosphere of the time. In the West and North, in particular, freebooting entrepreneurs began to challenge the more self-consciously genteel capitalists of earlier decades as exemplars of moral influence and discipline. As the veil of gentility lifted, the accumulative impulses that had always rested at the core of Canadian capitalism were both exposed and celebrated as never before. The market became more widely understood both as a test of character and as a significant measure of individual success — a success that could be displayed through the accumulation of possessions and the prompt servicing of personal desires.

Market pressures were exerting equally significant influences on the nature of leisure and popular culture in the lives of working-class and middle-class Canadians. Popular traditions of communal association, casual hedonism, and spectacle had long provided support for urban commercial entertainments that were consumed primarily by male working-class audiences, but by the early twentieth century many of these popular traditions had been incorporated firmly into market relations and subtly altered in the process. Although a small part of Canadian commerce had always played to popular dreams, hopes, and fantasies, increasingly the selling of these dreams, hopes, and fantasies to individual consumers was finding its way into the mainstream culture. As the twentieth century took hold, the idea of gaining self-satisfaction through consumption, the dream of vertical social mobility, and the understanding of market success as a measure of self-worth all emerged as powerfully interconnected elements in the definition of liberal and modern identities.

The turn-of-the-century belief in the prospects and promise of the "common man" also helped to sustain both older working-class identities and radical ideas about the difficulty of advancing the interests of "the working man" in a capitalist system. Even more notable was the extent to which turn-of-the-century Canadian culture retained a deeply rooted conservatism and antimodernism that identified with older European structures of privilege and with the apparent moral certainties of the early Victorian period. Reflecting these conservative cultural pressures, opinion leaders often struggled to articulate an identity for Canadians that struck a difficult balance: between, on the one hand, the uncritical embrace of "progress" and the advancement of individual rights and freedoms; and on the other the retention of older forms of paternalism — stability, duty, and respect for established authority.

In English-Canadian culture this attempted balance was clearly evident in the popular press of the day. In his book *The Making of the Canadian Media*, Paul Rutherford notes how editorialists and journalists of the era were generally inclined to "fix the identity of the Dominion as a 'Victorian commonwealth,'" a land of economic and industrial progress that was also one of "ordered liberty, moral rectitude and hard work, of class harmony and happy families."[1] But there also seemed to be a tacit recognition that this image of Canada often coincided in practice with persisting reactionary sentiment, conflict, and hypocrisy. The turn-of-the-century anglo popular press may have promoted the idea of Canada as an orderly and morally centred "Victorian Commonwealth," but while doing this it also played to the tensions and disorders of Canadian life and dramatized popular hopes and aspirations.

There was nearly a threefold increase in the number of newspapers published between 1874 and 1900, in large part due to the emergence of self-declared "people's journals" — like *La Presse* (1884) in Montreal; *The Telegram* (1874), *The News* (1881), and *The Star* (1892) in Toronto; and the *Herald* (1889) in Hamilton.[2] In contrast to expensive highbrow papers — or to other papers often directly sponsored by religious or Tory interests — the new "people's journals" typically adopted populist stances. They also operated increasingly as profit-driven businesses committed to reaching as many readers as possible. Following the examples set by Joseph Pulitzer and William Randolph Hearst in the United States, the most successful of the new popular dailies experimented with new layouts, increased use of pictures and photographs, dramatic headlines, and sensational stories. They expanded their coverage of sports and entertainment, added more cartoons and comics for children, and introduced new columns and whole sections for women; that is, something for everyone in the family.

All of this contributed greatly to already changing perceptions about what was significant and important in Canadian life. For a long time prominent bourgeois moralists writing in the "establishment press" had given a high profile to matters of politics, religion, self-improvement, and public duty to Dominion and Empire; this emphasis often contrasted with the attention paid by the popular press to pleasures and everyday enthusiasms situated in the realms of leisure, family life, and local culture. While rarely backing completely away from paternalistic invocations of duty and morality, the popular press nonetheless articulated a more democratized vision of social life that was comparatively open to popular-democratic interests as well as to middlebrow and lowbrow entertainments.

The growing representation of popular interests and pleasures in the daily paper had particular importance with respect to the new significance of advertising in Canadian culture. By the 1890s publishers throughout North America were gradually moving beyond their initial use of advertising simply as a means to supplement revenues derived from the sale of newspapers or periodicals. More and more they were beginning "to regard their publications not so much as products to be sold to readers, but more as vehicles that organized audiences into clearly identifiable target groups that could be sold to advertisers; the audiences themselves became the 'products' generated by the media industry."[3] Meanwhile advertising was becoming an industry all its own, with specialized copywriters and agencies devoting themselves not only to selling particular products, but also to selling the virtues of consumerism itself.

Notwithstanding the increasing attention paid to women and families, the core market for popular daily newspapers was made up of male wage earners and businessmen. Material designed for family audiences was scattered throughout the papers, especially in the weekend editions that were distributed by mail and train throughout the Canadian countryside. But the papers catered to perceived male tastes in their coverage of politics, business and labour reporting, and, above all, sports. By the end of the century most major Canadian dailies had substantially increased their sports coverage and created separate sports departments.

Despite this specialization, sports reporting remained strikingly similar to other forms of "specialty reporting" in the popular press. Paul Rutherford notes several important similarities between the sports coverage of the era and the press's increasingly specialized coverage of business.[4] In each case journalists celebrated the ideals of manliness and competition: sports writers glorified the ritualized drama and excitement of masculine physical contests, and business writers exalted the cult of competition in the free market. Sports coverage emphasized information designed to serve the athlete, the spectator, and the bettor — information like game schedules and detailed results — just as business coverage provided stock quotes and other information for investors. Both forms of coverage were meant to serve the active participant, yet both treated their subject areas as a grand spectacle. In addition, both business reporting and sports reporting defined their frame of reference beyond the local level by including items like British soccer results and information from the New York stock exchange. In this way, each conveyed a sense of participation in national and international communities of interest.

Like the sporting goods industry, the popular press helped to naturalize the idea of a "world of sport" in which the differences between high-level amateur and professional sport were becoming less important. People wanted news about *both* types of spectator sport, and even papers that tended to adopt a high moral tone ultimately couldn't ignore the public appetite for sporting spectacle. Sports coverage was proving to be good not only for building circulation, but also for opening up connections to new sources of advertising revenues from businesses interested in speaking primarily to male consumers. These businesses included beer, alcohol, and tobacco-product producers in addition to sporting goods companies, sports promoters, rail and tram companies, and hotel operators. In this context professional sports such as boxing, baseball, and hockey found active advocates among editorial writers across the country.

This is not to say that professional sport was universally accepted. Hostility to professionalism — and in many instances to spectator sport of any kind — had long been a familiar feature in highbrow cultural commentaries in Canada. As far back as the 1880s the establishment press had occasionally reflected upon the triviality or the "worthlessness" of sport and questioned the amount of time and money that Canadians were beginning to spend on it.[5] Patronizing attitudes towards sport appeared to harden further among Canadian intellectuals after the turn of the century, as more and more sports teams began to represent their communities and the popular obsession with sport grew.

Notably, some highbrow commentators began to worry that the attention lavished on sport was undermining new initiatives to build Canadian culture through the arts. Historian Maria Tippett mentions one Montreal commentator in 1907 who lamented that there was "seldom any excitement manifested over concert tickets" while it was "not unusual to see a line of men two blocks in length waiting patiently for the opening of the box office where tickets for a hockey match are on sale."[6]

Notwithstanding occasional editorial diatribes, most newspaper writing on sport between the 1880s and the late 1890s tended to be matter of fact and informational in tone. In its coverage of hockey the press focused attention on the participant by notifying club members of organizational meetings, practice times, and matches. Papers also reported game results, but coverage tended to be spotty, usually with little embellishment beyond publication of a brief game summary, the score, and, sometimes, a list of team rosters. Even as late as the 1890s there was "an almost complete avoidance of writing about personalities, as opposed to teams," and few sports journalists had perfected the larger-than-life style of reporting sporting spectacle that was to emerge to dominate sports writing by the early 1920s.[7]

A more sensational and star-centred style of writing in hockey began to develop in conjunction with new applications of the use of telegraphy. At first game highlights and results were simply taken to local telegraph offices to be transmitted by Morse code to interested parties in other locations. To save time and to create simultaneous coverage of hockey games, someone eventually had the idea of bringing telegraphers to rinkside. One account suggests that this practice began in 1896 because of the intense interest generated when the Winnipeg Victorias played the Montreal Victorias for the Stanley Cup.[8] Whatever the origin, the practice of stationing telegraph operators at rinkside or up in the press box with a sportswriter or a couple of knowledgeable hockey fans had become widespread by the late 1890s. At the receiving end, decoded game accounts were either read aloud to assembled fans, or transcripts were posted on bulletin boards. Hotel, theatre, and newspaper owners quickly came to realize the financial and public relations value of telegraphed accounts and made facilities of varying types available for fans to gather and "hear" the game. The popular press then routinely began to publish game reports, often including a transcript of the telegrapher's complete account.

The speed of hockey necessitated a terse style of game narration, but early telegraphers nonetheless tried to convey something of the atmosphere and drama of games in addition to describing the technical aspects of play. For example, commenting on Frank McGee's tie-breaking goal late in a 1905 Stanley Cup game, one of the telegraphers noted: "The rink had been in a furore but it burst into a veritable Niagara of sound now. Young and old weep with joy. Only 90 seconds to play."[9] Growing numbers of new fans not only wanted to know the score, but also wanted to hear and read about the flow of the game, the emotions of the crowd, and the character demonstrated by the players. Because people understood teams to represent distinctive community identities — associated with region, class, and ethnicity — hockey games were taking on a larger-than-life significance.

The demand for information about the results and details of hockey games seems initially to have exceeded the supply of information. Rinks in the early twentieth century tended to be small with little room for spectators, and teams of the era rarely played more than eight or ten games in a season. Together these factors meant that ticket prices for games involving the best teams were expensive. Few of the growing numbers of hockey fans in the biggest towns and cities were able to attend games with any regularity, if at all. A more self-consciously dramatic style of sports journalism emerged as a way of representing the excitement of contests that most hockey fans were unable to witness firsthand. The Canadian news media began to play a much more direct and important role in narrating and popularizing high-level sport than in the past.

A key element in this popularization was the way the daily press and the telegraph were combining to make "ordinary men" into heroes. As the new century unfolded there was more attention paid to individual players, to their skills, styles, and personalities. Telegraphers began to rely more heavily on players' names when telling the stories of game action. At the same time journalists began to write about the most skilled players in a mythic style of language that spoke to popular desires for larger-than-life events and personalities. Star players quickly developed big reputations that raised the hopes of fans anxious to become winners. The high salaries paid to early professional stars, and indeed to some "amateurs," added a further dimension to popular interest in players' careers. Senior amateur hockey and, then, the pro game were providing unprecedented opportunities for Canadian men from humble origins to achieve fame and financial rewards — to seemingly realize the promises of a modern, market-centred individualism — in a society still deeply influenced by older traditions of class privilege. Hockey, in turn, benefited immeasurably from the mystique of new sports heroes such as Frank McGee, Newsy Lalonde, Tom Phillips, and Fred "Cyclone" Taylor.

Not only did the press of the era help to popularize hockey, but it was also often directly involved in the promotion and organization of local teams and sporting associations. For example, two of the most high-profile figures in amateur hockey during the late 1890s were newspaper owners: the Toronto *Telegram*'s John Ross Robertson, OHA president from 1899 to 1905, and P.D. Ross, Stanley Cup trustee and publisher of the *Ottawa Evening Journal*. In addition, sports editors and reporters were often active participants in local teams and associations, sometimes taking paid employment as publicists or executive members. One of the best-known examples of this in amateur hockey was W.A Hewitt, sports editor at the *Toronto Star* and long-time secretary of the OHA. Notable examples in early pro hockey included Frank Calder, the sports editor of the *Montreal Herald* who went on to become the first president of the NHL in 1917, and Tommy Gorman, who was sports editor of the *Ottawa Citizen* before purchasing an interest in the Ottawa Hockey Club and becoming a founding member of the NHL.

Big-city sports editors in the early twentieth century typically maintained a wide range of contacts and affiliations to both amateur and professional sport. Increasingly they found themselves immersed in a world where the lines between the best amateur and professional teams had become blurred — a change clearly evident in the various types of ownership found in early professional hockey teams. At first the only clearly identifiable economic entrepreneurs in hockey were rink owners, promoters, and gamblers. And even rink owners — most of them struggling to make ends meet with ice carnivals and pleasure skating — were initially sceptical about the economic value of hockey. Many simply thought that renting ice time to hockey clubs was a nuisance. But as hockey soared in popularity, rink owners began to see the possibility of making money from the game. Some owners began to offer better rental terms if a prominent local club would agree to play all its games in their arenas. Others purchased teams so they could keep the entire gate and gain more control over scheduling. However, many of the best early pro hockey teams weren't owned by rink owners at all; they simply emerged out of the organizational structures of successful amateur clubs.

Small-Town Teams, Big-City Audiences, and the Founding of the NHL

While prominent amateur clubs of the day often offered money to attract good players and charged a fee at the gate, they operated as non-profit endeavours. These teams had begun to act like business organizations; but the promotion of community pride and the provision of opportunities for playing and watching high-calibre hockey remained their primary intent.

This was the case for several teams in Canada's two major amateur leagues, the Eastern Canadian Amateur Hockey Association (ECAHA) and the Federal Hockey League (FHL), before they allowed open professionalism in 1907. Within a year a number of prominent amateur teams such as the Montreal Wanderers, Montreal Shamrocks, and Ottawa Victorias simply declared themselves to be professional hockey clubs. A few others, such as the Montreal Victorias, attempted to remain in the league and play as amateurs, but dropped out within a season. As professional hockey came out of the closet after 1907 there was an almost immediate explosion of openly professional teams and leagues, some run by rink owners, others operated as outgrowths of amateur clubs, and some established by new entrepreneurs who simply organized teams to make money — they would try to take in more money at the gate than they paid out in wages, equipment, travel, and rink rentals. In the West a pro league operated briefly in Winnipeg in 1907-08, but the majority of new professional teams were located in western and northern Ontario, in the Ontario Professional Hockey League (OPHL) and the Temiskaming League.

Given all the new professional teams — in addition to large numbers of successful senior amateur teams — the market for audiences and skilled players was wide open. To overcome their disadvantaged position in the recruitment of players, small-town teams with big ambitions found they had to offer higher salaries than the big-city teams. This put immense strain on the resources of the local businessmen and professionals who generally ran small-town clubs, and it invited the participation of mining tycoons and local industrialists as patrons, sponsors, and, ultimately, owners. Nowhere was this better exemplified in the prewar period than in the community senior hockey team in Renfrew, Ontario. In 1907 the Renfrew Creamery Kings were a powerful senior team sponsored by a mining and industrial magnate, M.J. O'Brien, and managed by his son Ambrose. While there are conflicting stories about the elder O'Brien's motivations for sponsoring senior hockey in Renfrew, there seems little doubt that he was far less interested in making money from the game than in bringing a Stanley Cup to his home community.

Renfrew's directors had not been able to convince the Stanley Cup trustees to accept a challenge from the Creamery Kings, and the Eastern Canadian Hockey Association (formerly the Eastern Canadian Amateur Hockey Association) was not willing to allow Renfrew into the league. However, when infighting over rink sizes and gate receipts led the ECHA to expel one of its most established teams, the Montreal Wanderers, and to reconstitute itself as a new league called the Canadian Hockey Association (CHA), O'Brien was quick to seize the moment. Almost immediately he made a deal with Montreal rink proprietor P.J. Doran, the Wanderers' owner, to bring Renfrew and the Wanderers together in a new pro league, the National Hockey Association (NHA). In addition the new league included teams from Cobalt and Haileybury as well as a new club, the Montreal Canadiens, composed of francophone players only. Because the CHA had recruited an all-francophone club — the Nationals of Montreal — to play the 1909 season, the NHA executive wanted a comparable club of their own to compete head-to-head for French-speaking audiences. The extent of M.J. O'Brien's influence in forming and financing the NHA is readily apparent in the fact that he either owned or had an interest in every team in the league with the exception of the Montreal Wanderers.[10]

The advent of open professional hockey in Canada after 1907 created an intensely competitive market for skilled players, and it soon became common both for players to jump freely from team to team and for some clubs to offer players more money than could reasonably be recovered in gate receipts. In some small communities — Cobalt and Haileybury were prime examples — affluent club directors began to invest their own money to get top-notch players and simply tried to recover costs through side bets on the outcomes of individual games. However, with the creation of two powerful new pro leagues in 1909 the conditions were set for a salary war of unprecedented proportions. By the late fall the bidding for players had become frenzied. On a single day in December, player Lester Patrick received offers of $1,200 from P.J. Doran's NHA team, the Montreal Wanderers; $1,500 from the CHA's Ottawa Senators; and $3,000 from M.J. O'Brien's Renfrew Creamery Kings, also of the NHA. Understandably, he took the highest offer. Weeks later Renfrew signed star Ottawa defenceman "Cyclone" Taylor for $5,250 for a proposed twelve-game season — a sum that made Taylor the highest-paid professional athlete in North America on a per-game basis and stood in sharp contrast to the $35 per month he had earned as a full-time clerk in the federal immigration department.[11] Yet because this bidding war had no relationship to the revenue-producing abilities of NHA or CHA clubs, it simply couldn't be sustained. The salary offered Cyclone Taylor alone amounted to half of the gate receipts earned by the Renfrew team — now nicknamed the "Millionaires" — in the 1909-10 season.

Very soon after the season opened, in January 1910, some CHA clubs folded and the triumphant NHA absorbed the Ottawa Senators and the Montreal Shamrocks. But it wasn't long before the novelty of financing money-losing professional hockey teams wore off for the O'Briens and their co-investors. They folded the Cobalt and Haileybury teams after a single season and sold most of the players' contracts to a new Montreal Canadiens franchise that had been awarded to George Kennedy, a Montreal wrestling promoter. With an additional Montreal team entering the NHA, the O'Briens decided not to operate the original Montreal Canadiens franchise, choosing instead to look for buyers in Toronto. Meanwhile, in an effort to regain a measure of fiscal sanity, the NHA's directors moved to limit total salaries for the 1911 season to $5,000 per club, thereby reducing average salaries for sixteen games from somewhere between $1,500 and $1,800 to between $500 and $600. With the CHA out of business, and with salaries seemingly under control, the NHA entered 1911 as the premier professional league in the country. By the end of the season every team except the Renfrew Millionaires had made a profit.[12] The O'Briens finally withdrew the Renfrew team from the league, and the NHA's remaining directors moved to add two new Toronto teams.

When the NHA imposed salary caps in 1910, some players threatened to form a union to protect players' interests and there was even talk of forming a rival "players' league." But neither the union nor the rival league was ever organized. Because ice time at suitable arenas in Montreal and Ottawa was already committed to the NHA and to established amateur teams, it proved impossible to get a new league started on short notice. Furthermore, contracts were so flimsy and there was so much demand for skilled players from senior and new professional teams that only a handful of NHA players saw the need for a union. Between 1911 and 1912 a Maritime Professional League formed with teams in Halifax, Moncton, New Glasgow, Sydney, and Glace Bay; the OPHL split into two leagues with a total of seven teams; a professional Pacific Coast Hockey Association (PCHA) was started on the west coast by Joseph, Frank, and Lester Patrick; and similar initiatives were undertaken in Saskatchewan and northwest Ontario. In addition there were a number of professional and semi-professional teams and leagues in New York, Michigan, and Pennsylvania. Faced with all this competition the NHA was having difficulty getting its own members to follow league salary policy, and on more than one occasion owners within the league also threatened to pull out and start up rival organizations.

In analysing this initial stage in the commercialization of hockey it is important to note how a mix of wide-open entrepreneurialism and civic boosterism brought high-level professional and semi-pro hockey to small Canadian resource towns. But, paradoxically, this same process

also contributed to a scramble for players that contributed to the growing commodification of players' labour and to the broader incorpora-
tion of hockey into the exchange relations and patterns of uneven
development characteristic of Canadian society as a whole. It isn't surprising that small-town professional teams were highly unstable and
faced persistent financial problems. By 1910 increasing corporate concentration and U.S. investment in central Canada had substantially
weakened regional industrial economies, especially in the Maritimes.
With further pressures arising from a significant economic downturn
in 1913, and with the scarcity of players that developed during the
First World War, virtually all the professional leagues in the country
outside of the NHA and the PCHA soon collapsed.

In British Columbia the Patricks were both visionary and lucky
enough to be able to avoid some of these pressures when they started
the PCHA at the tail end of the prewar boom. Lester and Frank Patrick
had access to capital provided by the sale of their father's lumber business, and they had become experienced enough in the hockey business to know that pro hockey couldn't be profitable in the small resource
towns of the B.C interior. If pro hockey was to succeed in the West as
a profitable business it had to be constituted as a game for big-city
audiences. The problem was that the game could only be played on
the west coast in arenas with artificial ice, and only one Canadian city
in the region, Vancouver, had a population of over 100,000. With this
in mind the founding of the PCHA was anchored by the construction
of an artificial ice arena in Vancouver with a seating capacity of about
ten thousand, along with a smaller arena in Victoria. Franchises were
awarded to teams in Vancouver, Victoria, and New Westminster. In
1915 the PCHA gained instant credibility as a major pro league when
the Vancouver Millionaires won the Stanley Cup. The same year, when
the New Westminster franchise floundered economically, the Patricks'
pursuit of urban audiences led them to transfer the team to Portland,
Oregon. A year later they raided eastern Canadian clubs to set up
another U.S. team in Seattle.

For a few years openly professional hockey found it relatively easy
to exploit boom-time affluence and community. partisanship to build
an initial base of fan support. However, as pro teams in small towns
collapsed, and as hockey teams began to operate as profit-driven businesses, big-city teams faced the challenge of having to work harder to
build new and larger audiences of loyal customers. In the East the NHA
tried to make hockey more appealing to spectators by moving from
seven- to six-man hockey, placing numbers on jerseys to allow live
audiences and telegraphers to identify individual players better, and

switching from two thirty-minute halves to three twenty-minute periods. The league also sought to respond to pro hockey's reputation for uncontrolled mayhem — a reputation reinforced by press accounts of blood-filled contests and fan violence in tough mining towns like Cobalt and Haileybury — by bringing in tougher rules and penalties governing bodychecking and rough play.[13] On the west coast the PCHA retained seven-man hockey into the 1920s, but the Patricks introduced several innovations of their own, including blue lines that opened up a sixty-foot centre-ice surface for forward passing within the zone, and a penalty system that sent a penalized player off the ice for a specified time while his team played shorthanded.

The NHA and PCHA also tried to negotiate agreements to limit player raiding between the two leagues, but with little success. One thing on which the NHA and PCHA did agree was a deal with the Stanley Cup trustees that would essentially turn the "Dominion Championship" cup into a playoff trophy between the two pro leagues. Under the terms of agreement, Stanley Cup games were to be played in the East one year and in the West the next, an arrangement that would last until big-league professional hockey disappeared from western Canada in 1926. Nonetheless, despite all these changes, both pro leagues were barely surviving economically as they played through the early years of the war. Continued raiding back and forth kept salaries at a point where they often rivalled gate receipts. In addition, competition from senior amateur teams and the loss of players to the war effort hampered the recruitment of good players and the development of new "stars" whose names would attract fans. The NHA was also hurt by the fact that the league's directors kept fighting among themselves about future growth, expansion, league operations, and the scope of league authority over the property rights of individual owners.

These pressures in the NHA reached a critical point in November 1917. In an effort to rid themselves of a "troublesome" Toronto franchise owner, Eddie Livingstone, the NHA's other directors formed a new league, the National Hockey League, made up of the Montreal Wanderers, Montreal Canadiens, Ottawa Senators, and a financially troubled Quebec Bulldogs. The market values of professional teams had declined during the war years, and the cost of entry to the new league was low. Just months before the league's formation, Tommy Gorman and Ottawa rink owner Ted Day were able to purchase the NHA's Ottawa Senators for $2,500. Later the NHL's directors forced the Quebec franchise to sell its players to the league for a mere $700.[14] The Quebec players were distributed to the remaining teams and the NHL added the Toronto Arenas to create a new four-team league. The new NHL replaced the old NHA in the annual East-West Stanley Cup series, and in the league's first season the Toronto Arenas won the Stanley Cup. But even with a Stanley Cup win in its first season, the NHL remained a marginal organization with low franchise values, minimal profits, and an uncertain future. When Montreal's Westmount Arena burned down in 1918 the Wanderers were forced to withdraw, and the NHL became a three-team league with only two solid franchises, the Ottawa Senators and Montreal Canadiens.

NHL Hockey and the Emerging North American Consumer Culture

The fortunes of professional hockey improved dramatically with the end of the war and more stable economic conditions by 1922. Even during a brief period of postwar inflation that limited disposable incomes, large crowds turned up for the 1919-20 hockey season to watch prominent prewar players and a new crop of postwar stars compete in two major leagues, now with franchises only in established urban areas, including U.S. cities. The likelihood of finding large new audiences for pro hockey in the United States had increased markedly when the Stanley Cup trustees recognized the legitimacy of challenges for the Stanley Cup from U.S. PCHA teams in 1916. A year later the Seattle Metropolitans went on to capture the Stanley Cup, and the trophy formerly reserved for the "Championship of the Dominion" was now touted as emblematic of the "World Championship" of professional hockey. Seattle's "World Championship" helped raise the profile of pro hockey in the United States and attracted the interest of rink owners and sports promoters in northeastern U.S. cities. Before the war Canadian professional teams had followed the example of barnstorming amateur teams and had played occasional exhibition matches in cities such as New York, Boston, and Pittsburgh. In other cases Canadian pro teams participated in special prize-money tournaments organized by U.S. promoters and rink owners. In the early 1920s the Canadian pro leagues resumed the practice of playing exhibition games in the United States, only now with a view to testing U.S. markets for possible expansion.

The growing popularity and potential profitability of pro hockey after the war were clearly evident in the rapid appreciation in the market value of teams and franchises between 1920 and 1927. For example, after a financially disastrous season in 1919 the owners of the Toronto Arenas wholesaled their hockey club for $2,000, and the league charged the new owners a $5,000 admission fee for the new franchise, now named the Toronto St. Patricks.[15] The next year the old Quebec Bulldogs were reactivated, but after an unprofitable season they were purchased by a group in Hamilton for $7,500. Then, in 1921, with attendance increasing across the NHL, the Montreal Canadiens were sold for $11,000 to Leo Dandurand, Louis Letourneau, and a former NHA goaltender from the prewar years, Louis Cattarinich. A few years later, in 1924, Dandurand and his colleagues sold half their territorial "rights" in Montreal for $15,000 to a group involving Montreal brewery millionaire Ken Dawes and Jimmy Strachan, owner of the Canadian Arena Company.[16] That represented a threefold increase in the price of an NHL franchise over a five-year period, and it set the standard for franchise rights when the NHL finally launched its expansion into the United States.

The first U.S. NHL franchise was awarded to Boston grocery store magnate C.F. Adams in 1924, and a year later another franchise was sold to entrepreneurs in Pittsburgh, also for the $15,000 entry fee. That same year, with franchise fees still relatively low, the market value of NHL teams suddenly took off. The most notable example of franchise appreciation was triggered when players on the league-winning Hamilton Tigers had refused to play additionally scheduled playoff games not covered in their contracts unless they received an additional $200 per game. When the Tigers' management wouldn't pay the additional sum the players went on strike, prompting league President Frank Calder to suspend the players and issue each of them a fine of $200 instead of the desired stipend. Furious about the labour dispute, the Hamilton management became aware that investors in New York were prepared to pay an unprecedented amount for the team. After considerable negotiation, the team that had been worth $7,500 in 1920 was sold for $75,000 to a group led by Tex Rickard, the head of Madison Square Garden.[17] In the wake of the New York deal, entrepreneurs in several northern and northeastern U.S. cities started a frenzied round of bidding for NHL franchises that drove prices even higher. For example, encouraged by Tex Rickard, Major Frederick McLaughlin put together a syndicate that raised $150,000 to bring an NHL team to Chicago in 1926.[18] In 1927 Conn Smythe had to appeal to hometown sentiment and Canadian patriotism to talk the owners of the Toronto St. Pats down from an asking price of $200,000. He eventually paid $160,000 for the team that became the Toronto Maple Leafs.

The increased demand for NHL teams between 1920 and 1927 — and the accompanying increase in market values — can be explained by several interrelated factors. At the most general level, hockey was simply swept up in the growth and dynamism of the U.S. and Canadian capitalist development of the 1920s. Continuing corporate concentration, automated practices of mass production, new methods of organizing and managing labour, a rapid decline in labour militancy, easier access to credit, and new marketing initiatives all contributed to higher levels of production accompanied by reduced prices. In Canada the combined effects of high levels of employment, previous labour militancy, and pension and minimum-wage reforms led to a period of postwar stability in real wages that lasted through much of the 1920s.[19] One of the most significant effects of these tendencies was an increase in the free time and disposable incomes that could be devoted to consumption, including the consumption of commercial sporting entertainments.

The popularity and economic value of NHL teams were also influenced by the inundation of urban popular cultures with the images and values of modern advertising. Throughout the 1920s, Canadians and Americans experienced an array of innovative new design, marketing, and research strategies created by professional ad agencies to realize the sales targets of their major industrial clients — especially the producers of national brand-name household products, food, and automobiles. Advertisers began to move beyond their earlier emphasis on product claims to create symbolic associations between product use and popular desires and aspirations: success, modernity, and fame itself. One way of establishing these associations was to link advertised products with "successful" people: entertainers, businessmen, and athletes. Advertising's use of associations between success and heavily promoted products helped to turn these people into national celebrities and build national markets for the products.

Weekly magazines published by newspapers and nationally distributed mass-market periodicals were arguably the first media vehicles for the national marketing campaigns that began to emerge in Canada and the United States in the first three decades of the twentieth century. There were twenty magazines with circulations of over 100,000 in the United States in 1905, and in 1910 the *Saturday Evening Post* had a circulation of over two million readers. Similarly, in Canada, the biggest newspaper weekend magazines had circulations of over 100,000, and combined with new mass-market magazines such as *Maclean's* and the *Canadian Home Journal* they provided an early forum for Canadian advertising on a national scale.[20] These national magazines and some of the national brand names they advertised became familiar and characteristic elements in the national popular cultures that were beginning to emerge in both countries.

Canadians were also heavy consumers of U.S. periodicals and of the increasingly "national" American popular culture. The advent of the U.S. mass-market magazine — and branch-plant U.S. publishing — at the turn of the century increased the already heavy flow of U.S. periodicals into Canada. By the 1920s the importing and publishing of U.S. mass-market periodicals in Canada — and Canadians' exposure to U.S. advertising, products, pastimes, and consumer obsessions — were already well and deeply established. In response to these influences many of the images, styles, and messages associated with U.S. advertising and the mass consumption of "nationally branded" U.S. products simply blended into Canada's own emerging national popular culture. The Canadian national popular culture thus included new continentally distributed U.S. entertainment products such as network radio programs, Hollywood movies, and — most importantly for the discussion at hand — "major-league" U.S. professional sports.

We've already noted how sports coverage in Canada had a North American and international dimension as early as the turn of the century. Modern communications technologies such as photography and telegraphy — and thirty years of aggressive promotion by sporting goods companies and sporting associations in manuals, rulebooks, newspapers, and specialty periodicals — had laid a firm foundation for national and international audiences for major sporting contests. Nonetheless, sport at the turn of the century still tended to be closely attached to local cultures and traditions, and local newspapers usually gave their greatest attention to local teams and athletes. But by the 1920s sporting events and leagues perceived to be of national and international importance were receiving more and more coverage. The common interests of national advertisers and the producers of media and popular entertainments, and the popularity of new technologies like the automobile and radio, accelerated the breakdown of time and space, thereby undermining local popular cultures and their traditional communal forms of recreation.

Radio played an especially important role in glamorizing and popularizing "major-league" sporting events as a key component in the new national popular cultures of North America. In the early 1920s RCA first showed radio's commercial potential by broadcasting the Jack Dempsey-Georges Carpentier heavyweight championship fight "live" to astounded audiences in two hundred theatres across the United States. The subsequent lure of sports programming became an important element in early sales of radio sets. In an effort to further expand the sale of radios, RCA launched a National Broadcasting Network (NBC) in 1926. Within a year NBC had a rival, the Columbia Phonograph Broadcasting System (CBS), a network that was aggressively experimenting with new approaches to the commercial sponsorship of programming and the sale of national audience-listening time to advertisers. By 1927 U.S. radio was well established as an advertiser-driven commercial system with a major proportion of programming devoted to sports and light entertainment.[21] With the advent of national commercial radio broadcasting in the United States, the conditions were set for major-league professional events to emerge as the sporting equivalent to the nationally branded products promoted so aggressively in other media. Sporting events such as the World Series, the Rose Bowl, and the World Heavyweight Boxing Championships took their place as American popular cultural icons along with companies and products like Coke, Ford, RCA, NBC, and CBS. As this occurred, the public visibility of *all* seemingly major-league professional sports organizations and athletes increased remarkably and the larger-than-life character of sport was elevated to a new national-mythological level.

Acting in concert with radio, the U.S. mass press of the 1920s also helped to push major-league sports to the forefront of a popular culture that was increasingly national in its orientation. Intense competition in the newspaper industry had pushed many smaller U.S. daily papers out of business by the early 1920s, with the result that most big-city markets in North America were dominated by only one or two major dailies (circumstances paralleled in Canada). In these major papers the sale of audiences to advertisers had grown to the point where advertising revenues outstripped the revenues produced by circulation. Sports coverage was proving to be an even greater factor in building and selling audiences than in the prewar years. Because many newspapers were becoming more heavily reliant on wire services, there was a growing standardization of sports reporting; coverage became focused primarily on "nationally important" leagues, teams, and events. In addition a few sports writers were able to create such richly detailed and dramatic accounts of major-league sporting competitions that they became national public figures in their own right. Writers such as Paul Gallico, Damon Runyon, and Westbrook Pegler were centrally important in elevating major-league spectator sport in the United States to the level of national mythology.[22]

Hockey in the United States had only a small fraction of the popularity and visibility of baseball, boxing, or college football, but in the context of the burgeoning American obsession with sport in the 1920s it appealed to high-rollers in northern and northeastern cities — entrepreneurs wanting to build egos or to position themselves as leading citizens in their communities. Hockey was especially attractive for rink or arena owners such as Tex Rickard, who had a sharp eye for new ways to fill booking dates. Indeed, hockey had been played in New York, Chicago, and Boston for over two decades, and there had been positive reactions to the skills of Canadian stars when they had played in local tournaments or exhibition games. The possibility of manning big-city U.S. teams with Canadian hockey stars and of marketing "exotic" Canadian teams such as the Montreal Canadiens promised a level of fan support high enough to justify a substantial investment.

In addition, forward-looking sports promoters in both countries were beginning to glimpse how advertising could generate additional revenues beyond the gate. Commercial sponsorship of sporting teams and the selling of advertising in game programs, billboards, or through public announcements were not new to the 1920s. But in the mid-1920s radio advertising promised to substantially increase the economic value of hockey audiences, rather like the way advertising had so successfully added extra monetary value to the newspaper audience. Ironically, many owners of professional sports teams were initially suspicious of radio, believing that people would simply stay home and listen to games rather than attend games live. More visionary owners, like Conn Smythe in Toronto, felt strongly that broadcasting would help to popularize their teams with the effect of building the gate. Owners who took this view initially offered the broadcast rights to their games for free, but it wasn't long before they began to realize that advertisers were willing to pay for the rights to address the team's customers in radio broadcasts. Conn Smythe once noted that when Jack MacLaren of MacLaren Advertising suggested in 1929 "that we would get money for hockey broadcasts, it was then I believed the story about manna from heaven."[23]

Canadian Culture and the Americanization of Pro Hockey

By the early 1920s the stage was set for the NHL to emerge as hockey's single "major league." But during that decade the NHL faced significant competition for audience attention both from popular amateur teams and from a number of new professional and semi-pro leagues that had formed after the First World War. The most notable new pro league was the Western Canada Hockey League, formed in 1921 with teams in Edmonton, Calgary, Regina, and Saskatoon. The formation of the WCHL meant that the NHL suddenly had to compete for players with two other major professional hockey leagues, the WCHL on the prairies and the PCHA on the coast. One important result of this competition was that player salaries in the early 1920s soon became much higher than they had been during the war. To make matters worse for the NHL, the prairie teams demonstrated within a season that they could compete with the PCHA clubs, and the Stanley Cup trustees allowed the new WCHL to participate in determining a Western champion for the annual East-West Stanley Cup final.

When the PCHA's Seattle Metropolitans folded prior to the 1924-25 season, the PCHA and WCHL merged to form a new six-team league, the Western Hockey League (WHL), and at the end of the season the WHL's Victoria Cougars, coached and managed by Lester Patrick, won the Stanley Cup. The Cougars' win prompted no small amount of Western chest-thumping, but the WHL was having financial problems. Its teams were playing in smaller arenas and smaller markets than NHL teams and had difficulty matching NHL salaries. The Western League's difficulties were compounded by NHL expansion into large urban markets in the United States in 1924 and 1925, and the NHL was contemplating further expansion in 1926. Faced with the prospect of unprofitable teams and the lure of greater opportunities available in the eastern United States, the WHL owners folded their teams, and the Patricks began to offer players to NHL franchises (and franchise aspirants). Chicago arranged to buy the Portland team intact, Detroit negotiated for the Cougars, and Boston made a variety of offers for individual players. Fearing that this unregulated dealing for quality players would lead to warfare within the league, the NHL's governors voted to create a pool of all the former WHL players signed by Eastern clubs. In return for making WHL players' contracts available to the pool, the Patricks reportedly received over $250,000.[24]

By 1927 a new ten-team NHL completely controlled the Stanley Cup and had managed to put its major professional hockey competitors out of business. To finance the escalating cost of new franchises and the high salaries that had been necessary to outbid the PCHL/WHA, the NHL had nearly doubled the number of games in its season, from twenty-four games in 1921-22 to forty-four games in 1926-27. After 1927, with the PCHA/WHL out of business, the NHL moved to consolidate its hold over hockey's labour market, reign in salaries, and strengthen labour discipline within the league. Almost immediately it negotiated affiliations with a large number of senior and semi-professional clubs in Canada and the United States to reduce possible competition from "minor" professional leagues. These affiliations greatly lessened competitive bidding for player services in the late 1920s, and as a result — despite player protests and a threatened strike — average NHL salaries declined. Over the next few years team managements involving well-known hockey "builders" such as Lester Patrick in New York, Conn Smythe in Toronto, and Jack Adams in Detroit successfully used hockey's early traditions of team and community loyalty to hold down players' salary demands. Meanwhile the league as a whole did everything in its power to limit players' bargaining abilities, including a 1933 provision that gave the NHL president, Frank Calder, complete discretionary power to suspend any player who held out in contract negotiations.[25]

NHL owners had begun to realize in the 1920s that to maximize their individual profits they would have to collude to make the league as a whole profitable.[26] However, the collusion was far from complete. The NHL remained immensely fractious — filled with personality conflicts, backroom dealing, and vendettas that often surpassed the owners' commitment to the league as a profit-maximizing entity. After the powerful Chicago multimillionaire James Norris bought his way into the NHL in 1932, he once remarked that the NHL governors' meetings were like a "group of nasty little boys at each other's throats."[27] Norris was no angel either. When the original Chicago Blackhawks owner, Major Frederick McLaughlin, blocked Norris's attempt to buy the Ottawa Senators in 1928 and move them to Chicago, Norris set out to undermine McLaughlin by pumping money into the minor-league American Hockey Association and creating a strong AHA team in Chicago. Norris also quietly assumed control of Chicago's new $6.8 million, sixteen-thousand-seat stadium when the economic crash of 1929 threatened to bankrupt the project, thereby giving his AHA team, the Chicago Shamrocks, a "major-league" venue. The Shamrocks outdrew the Blackhawks on several occasions, and in 1932 Norris convinced the Stanley Cup trustees to accept a challenge from his AHA team. The NHL refused to let any of its teams take up the challenge from "an outlaw league" and the matter was postponed for a year, during which time Norris entered the NHL by purchasing the debt-ridden Olympia Stadium in Detroit and the NHL's Detroit Falcons. After this incident the Stanley Cup simply became the NHL's exclusive championship trophy. By the early 1940s Norris had managed to gain effective control over the league by virtue of having a majority interest in the Detroit Red Wings and the Chicago Blackhawks as well as Madison Square Garden, home of the New York Rangers.

The transformation of Canada's national winter pastime into a continental business largely controlled by ultra-rich Americans didn't occur without criticism. One area of concern was that the NHL's move to the United States threatened to take the game so far upmarket that pro hockey would be inaccessible to the "ordinary Canadians" who had long made up the bulk of fans for the various older leagues. For example, in a 1927 article in *Maclean's* one critic noted: "There is no Pacific Coast League today. Instead there exists a ten-club organization, with six of the clubs representing American cities, which will play this season to something like two million people. Millionaires back the organizations. Fine ladies in evening gowns with polite gloved palms, applaud the efforts of the skating roughnecks. Hockey has put on a high hat."[28] For Canadians with nationalist leanings another concern was that the Americanization of professional hockey appeared to be part of broader trends that threatened the very possibility of a distinctively Canadian national culture. During the 1920s the increasing influx of U.S. entertainments and ideas through mass-market periodicals, films, and radio was becoming a matter of great concern. Some commentators saw the apparent Americanization of pro hockey as one more example of the growing dominance of the United States over Canadian economic and cultural life.

Most Canadians, though, didn't seem overly worried by the NHL's move to U.S. cities. Nationalist concerns were softened by the fact that the NHL was still built on a Canadian labour market, and the sports pages of the day often reflected a sense of excitement about Canadian players becoming stars in U.S. cities along with famed American sports heroes like Babe Ruth or Jack Dempsey. In addition there was still a whole Canadian division in the NHL in the late 1920s; and with its head office in Montreal the NHL kept the impression of maintaining close ties to Canadian life.

The perception of the NHL as an essentially Canadian league was reinforced by the remarkably popular coverage of NHL hockey on Canadian radio during the 1930s. Radio coverage of hockey games in Canada first began when CFCA, a station created for publicity purposes by the *Toronto Star*, began to broadcast local amateur games in 1923. Over the next several years one CFCA announcer, W.A. Hewitt's son Foster, became the unofficial voice of hockey in Toronto. Hewitt went on to work out a partnership agreement with Conn Smythe regarding the production of hockey broadcasts in Maple Leaf Gardens, and in 1931 Smythe, MacLaren Advertising, and Hewitt laid the foundation for regular Saturday night broadcasts of Maple Leaf games to be sponsored by General Motors. On the first of January, 1933, General Motors extended its Saturday night NHL broadcast to a patchwork of stations that allowed the game to be heard coast to coast. NHL hockey became one of the first radio programs to address a national Canadian audience.[29]

In the following summer General Motors set out to consolidate this national audience, and to do so it purchased broadcast rights for the NHL's Montreal Canadiens and Montreal Maroons. That season, Phil Lalonde, radio director for CKAC (owned by *La Presse*), and Roland Beaudry, a Montreal sports editor, began broadcasting Canadiens' games in French. At the same time Charlie Harwood and Elmer Ferguson started doing English broadcasts for the Maroons. This set the stage for truly national hockey broadcasts, with Montreal games broadcast in English and French in Quebec and Toronto games aired across the rest of the country. By 1934 the national General Motors broadcasts were reaching over a million listeners. By the end of the 1930s the audience for *Hockey Night in Canada* — now sponsored by Imperial Oil — had nearly doubled to two million listeners.[30] Never had so many Canadians in all corners of the country regularly engaged in the same cultural experience at the same time. Stories and characters from NHL games emerged as the stuff of Canadian folklore: Red Horner "knocking people into the cheap seats," Eddie Shore's injury of Ace Bailey, the tragic death of Howie Morenz. *Hockey Night in Canada* began to create for hockey, and in particular NHL hockey, a deeply rooted, almost iconic place in Canadian culture, regardless of the fact that the NHL had become a continental league dominated by U.S. money.

Hockey's capacity to bring Canadians together around a common interest in the 1930s derived in no small measure from the game's roots in *both* English-speaking Canada and Quebec. Indeed, from the time the Club de Hockey Canadien established itself as Montreal's French team and initiated what would for many years be a firm control of the best French-speaking players, the Canadiens took on a representative significance that would have no counterpart in North American commercial sport. In particular, the Canadiens' rivalries with the Montreal Maroons and, later, the Toronto Maple Leafs provided for the regular dramatization of the French and English identities that were so much a part of the popular consciousness of the day. There was no other cultural form, no other popular practice, that brought the "two solitudes" into regular engagement with each other in quite the same way. Moreover, although millions of immigrants from other European countries had brought their own popular recreations with them when they moved to Canada, it wasn't long before their children and grandchildren were watching and playing hockey. Over the next thirty years, stars with names like Sawchuk and Bucyk, Mikita and Mahovlich, and Delvecchio and Esposito would become Canadian folk heroes.

Still, this popular enthusiasm for professional hockey did not find complete approval or support among Canada's intellectual elites. During the 1920s and 1930s Canadian culture continued to retain much of its earlier paternalistic imprint, and there was a notable concern about the apparent disruptiveness of modernity matched with a lingering suspicion of "excessive" commercialism in cultural life. This suspicion of commercialism was especially notable in English Canada, where the threat of Americanization was always felt more acutely than in Quebec. This resulted in a variety of efforts among the anglo-Canadian middle classes to respond to what the *Vancouver Star* called "the reeking cloud of lower Americanism."[31] This sentiment generated the first initiatives to constitute a public broadcasting network in the 1930s, and it encouraged the production of distinctly Canadian — and often highbrow — cultural alternatives to mass-produced U.S. commercial entertainments: Canadian art, Canadian literature, Canadian music, Canadian drama.

There was also a related current of patriotic discourse that continued to urge Canadians to collective self-improvement through participation in local voluntary associations such as choirs, book clubs, and dramatic societies. This discourse often maintained a gentrified tone through its continuing celebration of the Victorian ideal of the amateur artist, author, or actor; and for some of its advocates the Victorian ideal could certainly be extended to include participation in amateur sport. However, because most cultural critics of the 1920s and 1930s remained deeply suspicious of any form of mass-spectator entertainment, there was simply no way to find much that was socially redeeming in hockey, even for nationalists. Indeed, the alarmist criticisms directed at mass entertainment demonstrated how out of touch these critics were with the many Canadians who were happily incorporating the new continental popular culture into the rhythms of local and regional life.

To the degree that NHL owners cared to respond at all to highbrow stereotypes, they did so less by trying to "civilize" hockey than by playing up the idea that hockey had indeed "put on a high hat." In this regard Conn Smythe once noted to a writer for the Toronto *Star* that in building Maple Leaf Gardens in 1931 he wanted a place with "class": "a place to go all dressed up; [at present] we don't compete with the comfort of theatres and other places where people can spend their money. We need a place where people can go in evening clothes, if they want to come there from a party or dinner.... We need ... a place that people can be proud to take their wives or girlfriends to."[32] Such self-conscious attempts at gentrification may not have convinced many highbrows of the cultural value of hockey, but there seems little doubt that as hockey moved into new sports palaces in Toronto, Montreal, Chicago, and Detroit in the 1920s and 1930s it gained new levels of popularity and a larger share of urban middle-class audiences — which also began to include more women spectators.

The NHL gained this popularity despite the economic collapse of 1929 and the subsequent Depression. NHL teams were now in major centres and had larger numbers of upmarket fans, many of them not hit as hard by the Depression as people in rural areas and in working-class occupations. Furthermore, in Canada the combined influences of national radio broadcasts and an adoring popular press continued to expand the customer base of knowledgeable and enthusiastic fans beyond the home cities of Canadian NHL teams. The Depression reached its depths in Canada in the winter of 1933, precisely when NHL games were first broadcast to a national Canadian audience. It seems plausible to suggest that national broadcasts of NHL games found an audience hungry for inexpensive entertainment as well as a diversion from the challenges of difficult economic times. This isn't to say that every NHL team thrived during the Depression. After the crash of 1929 several franchises began to lose money, and two of the league's ten teams, including the famous Ottawa Senators, had dropped out by 1935. The Depression also created a situation in which the Montreal Maroons — lacking the Canadiens' strong connections to French-speaking audiences — had to withdraw from the league in 1938. When the New York Americans also closed down in 1942, the NHL was pared down to the six teams that would take the league through the next twenty-five years: the Montreal Canadiens, Toronto Maple Leafs, Boston Bruins, New York Rangers, Detroit Red Wings, and Chicago Blackhawks.

The NHL in the Early Postwar Era: Monopoly, Prosperity, and Television

The NHL was hit hard by Canada's entry into the Second World War. The enlargement of the armed forces through conscription in the summer of 1940 gutted most teams, forcing them to limp through the next five years with rag-tag teams primarily composed of players from the junior and senior leagues. But as the war ended the NHL found itself in an unassailable position. The Canadian government had allowed the league to operate during the war as a morale booster, and national radio broadcasts of NHL games on the Canadian Broadcasting Corporation were often subtly linked to patriotic themes and messages. In addition, the NHL emerged from the war years with the status of a cartel: it was now the only seller of major-league hockey in North America and the only significant buyer of major-league hockey talent.

One especially notable feature of the NHL's dominance of hockey after 1945 was the extent to which the league was successful in integrating not only new postwar minor pro leagues into its feeder system but also virtually all of amateur hockey. Some junior and senior amateur teams affiliated with the Canadian Amateur Hockey Association had developed close relationships with NHL clubs as early as the late 1920s, while others had to continually resist player raids from the NHL, minor pro teams, and the many independent industrial and semi-commercial leagues that could be found across Canada and the northern United States. Amateur hockey was immensely popular in the 1930s, often drawing gates that rivalled those of some pro teams, but as the Depression deepened the prospect of making even small amounts of money in hockey lured players away from amateur teams in droves. In 1935 the CAHA grudgingly responded to competitive pressures by allowing its teams to pay players and by welcoming former professional players back onto amateur clubs. Over the following year the NHL and CAHA struck an agreement in which the NHL promised not to recruit junior players and said it would compensate senior teams financially for players who made the NHL.[33]

The 1936 agreement paved the way for an even closer partnership between the CAHA and the NHL — a partnership in which the CAHA always negotiated from a position of weakness for fear that the NHL might call off its agreements and start recruiting senior and junior players at will. By the early 1940s, to make up for players lost to wartime conscription, the NHL found it necessary to recruit junior players and there was little the CAHA could do about it. By the end of the 1940s the NHL and CAHA had negotiated a new agreement that allowed each NHL team to sponsor two junior CAHA teams and to assume ownership rights to the players. Junior teams in turn received development money for players they sent on to the pros. The deal created incentives for junior teams to send players to the NHL, but it effectively marginalized the senior amateur leagues. Even more notably, the NHL earned the exclusive right to override any existing CAHA contracts, a provision that made it extremely difficult for senior teams to retain star players. Indeed, by 1947 the CAHA had become little more than a junior partner of the NHL; it couldn't even determine the eligibility of its own members or change its own playing rules without NHL approval.

These negotiations meant that NHL teams entered the postwar boom of the 1950s with unimpeded access to any prospective star playing in an amateur league in Canada. Moreover, the NHL's complete dominance of the hockey labour market ensured that players were relatively docile in salary negotiations, thereby contributing to windfall profits. Indeed, while salaries remained relatively low through the 1940s and 1950s the numbers of games in the NHL season jumped from fifty to seventy games. The NHL was entering a period of unprecedented popularity and profitability. The *Hockey Night in Canada* radio broadcasts had become well established as a Canadian national ritual, and a crop of new hockey stars such as Gordie Howe, Maurice Richard, Bobby Hull, and Bobby Orr helped to build even larger NHL audiences over the next two decades.

With postwar prosperity the earlier tendencies towards a media-based North American consumer society in Canada became more pronounced than ever before. Low unemployment, high disposable incomes, suburbanization, new levels of home and car ownership, and a massive increase in purchases of light consumer goods were all features of a postwar economic boom that lasted into the early 1970s. For Canadian working people in particular, postwar life and expectations came to be defined by unprecedented levels of geographical mobility, individualized consumption, home-centred recreations, and, significantly, the baby boom. The advent of televised NHL games with Foster Hewitt on CBC in 1952 and, later, René Lecavalier on Radio-Canada allowed an entire generation of baby-boomers to watch major-league hockey — the hockey in the news — every Saturday night from autumn to spring. By the mid-1950s the idea that NHL hockey was a significant part of common Canadian experience — and of the identities of postwar Canadians — had simply become a matter of course to this demographically significant generation.

Since 1952 it has become almost impossible to talk about the economics of the NHL without also talking about television. In 1949 the league president, Clarence Campbell, went on record expressing his fear that television coverage would hurt hockey by keeping fans in their living rooms. Later he would echo the fears of Canadian highbrows by calling television "the greatest menace of the entertainment world."[34] And even as savvy an entrepreneur as Conn Smythe was unsure: first about televised hockey's ability to compete with hockey on radio, and second about the possible threat of television to gate receipts. Smythe's concern about protecting the gate at Maple Leaf Gardens was the factor that led to early CBC broadcasts coming on air only after the first period of Toronto games had already been played. But it wasn't long before Smythe and the other owners realized that television too was offering "more manna from heaven." After an experimental year in 1952 in which he charged Imperial Oil virtually nothing for broadcast rights to Maple Leaf games, Smythe pronounced the experiment a success and asked for $150,000 over the next three years.[35]

Television revenues rose steadily through the 1950s and 1960s as the size of audiences grew in North America. Less than 10 per cent of Canadian homes had televisions in 1953, but by 1960 the number had jumped to 80 per cent. Almost immediately, *Hockey Night in Canada* became the CBC's most popular television show, drawing audiences as large as 3.5 million English Canadians and 2 million French Canadians by the early 1960s.[36] The value of these (largely male) audiences to advertisers increased strikingly through the 1960s, as television became the major publicist of the new postwar consumer society, educating people about new consumer goods and services and new consumer identities. It was the prospect of even greater television revenues that fuelled the NHL's first postwar expansion in 1967, and it was the lure of larger U.S. televison markets that influenced the initial awarding of franchises. It was also television that opened the door to the creation in the early 1970s of a new rival "major" pro league, the World Hockey Association — a league that briefly challenged the NHL's monopoly position in professional hockey and brought the pro game back to western Canada.

PART II

EXPLORING THE POSTWAR
HOCKEY SUBCULTURE

Chapter Five

The Work World of Pro Hockey

Over the last century professional hockey has developed as a form of wage work, similar in many ways to other forms of wage work that engage Canadians for much of their lives. Like other workplaces, pro hockey has bosses and employees, occupational friendships and rivalries, and performance pressures derived from the push for profit. By the same token, like workers in other occupations hockey players have moments when they love what they're doing and times when they hate it. They have times when relations with management seem invisible or almost familial and times when management seems like an oppressive yoke.

This is not to say that all forms of wage work are completely the same, or that the work of hockey is the same as flipping hamburgers or driving taxis. Pro hockey can be distantly compared with other "professional" occupations — law, medicine, drama, music, teaching, dance, or film — that are often the realization of a person's youthful dreams and sometimes offer the potential for significant rewards of money, status, or public visibility. Among these other professional occupations, hockey players' careers compare most closely with those of successful dancers, actors, and musicians. Like hockey, these occupations are part of the modern entertainment industries; they are geared to the selling of public performances.

Still, notwithstanding such comparisons, most people would consider pro hockey to be markedly different from other professional occupations in the entertainment industries. Two differences are particularly notable. First, our attitudes to pro hockey are often rooted in memories of the joys and challenges of childhood play. A large part of the appeal of a career in pro hockey lies in the (mostly male) dream of being paid to play a game you loved as a child. Former players frequently argue that even when hockey is most intensely competitive or callously commercial, those memories of play are rarely extinguished. The play metaphor is kept alive in popular language too. We go to see professional athletes "play" the game even though we know we are really watching them work. Nobody ever says, "I went to see the Canucks work against the Oilers last night."

Ironically, the idea that pro sport has its roots in play has also lent itself to more critical interpretations. In assessing the transformation from childhood play to the paid work and public spectacle of professional sport, some critics suggest that the innocence, joy, and freedom of play are lost. In the 1920s and 1930s similar arguments were occasionally made about professional dance or theatre — arguments that expressed lingering Victorian attitudes about the special status of the amateur in Canadian culture. In sport these arguments have persisted longer, with a uniquely powerful resonance. If play has often been seen as a civilizing social practice, or as one of the few truly autonomous areas of human expression, professional sport has often been seen either as a perversion of play or as its alienated expression in a money-mad society. Although these sentiments are far less common now than they were thirty years ago, they still occupy a place in the social memories of Canadians; and they've contributed to a longstanding tendency to view the work of sport as something qualitatively different than the work that goes on elsewhere in the entertainment industries.

This raises a second important dimension to popular understandings of hockey as a form of work. The mystique of hockey that developed in Canadian culture after the 1920s has brought a larger-than-life character to the pro game and its players that makes comparisons with other forms of work seem inappropriate. Undoubtedly, there are other larger-than-life cultural performers in Canada outside of pro hockey, and the game's mystique today may not quite be what it was in the 1950s or 1960s. But because few areas of Canadian life have been as consistently and heavily mythologized as hockey, we have tended to view our game as something that transcends "mere" work. There are few other occupations in Canada where "workers" have carried the hopes and dreams of communities in quite such a powerful and public way. Few other occupations, if any, have prompted so many young boys across so many generations to dream of professional careers.

For all these reasons, Canadians have chronically tended to either romanticize or misrepresent the nature of hockey as a form of work. On the one hand, some critics have reduced the work of the game simply to questions of money and power. They see hockey as a playground for a small circle of affluent men who treat their players like chattels and care about nothing more than the bottom line. On the other hand, for promoters and many fans the game is more about the romance of play and the passions of collective identification. Canadians know all too well that hockey is a business with its own occupational limits and pressures, but these limits and pressures have been downplayed as fans follow their favourite players and teams and indulge their "love of the game." Hockey's work relations have been viewed largely through the prism of media accounts in a celebrity-oriented culture. Broadcast commentators, fanzines, talk shows, and editorials all occasionally offer reflective commentaries on the work of the game, but on the whole these media exist only to keep the romance alive. In the end, neither the cynical view of hockey as nothing more than a glamorous sweat-shop nor the celebratory view of hockey as a commercial expression of the romance of play adequately captures the professional game's complexity: the pressures, fears, and satisfactions that construct its work world.

Working at the Game

On the surface the skills that today's professionals display in the arena are the same as those of backyard players: skating, passing, shooting, bodychecking, anticipating the play. Yet placing these skills together in league play, where players (and others) have a stake in the outcome, creates a far more intensely *competitive* emphasis. A former Chicago Blackhawk, Eric Nesterenko, once contrasted this competitive emphasis with his memories of the joys of unstructured play. "When I was a kid, to really *move* was my delight," he told U.S. journalist Studs Terkel. "The sweetness in being able to move and control your body. This is what play is. Beating somebody is secondary."[1]

Maybe so. But there seems to be a touch of idealism in this description of unstructured play. Men who recall the joys of childhood play often forget the high stakes involved in children's seemingly unstructured games. Indeed, most young Canadian boys quickly learn the implicitly competitive nature of their play. The pressure to play well, even in simple games of shinny, is felt in the agony of being picked last for a team in a pick-up game, in the need to have enough skill to win the respect of potential bullies, and in the shame of obvious physical ineptness. That said, Nesterenko's recollection captures something fundamentally important. As more and more factors are placed at stake in formal games — a game result, a playoff position, a trip, a championship, a scout's attention, a coach's job, a franchise's success, and ultimately a player's career and financial future — the pressures to perform increase dramatically.

Gradually (or sometimes very suddenly) the young player who aspires to be a professional is made to appreciate that beating his opponent — to the puck, along the boards, and ultimately on the scoreboard — makes *all* the difference between the "winners" who proceed in the game and those many others who simply have good skills. Professional teams, after all, sell the experience of winning to fans who themselves may not experience winning very often, at least not in the same clear and public ways, in their workaday lives. As a result, winners have been celebrated from the earliest days of pro sport, and losers tend to be forgotten. As young players apprentice for the professional game, they learn that the pressure to win changes coaches and teammates as well as themselves. Above all, players become subjected to much higher levels of labour discipline and surveillance from coaches and managers. Training regimes are more closely monitored, missed assignments are punished, friends who don't produce are cut. The pressure, moreover, is always there.

What management demands, and what most players have to develop if they are to survive in the pro game, is the habit of *unrelenting application*. This starts with systematic off-ice and off-season conditioning. It also includes dedication in practice as well as in games and, crucially, "coming to play every night." The recreational player and, indeed, the talented junior can have off nights, when they are not "up" for the game, not playing with the competitive intensity that is necessary to beat opponents who have that intensity. But it is part of the public's understanding of "professionalism" that professionals give "value for money" whenever they come to work. This is what people expect of the teacher and the surgeon. It is also, perhaps more analogously, what they expect of the actor and the musician, especially when these professional entertainers are highly paid.

It is arguable that only other performers can fully appreciate the extent to which performing at your peak requires being "psyched up."

It demands of the performer an adrenalin level that, for those who like it, is part of the thrill of being a performer. Most of us know these feelings of tension and excitement from special occasions. We also recognize that it is possible to be too keyed up to perform at our best. What is special about professional sport is the need to optimize the tension level, to play at a level of controlled arousal, so that skills are executed at a peak and in the face of determined opposition. The athletes we know as "money players" are the ones who manage this tension best, but for all athletes the fact of living with high adrenalin levels is a distinctive characteristic of their work. It is something they get used to, and mostly learn to like.

It is obviously difficult to sustain this maximum intensity throughout the long regular schedule that has helped to make professional hockey profitable. Every fan knows that mid-season NHL games can feature more than their share of lacklustre performances. Once the regular season is over the high stakes that attend success or failure in the playoffs produce an even higher level of competitive intensity, which is anxiously anticipated by hockey fans. Even in the regular season, the struggle to overcome other individuals in a continual series of personal contests — races for the puck, scuffles along the boards or in front of the net, one-on-ones — demands an intensity of application that is qualitatively different from, say, the effort required of a sales manager or engineer. The competition for NHL jobs is so keen, and differences in talent at this level so slight (except for a few superstars), that a player who can't sustain this intensity, or a sophomore who relaxes the work habits that made him a successful rookie, is unlikely to have a long career. A one-time St. Louis goalie, Rick Heinz, captures the effects of this stress in a story about teammate Larry Patey. Patey had enjoyed a long and fairly successful career with the Blues, but he told Heinz that he had never felt secure enough to be able to relax and enjoy his success. The point of the story, for both players, was that this insecurity was probably precisely why Patey had lasted so long in the NHL.[2]

The most obvious aspect of the work world of professional hockey is its sheer physicality: the levels of physical discipline, effort, and skill it demands, and the physical costs it exacts. Most work today outside of logging camps, mines, and construction sites is almost disembodied. White-collar or service-sector workers usually have to exercise if they want to feel good physically, or even to stay fit, and those workers whose jobs still involve physical labour quickly learn to pace themselves. But hockey players and other professional athletes are in touch with their bodies in a way that can only be appreciated by others (like dancers) whose work requires not only physical virtuosity but also continually pushing the limits of what bodies can do. To be a good athlete means knowing your body in a way that few others do. It means enjoying moving and stretching and doing physical things, "feeling good in your skin." For most players, performances of physical excellence are an expression of self, a side of themselves they miss when they leave the game.

This bodily knowledge and expressive capacity typically come at a price. The speed and strength required mean that professional players must continually *work* at fitness too, not only on the ice but also in the weight room and health club. Players today spend many hours working out — hours that their predecessors spent in other kinds of activities. Working out on weights and machines can be fun, but it can also be a mindless, mechanistic routine narrowly focused on self. Men who spend hours each day building up their bodily strength and refining highly specialized physical skills are seldom described as "well rounded"; nor are they always easy to live with. In occasional instances the desire for size and strength, as well as aggressiveness, can become so consuming that players have turned to virtually any lengths — including steroid programs — to give them an edge over their competitors. A former Toronto Maple Leaf, John Kordic, is one of the most notable examples of a player whose desire for strength, size, and aggressiveness led to steroid use; in Kordic's case it also led to a drug dependence that may have contributed to his premature death in 1992. Moreover, it is doubtful that Kordic's use of steroids was simply an isolated incident in hockey, particularly if we include junior hockey in the frame of reference. Junior players know that strength and aggressiveness are prized in the NHL, and it would be surprising if some of them didn't turn to steroids to help catch the attention of NHL scouts and recruiters. One former junior coach has estimated that in 1992 there were as many as fifty junior players on steroid programs.[3]

The intensely competitive arena in which hockey skills must be asserted also means that injuries are routine. Muscles strain and give way when asked to stretch beyond their capability, and bodies become the target of other bodies (and sticks). Players and fans alike know that injuries are a constant occupational hazard for professional athletes: they can mean weeks or months out of the lineup, or even an end to a career. For almost all players, seasons that start with an enjoyment of physicality give way to a series of strains, pulls, bruises, or worse. Professional athletes get used to playing with pain, and players who can't do this don't remain professionals for long. There are, of course, players who respond particularly well to the competitive demands of the professional game. They find more in themselves, physically and emotionally; and these "winners" — Bryan Trottier and John Tonelli come to mind — are widely respected, in the game and in North American society. Yet these demands get harder to meet as the years pass; and the hockey player who stops *wanting* to work at the game to this degree is soon pushed out.

Notwithstanding the need for strength, the elements of speed and skating ability are still the foundation on which other skills are built, on offence and defence alike. These requirements are obvious for offensive players, whether we are talking about the straight-ahead speed of an Yvan Cournoyer or a Jari Kurri or the finesse of a puck carrier like Mark Messier or Russ Courtnall. Speed is also essential to defence, in ways demonstrated by players such as Guy Carbonneau, Esa Tikkanen, and Bob Gainey. In *The Game* Ken Dryden emphasizes how speed forces opposing players to react before they have time to think or look: speed "robs an opponent of co-ordination and control, stripping away skills, breaking down systems, making even the simplest tasks seem difficult."[4] For some players it is the remarkable and unremitting speed at which skills have to be performed in the NHL that makes all the difference between minor-league success and big-league failure.

Still, size and strength continue to be of great importance in NHL hockey. Players who have played a punishing physical game have often been able to neutralize faster opponents, taking away not only the skater's legs but also his will to skate. The age-old techniques of bodywork and stickwork have been used to harass puckhandlers and playmakers, denying them the time and the space in which their skills can make the difference. Moreover, the offensive style developed by many teams in the postwar era began to place a premium on shooting the puck in and winning it again in physical struggles in the offensive zone. In these circumstances there were obvious places on team rosters for the big tough winger who could win the puck along the boards or stand his ground in front of the net for deflections or rebounds. Since the 1970s whole teams have been built around size and strength, and they have been able to win by imposing their own style of play. While some of the emphasis on size and aggressiveness began to soften after the late 1970s, even offensively minded stars like Wayne Gretzky and Mario Lemieux require the right supporting casts. Especially in playoff hockey, when winning and losing are (finally) *final*, determined defence can neutralize offensive flair most of the time. Intimidation and defensive systems are routinely deployed to take away the finesse player's edge; and this has meant successful careers for many players who are tough and disciplined but not prolific scorers.

Just as only the most talented teams have been able to win with a game based on speed and offensive flair (the Montreal Canadiens of the 1970s, for example), so too have teams built on size and toughness been beaten by teams who were tough *and* fast. The successful teams of the 1980s — the Islanders and the Oilers — each created their own blend of speed and size, of skill and controlled violence. Even a team as committed to offense and entertainment as the Oilers had to be able to defend its skill-players, to make it safe for them to work their magic. It also had to have forwards and defencemen who could gain the puck along the boards and who could defend their own goal against attacks built more around muscle than adroitness. Gretzky, Coffey, and Kurri "made the difference"; but given the style of play in the NHL in the 1980s they needed Hunter, Semenko, and Muni for their skills to triumph. Today every team still has a complex division of labour; every team struggles to find a blend of offensive and defensive defencemen, puck carriers and players who can get the puck for them, and snipers and protectors.

Playing a "role" on a team is a phrase that can subsume contributions of markedly differing importance. It can include players who are shuffled in and out of the lineup depending on whether the coach wants more speed or more toughness against a particular opponent. It typically includes the enforcer, the specialist penalty killer, and fourth-line players who participate (and are expected not to make mistakes) against opponents who use four lines. This last role is often accepted willingly by the fringe player or the young player who is happy simply to be in the NHL. But it is unsettling for a journeyman (a Mark Lamb, for example, or a Paul Fenton) when the next step may be out of the lineup, or when a young player placed in this role gets little scope to demonstrate his offensive skills. More important are the skilled role players who are the "backbone" of good teams, players like Edmonton's Craig MacTavish or Pittsburgh's Rick Tocchet.

These skilled role players do the regular, unspectacular work that every team requires to be successful. They rarely achieve the visibility or the rewards of highly skilled offensive players, and few of them play most of their careers on winning teams. But on losing teams the pressure to score is even greater, and management is often likely to go with young checkers in the hope that they will develop into consistent scorers too. So the career of the role player is always precarious, precisely because his contribution is less the product of artistry than of hard work. That contribution, therefore, can be made by other hard workers. Furthermore, because part of the role player's job is to "fit in," not only on the ice but off it, it has been more likely that he will come from an anglo-Canadian background. There has always been a place in the NHL for the star francophone player; and, until comparatively recently, the Montreal Canadiens provided a home for francophone journeymen. However, research suggests that francophones have been less likely to catch spots as role players; in other words, it appears to have been harder for the average or marginal francophone player to make an extended career in professional hockey.[5]

Finally, it is worth remarking on the rhythms that uniquely structure the hockey player's working life. On the surface the hockey player's annual rhythms look a bit like a teacher's. There is a new beginning every September, followed by eight or nine months of intensive, often emotionally draining work that builds towards a high-pressure series of tests in late spring, followed by a summer vacation. August, and with it the need to prepare for the next annual cycle, seems to arrive far too soon. Scratch this surface, though, and significant differences appear immediately. The most pervasive is that the "normal" rhythms of night and day, week and weekend, have little meaning in a professional hockey player's life. The role of working in an entertainment industry whose product is necessarily staged when most people are off work means that the hockey player, like the lounge singer or the stand-up comic, works "anti-social" hours that make it difficult to put time into relationships with others outside the game.

Moreover, unlike regular shift workers, hockey players have little regularity even within this pattern of life. Whereas most people live by clocks or calendars, in *some* kind of routine, for eight months a year pro hockey players live by a schedule organized around games, practices, and travel. Ken Dryden gives us a sense of what this schedule feels like when he remarks: "Awake half the night, asleep half the morning, with three hours until practice, then three hours until dinner; nighttime no different from daytime, weekends from weekdays."[6] The result is fragmented time, what Dryden describes as a "high-energy life" lived in short bursts. During these bursts players have to perform at their peak, while in between games and practices, and especially on the road, they have an oppressively large amount of time to kill.

Work Relations with Teammates

The work world of hockey is also very much contoured around being part of the team. Former players usually look back fondly on this aspect of team life: the golf and card games, the time spent eating and drinking and joking together. Journalists who have interviewed players or followed professional teams have remarked on the boyish banter, the playing around, and the camaraderie of the locker room, the plane, or the team bus. All of this provides time, as Pete Mahovlich once put it, for players "to act stupid together."[7] It is partly in such hours spent sharing fun — fun that becomes the stuff of stories that themselves become the stuff of team lore — that a group of individuals becomes a group of friends and a *team*. At the same time, though, the peer pressure involved in "being one of the guys" is hard to avoid, especially on the road. Younger players, in particular, feel pressure to follow the crowd and kill time with groups of teammates.[8] The regular rounds of card games and practical jokes, bars and health clubs, or shopping and watching television together can become an informal occupational obligation.

Such activities suit the rhythms and the mindsets of men who regularly face the prospect of having a few hours to fill. They are also typically fun, especially for younger players still somewhat star-struck about the opportunity to banter with players whom they may well have idolized for years. Some players recall, though, that while they enjoyed most of this aimless fun in the early years, towards the end of their careers they began to feel that time spent in these ways was wasted. Eric Nesterenko recalled how he began to see this killing of time as a loss and wanted to do something about it.[9] Yet he also recognized that after years of simply filling in time it was hard to change the pattern and learn to use time constructively. Commenting on his years with the Canadiens, Ken Dryden makes a similar point: "Always rebounding from one thing to the next, I'm always on the way to some place else; in contact with families, friends and outside interests, but never quite attaching onto any of them."[10]

This is also true when the player is "at home." We've interviewed young players who noted how the life of the young, single player in his home city is not unlike road life. With a schedule that isn't compatible with normal domestic routines, he is still apt to spend a lot of time with teammates whose hours of "work" and leisure are the same as his. This means "hanging out" together not only at the rink but also at health clubs and after-hours spots. For the married player the problems are similar at one level, but quite different at another. The hockey player with a young family comes home wanting to spend "quality" time with his family, yet winds up being not unlike the colourful uncle. He brings presents and is the focal point of special meals and outings. He is not so able to share in the daily crises and triumphs that become, cumulatively, a family's life together. Absent regularly for many things that other dads do, from helping with homework and settling fights to driving his children to practice or lessons, he soon comes home to a family that has learned, as Ken Dryden suggests, to cope without him.[11]

He misses the evenings and weekends that are other families' times to be together, and in the off-season and at the end of his career he finds himself trying to make up for lost time. The irony is that while at first glance professional hockey players appear to have plenty of free time, on closer inspection this time seems far less free. Most notably, the rhythms of the work make it hard to participate in any dependable and regular way in the projects and lives of people beyond the team.

All of these pressures tend to reinforce a perception of the team as a kind of surrogate family in which people come to depend upon one another both during regular work hours and after the official work is done. Even the most independent and iconoclastic players deeply feel the need to "belong" to their occupational group. For instance, in many ways Ken Dryden was an outsider on the Canadiens: a goalie, a university player, an intellectual, and an anglophone on a team that in the 1970s still had a francophone core. Yet it clearly mattered to him that he was a part of the team. He needed to feel that the team depended on him. In *The Game* Dryden uses a story about Bob Gainey to illustrate the sense of interdependence and the commitment to one another that develop on successful teams. Gainey recalled hearing Roger Neilson, his junior coach in Peterborough (and later an NHL coach), tell a team without stars that to succeed in the playoffs, "They would have to play as a team, working for each other, *depending* on each other."[12] It worked, and for Gainey it was an enduring lesson. He discovered that he could accomplish more as a member of a successful team than he was ever likely to accomplish by himself. He also found a greater satisfaction and joy in this collective and shared achievement than he had ever known in individual triumphs.

This, in Dryden's view, is the lesson of team sports. Others use different words; but the experience of interdependency is the same, and the power of the bonding it creates comes through. For example, Don Saleski of the Philadelphia Flyers of the 1970s recalls: "The word 'respect' comes to mind. We respected each other's roles and each other's abilities. There was a real good feeling for each other's shortcomings, strengths and weaknesses. That enabled us to play off each other."[13] On the Flyers this fellowship meant standing together physically, too. The phrase "if you fought one Flyer, you fought everybody" became one of the popular clichés of the 1970s. Cliché or not, the sense of protection and mutual aid embodied in the phrase was an important part of the Flyers' successes. Eric Nesterenko gives a somewhat different and less antagonistic meaning to being able to count on teammates: "There have been times when I knew what the other guy was thinking without him ever talking to me. When that happens, we can do anything together."[14] This is a special experience, but it can be difficult to translate into other contexts — that is, for men who subsequently find themselves "just individuals," in a society that offers few other opportunities to experience this kind of fraternal closeness.

Yet we immediately need to add a note of caution here. Dryden, Gainey, Saleski, and Nesterenko are all talking about the team feeling generated on *winning* teams. Sports fans will be familiar with the public name-calling and tension that often surround losers. Some offensively minded players are accused of floating and of being more interested in personal statistics than team success. Meanwhile, role players are shuffled in and out of the lineup in a way that makes learning to play with and depend upon others nearly impossible. However, the experience of being part of a team is forged off the ice as well, especially on the road; and the camaraderie is cited time and again by retired players as what they miss most from their hockey years and value in their hockey memories. It is cited by players who spent their careers with losing teams as well as successful ones, and even by players who played most of their years in the minors.

Part of what is remembered most warmly is the humour of a team, the aspect of making fun at others' expense: in the dressing room, in hotels and restaurants, on planes and buses. It is quick humour and often aggressive, in the sense that personal idiosyncrasies become the butt of constant jokes, typically without malice. It tends to be a theatre of give and take in which players make it *fun* to be on a team, precisely because they can be relied upon to play the "characters" that become assigned to them. Jock humour in these circumstances is a zany flow of quips and digs and practical jokes whose manifest purpose is entertainment, but whose side effect is to bring the team together, as familiar roles are rehearsed and enjoyed. It is a way of sparring and making fun that is characteristic of many male subcultures; and it is something that many men miss when they leave sports for work environments where humorous bantering — which is funniest and has the most meaning in groups whose members know each other very well — is less likely or possible. This is not to say that players always enjoy the aggressive bantering and teasing associated with jock humour, especially when it slides into the humiliations of hazing or the lower reaches of adolescent sexism. For instance, Rick Heinz remembers that Jorgen Pettersen never became comfortable with this style of humour and had a miserable time on the St. Louis Blues. In the years when European players were still a rarity in the NHL, it wasn't uncommon for them to experience such difficulties before learning the ropes of North American hockey's masculine subculture.

This masculine subculture can also have a far darker side. The allegations in 1991 of sexual assault against several members of the Washington Capitals, as well as similar allegations concerning college teams in both Canada and the United States, arguably provide a glimpse of a misogynistic dimension to hockey's rituals of mateship and male bonding. There have been enough of these incidents in college and professional sport in recent years to raise questions about relationships between the group maleness and cult of the celebrity that meet in many sporting subcultures, and the problem of sexual assault. Undoubtedly, some sport subcultures allow for the rehearsal of male anxieties and aggressiveness in ways that celebrate sexual adventure and conquest as necessary components of masculine identity. Opportunities for such adventures are amply provided by the groupies who hang around the social fringes of professional sports. The news accounts of professional athletes' sexual liaisons that followed Magic Johnson's disclosure of his positive HIV test highlighted the extent to which casual sex can be a part of the celebrity athlete's lifestyle. Canadians received another reminder of this in the case of the Montreal woman who told her doctor before her tragic death from AIDS that she had slept with over fifty NHL players.

In the case of groupies or steady girlfriends, the sex is normally consensual. Yet there is evidence to suggest that male athletes who have been treated as celebrities, whether they are big-time stars or small-town heroes, have sometimes come to expect sex from women as part of their sense of celebrity privilege. This sense of privilege may lead some players not to grasp that "No means no." A highly publicized airing of this attitude occurred during the rape trial of boxing's heavyweight champion, Mike Tyson, but there have been other instances as well, including two Canadian cases involving Jr. A and university hockey players, which may lend a measure of support to the argument that a misogynistic streak runs through the culture of male sport.

This argument needs to be qualified immediately by noting that allegations of sexual assault on the part of athletes, let alone convictions, remain very rare. Furthermore, it is clear that "date rape" and other forms of sexual assault involve differences in power and problems of perceived masculine privilege that go far beyond the world of sport. Moreover, because individual athletes all respond differently to the peer pressures and the opportunities that attend their way of life, it is difficult to make sweeping generalizations about aspects of misogyny that may be evident on any particular team or in any given sport. However, even if the darker possibilities are rare exceptions, there appears at minimum to be widespread acceptance in the subcultures of many sports of a view that objectifies and denigrates women.[15] At various levels of the hockey subculture this view surfaces in initiation rites that rehearse juvenile forms of sexual exhibitionism, the ready circulation of tales of sexual conquest, a latent contempt for groupies and prostitutes, and the sexual innuendo typical in comments made from the bus, the cab, or on the street to women who simply happen to be passing by.

Relationships With Fans

The issue of celebrity privilege relates as well to another set of important social relationships in the work world of hockey: the player's inevitable relationships with fans in general. As stars in an entertainment industry, hockey players are public figures as well as employees. Public relations are a part of their job, albeit a minor one; and in many informal situations players are frequently recognized, deferred to, and treated as celebrities. For almost every player this is a source of pleasure and pride, at least initially. Fame is part of the dream. And fame isn't just signing autographs. Fame is also about perks, many kinds of them: repeated favours from fans and local businesses; free memberships in clubs; special treatment in restaurants and bars, attention from women. All these things, and more, come with the life of the sports celebrity.

Yet celebrity life can also be constraining. The most obvious constraint, perhaps, is attention when you don't want it. Eric Nesterenko describes how he had easily learned to wear the off-duty role of the professional athlete. "Laughing with strangers. It doesn't take much. It has its built in moves, responses." As he got older, though, it became a role he shied away from. No longer willing to respond to a fan's desire for the sort of banal friendliness that would allow him (or her) to say, "I met Eric Nesterenko last night. He's a good guy," he found himself brushing more fans off; and he could see their hurt at his refusal to give them this story to tell, this little bit of status. Star players, in particular, have to learn to live with this constant attention and deal with it gracefully. People often stare at them, occasionally try to touch them, slap them on the back, or confront them with requests or bonhomie. The public lives of most NHL stars regularly overshadow their private lives.

At one level such fame is the measure of the media and marketing efforts of people in the sports/entertainment industries. The public desire for larger-than-life personalities, for winners, and especially for those who carry it off with flair and remarkable skill provides plenty of grist for the star-making machinery of these industries. At another level, the fame of some athletes touches something in the popular imagination that transcends marketing. For example, for many people in Quebec Guy Lafleur is more than a sports celebrity, he is a francophone hero — someone whose flair, skill, and success on the ice with the Canadiens in the 1970s came to symbolize the abilities and qualities of a people struggling to assert their "distinctiveness." The thunderous standing ovation Lafleur received in Quebec City at the opening of the '91 Canada Cup — set in the context of Eric Lindros's refusal to play for les Nordiques — powerfully dramatized the scope of Québécois affection for their hockey legends.

The pressures to live up to this level of fame are immense. Too often people expect that because athletes are good and graceful at sports, they are automatically going to be good and graceful at other things. At the very least many fans expect their sporting celebrities and heroes to be exceptionally nice, articulate people. Sometimes, as in the case of Jean Beliveau or Wayne Gretzky, they are; and in these fortunate cases the hopes of fans are fulfilled and the players find many kinds of doors opening easily for them. In rarer cases, like Ken Dryden, professional athletes are not just articulate; they are also highly educated individuals whose demonstrable intelligence and thoughtfulness appear to fulfil at least some of the "good and graceful" ideal. Others are simply bright people with a natural intelligence and passion about the world around them.

In many cases, though, the public's expectations of athletes as heroes and role models are not fulfilled. Professional athletes are people we take an interest in because they do one thing wonderfully well. Furthermore, what they do seems remarkably glamorous and often provides significant points of identification for individuals and communities. Yet professional hockey players, like other prodigies, are often young men who have often done little else in life besides train to play hockey. There is little doubt that hockey players have a capacity for wider experience and have a discipline and focus that, had they led different lives, might also have brought accomplishment in other areas. But from the time they formulate the ambition to be hockey stars, young players usually have to focus on hockey to such an extent that other interests and talents remain undeveloped and perhaps unknown. They are successes in their chosen field, but they've succeeded in a subculture where the dominant mindset is that hockey is much more important than anything else. For that reason hockey fans are often disappointed to find that their heroes usually don't have a lot to say about topics outside of hockey. Certainly, things are changing as more and more players have higher levels of education. However, the path that most players have followed to pursue their hockey careers simply hasn't provided them with the breadth of life experience that enables charming conversation and easy participation in social gatherings.[16]

Work Relations with Employers

Because professional hockey is a form of wage work, the whole experience of playing is shaped by the relationships that players have to their employers. We've already noted how between the late 1920s and the 1960s NHL hockey players were subjected to extremely paternalistic, often autocratic forms of labour discipline. As the NHL gained progressively greater influence over its labour market, players lost most of whatever control they may have once had over the conditions of their work and the wages they received. A significant number of hockey's early owners and managers understood themselves as hockey people first and business operators second, but all owners understood the extent to which profitability depended on gaining complete control of their labour market. In addition to creating rules restricting player movement within the league, and struggling to ensure that no rival league developed to compete for player talent, the NHL also developed an approach to employer-employee relations that can be summarized in the adage, "Managers should manage, coaches coach, and players bloody well play." Managements around the league promoted the idea of the team-as-family, and they were often quick to castigate players who wanted greater control over work conditions or salaries as selfish malcontents who put their own interests ahead of "the good of the game." At the same time, team managers had immense discretionary power to make or break a player's career.[17]

In this context most NHL players developed a strategy of concentrating on their game, treading softly with management, and keeping their "heads down." When management was the primary source of information about the business of hockey, players had few options other than to simply put their faith in their bosses' decisions. Furthermore, the seductiveness of the idea of the team-as-family induced some players to identify strongly with management positions. Managers were often colourful figures from the game's past, and their love of hockey and apparent attachments to their players made close identification with them highly appealing. In any case, players were usually sufficiently intimidated to know enough not to take too active an interest in the financial affairs of the team or league. And when players did try to organize or make collective demands of any kind their efforts were met with hostility and reprisals. For instance, in both 1957-58 and the mid-1960s managements in Toronto and Detroit waged punitive campaigns against players who attempted to form players' associations. By demoting or trading away all the "troublemakers," the managements of the Leafs and Red Wings crippled their teams for years.[18] Still, the teams continued to be profitable through the 1960s and 1970s because of loyal fans and the fees paid by new expansion teams.

A whole series of developments from the late 1960s to the present day have put greater pressure on managements to become more accommodating to players' interests and demands. Examples include Alan Eagleson's successful formation of the National Hockey League Players' Association (NHLPA) in 1966-67, the growing use of agents, the brief existence of the World Hockey Association in the 1970s, and the greater willingness of the courts to intervene in professional sport. All of these things have challenged the NHL's ability to exert complete control over its labour market. Today's joint management-player arrangements like the collective agreement and the pension plan, despite significant flaws, have given established players greater financial security, and the very existence of the union and of agents constitutes a control, of sorts, on the arbitrary and punitive exercise of managerial prerogatives.

Despite these factors, management attitudes in hockey have changed only slowly and grudgingly, with continuing effects on players. Indeed, in most professional sports managerial tantrums that would be unacceptable in other lines of work are still seen to be acceptable — and are sometimes even admired. Hockey is certainly not the only sport in which a manager's personal feelings can have a greater impact on a player's career than is normal in workplaces where the effects of unions and of grievance and salary procedures are to depersonalize employer-employee relations. But in hockey, autocracy and paternalism have been particularly resilient. Agents and NHLPA representatives can and do seek to act as intermediaries in disputes, but managers still wield enough power in the business that one general manager's reported threat to bury a player "so far in the minors that the *Hockey News* won't be able to find you" remains the kind of thing that players have to take very seriously.[19]

It is quite remarkable how recent it is that new ideas about marketing, promotion, and public relations, let alone labour relations and coaching, have made any headway in professional hockey. The NHL competes as a business with other professional sports organizations (notably, the NBA and the NFL) that have shown much more imagination in their strategies for cultivating new markets in continental North America and Europe. The NBA, in particular, has also been far more innovative in its approach to labour relations. By contrast the

NHL has been a highly conservative subcultural world in which "tradition," measured through "experience" (and indeed NHL experience), has counted for more than anything else, a world in which newcomers are likely to be greeted with suspicion and resistance unless they operate in the same old ways. This helps to explain why coaches from universities have often been unsuccessful in the NHL, and why the hiring of a European assistant coach like Alpo Suhonnen in Winnipeg was publicly ridiculed by NHL insiders.

More importantly, this reliance on "tradition" also helps to explain some of the events surrounding the unprecedented 1992 players' strike — notably, the owners' initial intransigence and their apparent misreading of the players' new resolve. It also helps to explain the depth of player resentment with the league's traditional approaches to labour-management relations and what was really at stake from the players' point of view. Professional sports have been one of the last preserves of the mogul, the very rich "hands-on" owner, who is himself part of the show and is accustomed to running things. But perhaps more than any other major professional sport in North America, hockey has remained dominated by a backward-looking handful of eccentric entrepreneurs — men who have fiercely guarded their property rights and have often put their own vendettas and personal values ahead of anything else.[20]

Through the 1970s and 1980s Harold Ballard was the archetype of this sort of owner. His well-publicized antipathy to certain individuals and nationalities and his loyalties to others who embraced his own prejudices undoubtedly hurt the Leafs over the years. Ballard, in turn, was simply following a style of ownership that had been set by earlier idiosyncratic owners such as Conn Smythe and the generations of dynastic family control associated with the families of James Norris and Arthur Wirtz. Ballard is gone now but his brand of truculent conservatism, complete with its quasi-feudal view of labour relations, continued to be powerfully represented by Bill Wirtz, president of the Chicago Blackhawks and, until recently, Chair of the NHL Board of Governors. In the negotiations that led up to the 1992 strike, Wirtz was not only the leader of the hard-line governors who opposed any concessions to the players. He also hardened the negotiating atmosphere through public boasts that his team would be stocked in the 1992-93 season with replacement players from the minors and Europe. In addition Wirtz arrogantly threatened that any season ticket-holder who didn't want to pay NHL prices to watch replacement players might not get their seats back when the strike ended: not just hardball with the players, but hardball with the fans too.[21]

It was the accumulated years of precisely this sort of authoritarian bravado that had instigated a showdown in the first place. Players willing to talk publicly during the strike, including Tom Barrasso, Mark Recchi, Guy Carbonneau, and Jyrki Lumme, emphasized that the underlying issue was the need to establish the basis of a new relationship between owners and players — a partnership that would promise a more "professional" relationship between both parties. Indeed, today's generation of players is better educated than ever before. In the 1992 strike they were far better informed about the issues and less easily conned by self-serving arguments about "the good of the game" than previous generations of players. In any case, there was a longstanding set of more tangible financial issues surrounding free agency, pensions, licensing arrangements, and schedule and contract length that provided the grist for the actual negotiations that led up to the strike. Players were particularly troubled by the fact that NHL salaries had slipped markedly behind those of other major professional sports during the 1980s. For example, in 1977 professional hockey players made 77 per cent of what professional basketball players made. By 1988 the average salary in hockey had fallen to 38 per cent of the average basketball salary. This relative decline in NHL salaries occurred during a time when the NHL was experiencing a period of significant economic prosperity.[22]

Many commentators have noted that NHL management had not appreciated the extent of player anger and mistrust — a condition enhanced during the negotiations by the owners' provocative actions on the issue of playing card licensing. Owners also misread the players' increasing sense that hockey was being left behind as labour relations in other professional sports were moving away from managerial paternalism. Nor had owners expected that the solidarity of the new NHLPA, now under Bob Goodenow rather than Alan Eagleson, could be maintained as long as it was. The strike vote of 560-4 — taken just before the 1992 playoffs when, as player-negotiator Mike Liut put it, "The hockey player inside each of us wants to play the games" — was a startling indicator of the extent to which players wanted a change. It was also a graphic indicator of Goodenow's unprecedented success in informing the membership about the issues.

The position of the Players' Association had never been stronger. It was as if John Zeigler and the NHL Board of Governors were so confident that the players' traditional "heads down" mentality would never change that they allowed negotiations to continue right up to the point where a strike would hurt the league the most. This managerial bungling continued through the negotiations, when the league kept crying poverty but would not open the books to prove it. The owners' position was that the increased salary demands that would surely follow upon any significant relaxation of the conditions of free agency would lead to the bankruptcy of many franchises and to a steady flow of star players away from the poorer, small-market franchises. This is indeed a highly plausible scenario — *if* the league's revenues were to remain at 1991 levels, and *if* there were to be no move towards some structure of revenue sharing, as is done in the NBA.

The difficulties faced by small-city franchises, in particular, are graphically illustrated in Peter Pocklington's willingness to part with the core players of three championship Edmonton Oiler teams. Nonetheless, the same group of owners who cried poverty in their bargaining with the NHLPA must have painted a very different picture of the money to be made in hockey when they convinced investors in Ottawa and Tampa Bay in 1991 to pay $50 million for franchises.[23] What makes the difference is that there is most likely much more money to be made in professional hockey if and when potentially lucrative new sources of revenue are actively developed and when the richer teams agree to additional revenue sharing.

For the union, the 560-4 strike vote marked a turning point in a sport with a history of union-bashing and considerable player suspicion of collective action. Certainly, the NHLPA from its beginnings in the 1960s constituted a step away from the days when individuals who complained could be harassed out of hockey altogether. Under Alan Eagleson, the Players' Association was also run in an often autocratic and paternalistic fashion. There were certainly tensions in the negotiations of earlier collective agreements in the NHL, especially those leading up to the first revenue-sharing initiatives associated with international play, but it often seemed that Eagleson represented his own as much as the players' interests. Indeed, it has been suggested that much of Eagleson's influence with NHL managements was a direct result of his ability to "deliver" the players and keep them in line.[24]

In contrast, in the period leading up to the 1992 strike, players were included in discussions of strategy, and information was disseminated widely. Player representatives were encouraged to hold discussions with their own teams, so that everyone would learn about issues and strategies. One result of this was a much greater understanding of how players had been taken advantage of in the past and of the owners' tactics in the most recent negotiation. Another result was an unprecedented determination to retain solidarity and resist any attempts by the owners to bust the union and discredit its new executive director.

Certainly, too much could be made of the players' solidarity during the strike. Hockey's paternalistic traditions run deep throughout the sport, and they are not likely to be overturned in one militant episode of collective bargaining. Similarly, the basic structure of work relations in professional hockey continues to be unchanged. But there does appear to be a new awareness among NHL players that their conditions and quality of work are best negotiated collectively rather than individually. There is also a new understanding of the money to be made in hockey and a growing desire on the part of some players to see the kind of free-agency provisions in hockey that have so dramatically escalated salaries in baseball. During the strike, some players interviewed in the Toronto media even suggested that owner attitudes were compromising the future economic prospects of the league. This, in part, is what was behind the NHLPA's talk about the necessity of the players becoming "partners" in the hockey business. Financial restructuring that included the players more directly in the operations of the league, the argument ran, might rein in the profiteering of individual owners enough to strengthen the whole league as a unit for profit-maximizing behaviours. In this way, small teams (like the NBA's Portland Trail Blazers and Utah Jazz) could continue to be competitive in the NHL, and the league might be better positioned to capitalize on players' marketing power.

Opinions differ about who actually "won" the players' strike of 1992. In one reading the players made important gains in the areas of pensions, playoff money, insurance, and arbitration; they also held on to the status quo with respect to playing card revenues, which the owners wanted to share, and salary caps, which the owners wanted to introduce. Conversely, on the most important financial issue of all — the rules regarding compensation for free-agent signings — the changes did not open the doors to free agency very wide, and many players were reportedly unhappy that their "final" offer had already conceded too much. The owners also held firm in their demand that the 1992 agreement be for one year only. Thus, as one observer put it, "They lived to fight another day."[25]

The most important agreement to emerge out of the 1992 strike was not financial at all, but one in which players and owners agreed to form joint committees to look at the financial structure of the league, as well as at marketing and promotions. New marketing and promotions initiatives are already a significant part of the NHL's strategy for the future. New agreements with regional and national U.S. cable networks, pay-per-view services, and European television will be another part of that strategy. The replacement of John Zeigler with interim president

Gil Stein and the subsequent hiring of the NBA's Gary Bettman as league commissioner arguably point to a new direction both in league marketing and promotions and in labour relations. Significantly, some owners, including the new chair of the league's Board of Governors, Bruce McNall, have begun to speculate publicly about a new vision of the NHL's future. If taken at face value, that vision includes involvement by the players in profit-sharing and in the pursuit of marketing opportunities made possible by new communications technologies and international changes in the entertainment industries. If this new thinking prevails in future negotiations, we may well see the beginnings of significant changes in the social relations of the hockey workplace.

Chapter Six

Careers, Myths, and Dreams

Despite widespread changes in Canada since the early 1950s, hockey stars continue to occupy a significant place in the popular imagination. For instance, in their different journeys to the big time Wayne Gretzky and Mario Lemieux have embodied and renewed deeply rooted themes in Canadian popular culture about social and geographic mobility. To become an NHL star is to leave behind the corner rinks, local arenas, and relatively quiet life of small-town or suburban Canada for urban affluence, the national stage of *Hockey Night in Canada*, and the glitter and huge crowds of Toronto and Montreal, New York and Los Angeles. Hockey stars have articulated the dreams of generations of young Canadian men about stepping out from the familiarity and rootedness of hometown lives towards the beckoning bright lights and brighter opportunities of new careers — careers that hold the possibility of fortune, and sometimes fame.

Careers are by definition individual journeys, and they almost always involve some degree of geographic and social mobility. Of course, hockey is simply one of many careers in Canada that have fuelled youthful fantasies of fortune, fame, and travel. The local rapper and the members of the suburban garage band, the budding concert pianist and the aspiring actor: they too have their fantasies. But in Canada none of these careers has been as deeply intertwined with popular myth as hockey. Moreover, only a few other performance careers are likely to end well before middle age. When the cheering stops, hockey players must abruptly confront personal adjustments and changes of direction that are challenging and sometimes painful.

The connections between hockey careers, Canadian myths, and dreams have been so close that it is often difficult to disentangle them. To begin to consider these connections we should explain what we mean by the idea of "myth." The word *myth* is most often used to suggest something that is essentially false. It implies a contrast between the world of fable or superstition and a "reality" that the fables often disguise. In his influential book *Mythologies*, the French literary theorist Roland Barthes took this general notion and modified it in a thought-provoking way.[1] For Barthes, myths are not so much a denial of some actually existing truth as they are a form of cultural discourse — a way of speaking — about the world people live in. The problem is that myths tend to speak a conservative language: their language is static and intransitive; they represent the social world as something "natural," a fixed set of relations without a history. Barthes argues that to avoid this tendency it is necessary to develop a way of representing the world that has a more active character — a discourse that depicts human beings as makers of a world that can be continually changed.

The myth of hockey as a "natural" adaptation to ice, snow, and open space is a particularly graphic example of what Barthes is alerting us to — about how history can be confused with nature. The myth is circulated throughout Canadian popular culture by means of signifiers that continually link hockey to the physical environment. A magazine ad for Canadian Spirit Whiskey announces, "Hockey is as much a part of Canada as the cry of a loon at dusk on a Northern Ontario Lake or the flame red sunset over a peaceful Prairie town" — only one of innumerable examples. This discourse of nature creates a kind of cultural amnesia about the *social* struggles and vested interests — between men and women, social classes, regions, races, and ethnic groups — that have always been part of hockey's history. Hockey has become something whose lore, traditions, and major organizations themselves seem "natural."

This naturalization of hockey, along with its lore, traditions, and major organizations, has been easily manipulated by people with an interest in defending hockey's status quo. For example, the related discourses of the "team as community" and "the good of the game" in professional hockey have frequently obscured the different interests of owners and players in the NHL and have subtly naturalized the exis-tence of the NHL's dominance over the game. As people began to lose a sense of the history of the struggles that surrounded the NHL's rise to power in hockey — struggles between amateur and professional visions of hockey, and between different visions of what professional-ism might entail — NHL dominance began to seem natural. At the same time, the related idea that what was good for the NHL was also good for "The Game" came to be widely repeated, and widely believed, as common sense. This common sense was routinely expressed in pro-grams handed out at games, in pictures and stories in local papers and magazines, and in interviews on *Hockey Night in Canada*. Through these various representations, the myths surrounding "The Game" were connected to a specific power structure — that of the NHL — in an implicitly conservative way.

There is also another way of understanding myth — a mode of under-standing that cautions us against equating mythology only with mean-ings that serve dominant interests, with ideology.[2] For while myths have the capacity to confuse history with nature — thereby natural-izing one group's vested interests at the expense of another's — they can also have a more open-ended, metaphoric character. From this perspective, myths are stories that dramatize important themes and tensions in a culture. People interpret their culture through such mythic stories. They tell the stories over and over again, inflect them with dif-ferent meanings, and interpret them against different "truths." In this way popular myths are an important part of a people's basic stock of cultural knowledge. They also serve as an important source of routine narrative pleasure. This means that mythic stories can't be reduced to ideology in every instance.

Public Meanings, Hockey Careers, and the Myth of "Making it"

The symbolic role of hockey as a "field of dreams" for young Canadian boys and men is mythical in both of the senses described above. And no contemporary player's career is as mythologized as that of Wayne Gretzky. His case profiles virtually every mobility theme embodied in the popular dream of "making it to the big time" — and then some. The son of a railway worker in Brantford, Ontario, Gretzky is one of those international figures, like Mohammed Ali and Michael Jordan, whose name becomes, in some ways, bigger than his sport, known even where the game itself is not played.

Gretzky gives real meaning to devalued phrases like "franchise player" and "superstar." He has set scoring marks far beyond his peers or anyone before him. He helped turn two losing teams into winning ones and took on a larger role as ambassador for the game. His marquee name and saleable image were used to sell the game to new fans in southern California and beyond, in the large U.S. entertainment market. By the early 1990s he was justifiably one of the two highest-paid players in the history of hockey. With his Hollywood home, appearances on TV programs such as *Saturday Night Live*, and his marriage to movie actress Janet Jones — a union referred to by more than one journalist as Canada's "royal wedding" — Gretzky is both the working-class boy who made good and the Canadian who made it onto the huge stage of the American entertainment industry. Indeed, the Gretzky story is one of "making it" in so many ways that even the dream merchants of "boys' own" fiction could scarcely have made it up. In Wayne Gretzky, life surpasses the normal limits of fiction.

Gretzky's fairytale story is not yet over, as he proved once again in the 1993 playoffs. At the start of the 1992-93 season he had been sidelined with a back injury that seemed likely to end his playing career, or at least his superstardom. But he came back much earlier than expected, to play most of the second half of the season. Then, in the heat of the playoffs (after taking some abuse from the press) he scored the overtime winner in the crucial sixth game of the semi-finals against the Toronto Maple Leafs to tie the series at three games apiece. Even better, in the seventh game he almost singlehandedly (it seemed) led his team to victory. The myth continues: according to L.A. coach Barry Melrose, interviewed shortly after the game, " Wayne Gretzky just said 'I'm winning,' and that's all there is to it."[3]

Like many famous Canadian expatriates in the entertainment industries, Gretzky appears to have settled happily in California, even though the 1993 season ended with rumours of tensions with the L.A. management, a possible move, and speculation about his retirement. When he does retire from hockey he will be able to turn to managing his extensive business interests. During his years in Edmonton Gretzky invested in real estate and purchased the Hull Olympiques junior hockey team. Since his arrival in Los Angeles he has been involved in several ventures with L.A. Kings owner Bruce McNall, including a stable of racehorses and the well-publicized purchase of a coveted Honus Wagner baseball card for more than $400,000. Furthermore, in partnership with McNall and comedian John Candy, Gretzky purchased the Toronto Argonauts of the Canadian Football League; other joint ventures in sports ownership seem likely to follow.[4] It is difficult to imagine, say,

Gordie Howe, Bobby Orr, or Guy Lafleur in a similar role during their playing days — which is partly a mark of how much the salaries of hockey's stars rose in the 1980s-1990s, and how hockey became more closely integrated into the core of the U.S. entertainment industry. A small number of former players from the 1950s through the 1980s went on to own minor-league sport franchises — Phil Esposito and Mike Vernon, for instance — or became directors of major-league teams. But nobody has made the transition on the scale of Wayne Gretzky.

A social critic might argue that public celebrations of Gretzky's story, and those of other sports superstars, merely rehearse the themes of possessive individualism and upward mobility through skill and hard work that are part of the ideological core of Western capitalist societies — societies whose cultures and institutional structures impose significantly different pressures and limits on the life chances of men and women, and of people belonging to different social classes, races, and ethnic groups. Furthermore, it could be argued that the dramatic success stories of Gretzky or Mario Lemieux tend to capture the popular imagination so completely that they deflect attention away from the barriers that hold many other people back in their lives and careers. Moreover, in such stories "success" often tends to be defined narrowly, in a manner that uncritically rehearses the values of a celebrity-centred consumer culture.

There is a great deal that rings true in this kind of critical reading, but it would be wrong to suggest that these are the only meanings to be drawn from the myths associated with the careers of sports stars. For example, for many fans Wayne Gretzky is simply a remarkable performer whose complete mastery of his game brings an aesthetic pleasure comparable to observing the work of the greatest actors, musicians, and painters. Every story, every photograph of Gretzky working his magic potentially allows fans to relive the experience and intensify the pleasure. Even people who dislike the commercial imperatives that drive professional hockey — the greed, the hucksterism, the arbitrary whims of owners, the star system — frequently put this understanding to the side to savour the seemingly transcendent moments a player like Gretzky makes possible. We've talked to people who say they've seen something in Gretzky's performances that dramatizes the importance of reconciling individual artistry with broader collective needs. They say that through a combination of unselfish play, magnificent individual skills, and a remarkable sensitivity to teammates' styles and abilities, Gretzky has shown how, even for a superstar, "making it" can be viewed as a collective project. With this dramatization, for a fleeting moment, people glimpse a quality of human productive relations rarely found elsewhere in social life. In contrast to sport's obvious dramatization of possessive individualism, players like Gretzky also offer the potential to articulate more subtle collectivist myths as well.[5]

Organized hockey has always acted as a kind of popular theatre that circulates myths in compelling ways. The game's ability to dramatize collective hopes and aspirations has been readily evident from the moment amateur teams first began to "represent" their communities. As pro hockey took off and gained public visibility in the early years of the twentieth century, professional teams and players emerged as the standardbearers for these collective hopes and aspirations. With the advent of radio and then television, the representativeness of specific teams was broadened beyond their original anchorage in specific geographical communities. Coverage of hockey — or more properly, (re)presentations of hockey — in these media provided an expanded range of popular identifications. In the 1950s, for example, with only two Canadian cities represented in the NHL, it was easy to interpret games between the Toronto Maple Leafs and Montreal Canadiens as a dramatization of anglo versus francophone hopes and aspirations and cheer accordingly. Or, when listening to the Leafs or Canadiens play New York or Chicago a fan might pull for the Canadian rather than the U.S. team. The fact that almost all the players on the U.S. teams were Canadians mediated such nationalist interpretations. Even more notably, in the 1950s and 1960s nationalist interpretations of games between Canadian and U.S. NHL teams were further offset for younger fans by the continental reach of the CAHA/NHL feeder system. If you played minor hockey as a boy in Winnipeg you knew that your future "playing rights" were owned by the Boston Bruins. In Fredericton you knew you "belonged" to the Chicago Blackhawks.[6] For that reason there was an incentive for young boys across the country to snuggle up in front of the television and follow the fortunes of "their" team, even if that team played in the United States.

With pro teams and players acting as symbolic representatives of all these different communities and interests — coupled to the apparent glamour of public adulation and the prospect of considerable financial rewards — hockey could articulate an extremely wide range of collective attachments and individual fantasies. The fortunes of national amateur teams in international competition provided even more opportunities for collective identification and the celebration of skilled players. Hockey increasingly became our most popular cultural forum for playing out the central themes of Canadian life: French and English, East and West, Canada and the United States, Canada and the Soviet Union. The game also dramatized longstanding tensions between commerce and culture in Canada, the changing dynamics of rural and urban life, the postwar tensions between capitalism and communism, and, of course, the timeless Canadian struggle with winter.[7] Beyond these uniquely Canadian themes, hockey's mythic structure in Canada has also drawn upon a number of more universal Western cultural themes: individualism versus collective responsibility, competing understandings of success and failure, the comparative virtues of brain and brawn, and the apparent contrast between homespun innocence and big-city corruption.

The scope and power of hockey's representational character are key factors in the game's important role in Canadian popular culture. This representational character has prompted intense attachments to particular teams and players and fuelled popular fantasies and myths about the game, its lore, and its legends. It was this intensity of attachment that drove Montreal Canadiens fans into the streets in 1955, in a riot protesting NHL president Clarence Campbell's suspension of Canadiens' superstar Maurice Richard. This intensity has remained in Montreal, where the Canadiens have achieved a legendary status as defenders of civic self-esteem. There are also fans in Quebec City, Toronto, Vancouver, Winnipeg, Calgary, Edmonton, and Ottawa who identify strongly with their teams, but in every one of these cities — even in Montreal — popular identifications with NHL hockey teams have never simply arisen on their own. These identifications have been greatly influenced by the shared interests of NHL promoters and myth-makers in the media. Over the past thirty years or so, and especially during the 1980s, the dominant form of story-telling in and around the game seems to have become increasingly dominated by the language and the imperatives of marketing.

So despite the great range of cultural themes and issues that continue to be dramatized by hockey, and despite the wide range of interpretations that can be given to the skills and careers of players who have "made it" to the top of their game, hockey myths today are best viewed in relation to the continued growth of what Canadian cultural theorist Andrew Wernick calls "promotional culture."[8] At one level the idea of "promotional culture" simply refers to the pervasive yet still growing presence of promotional discourse and marketing activity in contemporary life, all of it seeking to create receptive audiences not only for products but also for politicians and even ideas. What is of greater significance, though, is a subtle shift in the content, and indeed the structure, of promotional discourse: away from making direct claims about the items being promoted and even away from (rational) argumentation, and towards a reliance on visual images, on stylistic connotations, and particularly on symbolic associations.

In this context, because of the omnipresence of popular entertainment in contemporary culture, the superstar athletes like Wayne Gretzky, Michael Jordan, Joe Montana, or Dave Winfield, as well as the superstar entertainers, such as Madonna, Michael Jackson, Arnold Schwarzenegger, and Jack Nicholson, offer the greatest possible name recognition, the widest reach into uncommitted audiences, and the most positive (if vague) symbolic connotations and associations. Even the distinctly promotional appearances of such athletes and entertainers have come to be understood as entertainment on its own terms, until the lines between entertainment and promotion — and sport, popular music, film, and advertising — have become blurred beyond recognition. When Michael Jordan appears in a Nike promotion he is also promoting basketball, the NBA, and, not least, himself, by adding to his own visibility. The superstar celebrity athlete — and only a few can create and sustain the aura — thus becomes a promotional signifier of unprecedented influence and value. This adds a further mythic dimension to the legends that the superstar athlete creates on the basketball court, the playing field, or the ice. Wayne Gretzky's image in subways, magazines, or on roadsigns signifies both the centrality of the big sell and the privileged role of commerce in Canadian culture at the very moment that it articulates other myths more directly related to hockey, personal identities, and physical performance. Most young boys who dream of "making it" in hockey would be satisfied simply to get to the NHL and to play well there. But in contemporary culture the myth of "making it" has also become indissolubly connected to the player's public visibility as a celebrity, marketability as a promotional vehicle, and ultimate financial success in business endeavours beyond the sport.

Myths of Demotion, Failure, and Tragedy

Not every aspiring young hockey player achieves the goal of playing in the NHL, and among those who do make it, only a few become stars, let alone superstars. Moreover, even players who have achieved reasonable levels of career success tend to slide into obscurity in their retirement. More notably, many players reach retirement only after going through a painful process of downward mobility.

In a 1975 study of player mobility from the 1950s through the early 1970s, Michael D. Smith and Frederic Diamond found that about 70 per cent of all NHL players in that time period finished their careers in the minor leagues.[9] Most of those players also moved from one team to another an average of seven times during their careers, and the average age at retirement was thirty-three, following an average pro career of twelve years (typically, six years in the NHL and six in the minors). Smith and Diamond point out that slightly fewer players who retired after expansion in 1967, and before 1972, ended their careers in the minors. Furthermore, they remind us that in the days of the six-team NHL, aspiring pros from all across North America were competing for less than 170 jobs. Job security was fragile at best in this intensely competitive environment, and the top minor leagues had large numbers of extremely skilled players, many of them staying on to complete successful (although modest by NHL standards) careers in places like Rochester, New York, and Springfield, Massachusetts.

In the 1950s and 1960s the minor leagues were something more than the strictly development leagues they later became, and it was far less of a stigma to extend a playing career by spending several years in the minors. Still, virtually all players aspired to the NHL, and the minors offered less money and far less glamour. During the 1960s Rochester of the American League was an example of what it was like at the apex of the minor professional system. The team had loyal hometown fans, it was the player source most likely to be tapped by its NHL parent, and the team even travelled on an old DC-3 while others in the American League went by bus.[10] At the other end of the scale was Yorkton, Saskatchewan, in the Prairie League, where former Maple Leaf player Gerry James played out his career. There, he recalled, "Everything comes hard. Meeting a payroll. Getting ice time for practice. Hot water for showers."[11] So why bother? Love of the game and the inability to imagine another life are the reasons given by many former players. But there was also the simple issue of the limited range of options open to them. As late as 1970 the average NHL salary was still only around $24,000. At a time before big salaries and the widespread use of player agents and investment counsellors, the most likely alternatives to minor hockey were the hometown fire department, the car lot, or the insurance agency.

A key part of the problem was that before the 1980s, few hockey players had completed their education. Only 17 per cent of NHL players who played in the era of Bobby Hull, roughly the late 1950s to the mid-1970s, had finished high school.[12] The "Golden Jet" himself dropped out of school in Grade 10. Few players thus had the opportunity to develop marketable skills that would increase their possibility of financial security after retirement. Moreover, the original NHL pension plan, initiated by the league in 1947, did little to ensure that players from the early postwar era had enough money to live comfortably after retirement. Even the pension money drawn by star players of that era turned out to be remarkably paltry. After twenty-six years in the NHL, Gordie Howe drew a pension that paid him $13,000 annually. After sixteen years and 964 games, Bob Baun's pension amounted to a mere $7,622 a year.[13]

Current NHL players are in a considerably stronger position. Not only are their incomes vastly larger than those commonly paid even to stars in the old six-team league, but pension provisions also improved noticeably between the late 1970s and mid-1980s. During the 1992-93 season *The Hockey News* estimated the average NHL salary at $379,000.[14] In addition, under pension terms negotiated in 1986 any player with four hundred games of NHL service is eligible for a lump-sum pension of $250,000 at age fifty-five. Still, we need to remember that figures depicting average hockey salaries — especially after the mid-1980s — tend to be skewed upwards by the huge sums paid to a small group of superstars. Similarly, the current pension benefits do not offer any guarantee of financial comfort. Considering inflation, the $250,000 likely to be collected sometime in the early twenty-first century will be far from a fortune. The tax consequences of a lump-sum pension will potentially reduce the amount even further. Furthermore, there has been considerable uneasiness among NHL players — especially pre-expansion players — about irregularities in the operation of the pension plan and the lack of accountability of the fund's administrators. In 1991 a group of older retired players and supporters — led by Carl Brewer, Eddie Shack, and Bobby Hull — filed a lawsuit to recover what they alleged was a large pension surplus that had never been passed on to the players entitled to it.[15] In the winter of 1993 there was a flurry of publicity about pending investigations into the operation of the fund and into Alan Eagleson's personal business dealings.

Notwithstanding the problems with the financial terms and administration of the pension fund, the four hundred-game qualification requirement remains a challenging target. It essentially means playing five full seasons with virtually no time lost to injuries, suspensions, or demotions. At the end of the 1980s the average length of playing careers in the NHL was about four and a half years.[16] So under the terms of the 1986 pension agreement many players will leave hockey without qualifying for the $250,000. The NHL's expansions in 1992 and 1993 may end up extending a few careers, but increased retirement security in professional hockey — especially for journeyman players — is likely to be achieved only through a combination of profit-sharing, increases to current salary minimums, and continuing improvements to the pension plan.

The saddest and most abrupt cases of downward mobility in hockey are often those for whom life in the fast lane has led to serious problems with substance abuse: usually, though not always, alcohol. The NHL has never admitted that alcohol is a problem in professional hockey — perhaps because of the involvement of major breweries in team ownership or a more general concern about the game's "image." However, hockey insiders frequently admit in private that alcohol has cut short many careers. It is certainly easy to understand why alcohol and drug use can become a part of the lifestyle of the professional player. Beer and bars are a large part of the life of many young men in Canada to begin with, and professional hockey players experience many opportunities and pressures to drink. They have large salaries, they often have a great deal of time to kill, and there are strong pressures on them to be "sociable." There are also the pressures of the job itself, and the expectations and self-expectations that attach to the very notion of "celebrity" in a promotional culture. These are realities that all players must deal with, and most players manage them successfully. But the problems attached to the life are real, and the results are saddest, perhaps, when the careers of promising young players (Bob Probert and Bryan Fogarty are among the most publicized) are threatened or cut short, just when they looked like they had "made it," before they had achieved the financial security that seemed within their grasp. For such young men, life after hockey comes to look very different than it did only a short time earlier. For other well-known players (for example, Dave Semenko, Dave Hunter), facing up to the reality of an alcohol problem and beating it became one of the first challenges of life after hockey and formed a necessary condition for going on to other careers.

Hockey myths tend on the whole to celebrate and dramatize positive possibilities and outcomes. Myths associated with the dream of "making it" are far better and more frequently articulated in Canadian culture than myths of failure or of losing success just when it seemed within grasp. Nonetheless, the myths of "making it" only have their evocative power in contrast to parallel myths that embrace the ever-present possibility of failure, even tragedy. In this regard Peter Gzowski reminds us that Canadians have not been overly kind to their hockey heroes.[17] There is so much expected of professional hockey players, they are raised to such an exalted status, that fans can feel let down, cheated, even hurt, when players prove to be merely mortal. As a result, yesterday's heroes can be quickly left behind in the wake of injury or simply from a failure to live up to what fans expect of a high salary. Grant Fuhr, Dale Hawerchuk, and Gary Leeman are all examples of formerly popular players who were booed as their careers appeared to go into decline.

Part of this rejection is clearly connected to the public's sense of strong disappointment when highly paid players don't do what they're ultimately paid to do: send their fans home "winners." This sense of disappointment, however, goes far beyond the question of value for money. Sports fans have been hard on their heroes since long before the days of big money in sport. The high level of emotional (and, sometimes, financial) investment made by partisan fans in their favourite teams has always created considerable potential for resentment. Indeed, the twentieth-century male sports hero has arguably become the modern successor to the masculine heroes of ancient Western mythology, the exemplar of all that is perceived to be best in warrior-men, the individual who triumphs when it matters most and when the forces arrayed against him seem most daunting. These are precisely the kinds of expectations that are built up around our best-paid hockey stars, both by many of the fans who follow them and, especially, by the myth-makers in the contemporary media and entertainment industries.

Yet when sports stars prove human, when they show faults, or when their aging bodies no longer have the magic, the journalists, broadcasters, and writers who narrate their stories in popular culture will sometimes shift focus from the selling of heroic adulation to the selling of pathos and irony. In such circumstances "the story" can suddenly become how the player will hold up as a person. Will he maintain the kind of style, grace, or tenacity outside the game that distinguished his career on the ice? Or will he prove simply to be ordinary, perhaps even pathetic? A growing concern with players' private lives is a manifestation of a broader tendency in contemporary journalism in which the private lives of public figures have increasingly come to be regarded as news. The exemplary images maintained by older generations of heroes always depended upon a careful separation between public performer and private life, in which "backstage" behaviour — including relaxation and ordinariness, as well as slips and flaws of character — were well shielded from the public eye.[18] By contrast, since the mid-1960s journalists have become more willing to play a role in the selling of access to the private lives of celebrities. Part of this emerged out of the Vietnam War and the post-Watergate enthusiasm for investigative journalism. In sport, part of it has come about in response to the growing recognition that pro sports are businesses more than magic islands of play, and part is simply the tendency to increasingly "personalize" celebrities, which has been one of the apparent cultural legacies of television.

If a hockey player in decline can't cope, or if he experiences some kind of related personal hardship, stories of his fall from grace and debates about his skills and "character" circulate and recirculate until they become firmly established in the popular memory. The hard realities of hockey's labour market, juxtaposed against the power of the dream of "making it," have guaranteed a ready supply of stories of success and tragedy in hockey. Almost every Canadian community that has ever had a junior or senior team has an inventory of such stories. But over the past two decades these stories appear to have circulated more widely than ever before. One of the most heavily publicized stories was the death in late 1992 of John Kordic, after an incident in which the former Leaf player had to be subdued by nine police officers. Investigators later found forty unused syringes and several boxes of anabolic steroids in Kordic's motel room, and stories of longstanding problems with alcohol and drugs filled the press. Another well-known hockey tragedy is that of Brian Spencer, murdered after living in squalor on the margins of the Florida underworld. But these are simply the most sensational examples. The personal problems of many past and present players, such as Derek Sanderson and Bob Probert, have been widely publicized and discussed, forming the stuff of our national soap opera. Then too there are the innumerable stories of former small-town heroes who return to their home communities and run afoul of the law or become prominent town drunks trading on their past successes for free beer and conversation with strangers. These narratives of decline into tragedy are woven together and fictionalized brilliantly in Roy MacGregor's depiction of Felix Batterinski in *The Last Season*.[19]

Clearly, the examples such as Gretzky and Lemieux, and Kordic and Spencer, are the extremes — the myths of success and stardom versus the myths of failure and tragedy. Between these extremes, the hockey player who achieves a stable career in the NHL of the 1990s has gained the opportunity to live out the dreams pursued by thousands of others like him. He has enjoyed success at an intrinsic level, as well as the money that comes with success in the entertainment industry. Even if he lasts only three or four years in the pros and therefore leaves the game in his mid-twenties to late twenties, he will usually have made well over half a million dollars in after-tax earnings. This figure doesn't take into account living expenses, of course, and players who have enjoyed the celebrity lifestyle may end up spending quite a bit of the total amount. Unless he has been reckless, though, the player will retire from hockey with considerably more capital than most people under thirty are ever able to save. At the same time, unless he has been one of the elite stars, it is unlikely that he is set for life, in a position to relax and live off his investments. Most NHL players, in other words, have to find other forms of work after they leave the game.

Life Advantages and "Hidden Injuries" of Hockey

Some players try to pursue other careers within the game. Clearly there are attractions in remaining part of the hockey subculture, and these attractions are especially powerful for players who haven't completed their formal education or established business interests in their off-seasons. These former players may feel there is nothing else they know but hockey. Others may find it difficult to break free of dependencies created through years of immersion in the game's paternalistic sub-culture. Some former players become successful as coaches and general managers while others do well for themselves as broadcasters or commentators. But there are only a few of these jobs available at the NHL level. Some former players remain around the game in more marginal roles, as minor-league coaches or as scouts. But most of those jobs are precarious and poorly paid in comparison with players' salaries, and they are limited in numbers. The alternative that most players have to face up to, therefore, is working outside the game; and what literature there is indicates that this requires a complex set of adjustments.

Interviews with former players suggest a "transition period," in which individuals often find themselves disoriented and even floundering while they try to establish a new way of earning a living.[20] This is followed, in most cases, by a relatively successful adjustment to retirement, with occasional sad exceptions. The majority of these difficult experiences go back to the time before large salaries and the improvements to the NHL pension plan that were negotiated in the 1970s and 1980s. Most pre-expansion players gave their best years to careers that ended before they were thirty-five, and they usually didn't earn enough to establish themselves in new careers and businesses.

Even today, when money is less likely to be such a pressing issue, players report that the transition period between playing hockey and establishing a second career is probably one of their toughest and most personally challenging periods. In some ways the transition is easiest for those who never really "make it" at the top level, or do so only briefly. They are not famous enough to be able to trade on their hockey "names," and they will not have put away much money. They simply have to get on with establishing themselves in some other line of work, and because they haven't had much time to take celebrity status for granted, they can more easily become an ordinary person once again. They are also more likely to find themselves out of hockey at an early age. In his book *Life After Hockey* Mike Smith offers several accounts of players who, although successful in junior and Olympic hockey, never really established themselves as major-league professionals. After two or three years in the minors, or as fringe players in the NHL, they left hockey to pursue other careers: in law, business, the academic world, even the priesthood. None had any regrets about their time in hockey. However, all of them clearly felt fulfilled in their subsequent careers and thought they had made what was for them the right choice.

Ken Dryden's transition was more complex. With his credentials already established in a potentially lucrative law career, and with his varied work experience already established outside hockey (government advisory committees, consumer advocacy work, media work) — along with the contacts associated with these experiences — Dryden's posthockey life seemed to promise interesting and rewarding possibilities. Yet Dryden knew, too, that he was stepping into the new and highly competitive field of law a little late and still had to learn many things that lawyers his age already knew: "And now I am beginning to learn the choice I have made. When I was twenty-four or twenty-five, I did more interesting and challenging things, more exciting and remunerative things, than every other twenty-four- or twenty-five-year old I knew. Three or four years out of college, my friends started in the middle, working slowly up the corporate ladder.... I am beginning to feel I am missing out."[21] At age thirty-one, Dryden recognized that the tables had turned. His friends had progressed to the threshold of real influence and success; their careers were taking off, while his was winding down. What seems most important in Dryden's exploration of his impending retirement was that he was *accustomed to being a success*, and he knew enough about success to understand clearly the disadvantages he now had to overcome.

If this disjuncture between a past of successes and a future of uncertain prospects can pose problems for someone as "qualified" as Dryden, it can be all the more daunting for players who haven't got other credentials or experience. NHL players start life after hockey with the advantages that a public persona and a good bank balance can offer. They also usually have a confidence grounded in repeated success and in having learned that perseverance can produce success even when failure seems likely. But they still have to turn these advantages into enduring careers, before any or all of them are dissipated. They also have to learn to adjust their expectations as they cast around for things to do that are as rewarding as the life of a hockey player.

In some ways the financial adjustments are the easiest, if only because they are unavoidable. Once the ex-player starts seriously looking for other work, he finds himself starting at the bottom in businesses that other people know. Former players often note the surprise of looking for work and finding that the salaries they can command in "the real world" are nowhere near the levels they had been at in hockey. For example, former Philadelphia Flyer Don Saleski noted how he had to accept a position after retirement from hockey that paid him less than half his former salary. More strikingly, a former Boston player, Tom Williams, commented on his shock at realizing that he had made less in his first year in the construction-pipe business than he had paid in taxes in his last year in hockey.[22] Significantly, as salaries rose in hockey through the 1970s players of working-class and rural origins often found themselves developing lifestyles more often associated with the urban professional and business classes. In this regard hockey players have not been much different from other young men in professional careers who experienced social and geographic mobility through the years of the postwar boom. However, what makes hockey careers different is the fact that they usually come to an early end and offer few prospects for the future. The result, in many instances, is that lifestyles and tastes developed during a player's days in the NHL can no longer be sustained in retirement.

Both Don Saleski and Tom Williams soon got over the shock of their low salaries and realized that if they wanted to live in the accustomed manner they would have to apply themselves to succeeding in their new businesses. Both made rapid progress in sales, once they had learned the ropes of their products and learned about their customers' needs; today they have lucrative positions in sales management. Yet there is a trap that they and others warn about — of a player expecting that after leaving the game his hockey name alone will produce success in sales and public relations positions. Often the name *is* enough to get former players an interview, and even a first job. But the player still has to do that job, diligently and knowledgeably. Some former players tell about how they kidded themselves at first that chatting with customers about hockey was enough to make a sale, perhaps even enough to build a business. As Don Saleski recalls, "Quickly, I found out that companies rarely do business with an individual because he's a nice guy."[23]

Many former players get by for a little while in fields like car sales and insurance, wooing customers who may or may not be hockey fans.

Here, too, retired players learn that they have to make the calls, know the products, and give good service. Trading on the past just doesn't count for much when people are making significant financial decisions. To become a success at something else, indeed, most players have to learn the lesson that they are no longer celebrities. This recognition is extremely difficult for some players, producing "rough" transition periods featuring disorientation, resentment, relationship problems, and greater or lesser crises of identity. All their lives they've defined themselves as hockey players, first and foremost, and when hockey is over they feel a loss of self-esteem.[24]

Former professional hockey players, in short, have to cope with an immensely disruptive occupational and personal transition. In addition to other necessary adjustments, the time structures of their lives are turned upside down; instead of having time on their hands they have to adapt to normal working hours, with only a few weeks of holidays a year. The former professional player also typically misses the "occupational community" that used to provide friends as well as colleagues. He is now "at home" with spouse and children, instead of being the visiting celebrity just back for a visit. Ideally, this means that he can participate in the routine responsibilities and pleasures of family life, in ways he couldn't when he was on the road so much. Some players, indeed, talk movingly of the support their spouses gave them during their transition periods. Still, the father who has learned to feel comfortable with life on the road can experience difficulties fitting into new family routines. And some players make these adjustments more difficult by clinging to their old haunts and habits, especially time out "with the boys." Conversely, some spouses who thought they had married celebrities find it difficult to adjust to living with ordinary men on ordinary incomes. Given all these changes in circumstances, it is not surprising that relationships undergo strain, and that divorce, already common among pro players, is an increased possibility in the early years of retirement. The former pro player is obliged to become a different person, and the remaking of family and other relationships is a necessary and sometimes painful part of this process.

Moving into second careers can be especially difficult for men whose identities are tied to their original work skills. At one level the former pro player has to come to terms with a loss of physical skill that is simply part of aging. He is different from many other men, though, because his livelihood has depended upon his physical prowess. While still relatively young, he has been pushed aside by younger men who are stronger and faster. His new life will depend less on his physical virtuosity, and anyone who has been in touch with their bodies in the way that good athletes usually are is likely to experience a sense of sharp physical decline. Many hockey players, moreover, will experience aches and pains from old injuries, aches that will increase as they get older and further diminish the pleasures they once took in physical pursuits. Players who have had severe injuries or multiple knee operations — Bobby Orr is an obvious example — may even live their later years with reduced mobility or considerable pain.

Another adjustment surrounds the relative value placed on the retired player's new skills in comparison with his former ones. For the first part of a player's working life he has been a principal beneficiary of a celebrity-oriented promotional culture willing to pay entertainers more money than school principals and scientists. In an affluent society we are willing to pay enormous sums to people (musicians and actors, as well as athletes) whose skills can entertain and excite us, who can (however temporarily) take us beyond our daily routines, who can *move* us. Many people do "socially valuable" things, and many more make and sell the things that create wealth in more conventional ways. But the ability to entertain, to make people hope and laugh, dream, and feel a part of something, has always had a very special place in modern Western cultures and economies.

When former players talk about the options open to them after hockey, our attention is drawn to factors and issues that take us beyond the limelight. The simplest of these may be that professional athletes have experienced being *really* good at something. Former players express great satisfaction in "having reached the top of their profession," or some version of this experience. The reality of many other jobs, though, is that we have only to perform them at a "good enough" level to get by. Even when we are working diligently, moreover, effectiveness in many jobs is hard to measure; and success in most jobs is almost always less conclusive than it is in sports. It is also more dependent on factors outside our own control. Last year's success as a stockbroker or real estate salesman may fail this year, when markets turn downwards, and it is rare in the circumstances of social work to experience many "successes." Indeed it is difficult in most "ordinary" jobs (however we may try to kid ourselves) to *know* that we are really good, to know that our being there has made some difference. The temptation for the athlete, then, as for the rest of us, is to keep score by the amount of money earned.

Some players eventually achieve substantial financial rewards in their new careers. These individuals express a special kind of pride in the knowledge that they have succeeded outside the game, just as they did inside it. Few former NHL players, though, can make as much money as they did in hockey, so once outside they are left with the feeling of being less successful.

This sense that the rest of life forms an anti-climax can be heightened if the former player finds it difficult to respect the work available to him. Ken Dryden was not attracted, by his own admission, to the practice of law itself. Eric Nesterenko quickly became cynical about his try at stockbroking, "persuading people to buy things they don't want" — the stuff of most sales work. He took more satisfaction out of working on construction, building real and visible things, before moving on to become a ski instructor. Likewise, Guy Lafleur was apparently less than happy in the public relations work he was given by the Canadiens after his first retirement.

What these former players experience is not unlike the ambivalence that a great many working-class men experience when they move from blue-collar to white-collar forms of work. Many men who work with their bodies in industrial settings, often under hard and dangerous conditions, want to be able to find work that leaves danger and physical exhaustion behind. They also want the respect, status, and financial rewards that attach to many forms of white-collar work in Western societies. Yet, ironically, once they get into the office — into inside sales, junior management roles, technical positions requiring "qualifications" — many of them do not feel they are doing much that is worth being proud of. The resulting problems of self-respect are central to what the authors of one classic sociological study have called the "hidden injuries of class."[25] As people who have also done physically demanding, skilled work, many professional athletes similarly find it hard to take the same pride in the kinds of work available to them after retirement.

Yet it is precisely these kinds of work in sales, public relations, and administration that make market economies go round. What is thrown into relief in so many personal accounts of the contemporary workplace is just how rare it is to be paid well for work you love and take pride in. A great many former hockey players talk of loving the game itself, even when they became cynical and resentful about their status as chattels in the hockey business or felt they were not being paid in a manner commensurate with the profits being made by the owners. And while athletes are by no means the only people who tend to speak positively about their work, what stands out clearly in their personal and occupational biographies is the sharp contrast between the work they feel they fully expressed *themselves* in and the work available when they left the game.

Careers, Satisfactions, and Myths of Community

Playing professional hockey demands a total commitment of self: emotional, mental, and physical. Not every player gives this every night, but most good players recognize the differences. Almost all players at this level know what it means to play the game with passion and adrenalin, and they know how good it feels to be "up" for a game, individually and as a team. By contrast, in the jobs that most other Canadians do, and that most hockey players do after their sports careers are over, it is much harder to talk about "giving it all you have." There is certainly a lot of talk about this in sales meetings and motivational seminars, but much of this is readily identifiable as a managerial charade. Many Canadians take pride in a job well done, no matter what the job, but the idea of getting psyched up for a complete commitment to a retail chain's "game plan" in a job that pays eight dollars an hour, with little chance for promotion, is often hard to swallow. Likewise, many physical jobs in industrial production, while often demanding, virtually require workers to leave their minds and spirits at the gate. Some professional jobs may be intellectually challenging; others, in education, in the "helping professions," and in management, make different but still very real emotional demands on people. Yet these jobs also use only parts of the whole person, so much so that the workers risk becoming fragmented or one-dimensional men and women. Although they feel drained at the end of a long day or week, many people see no irony in seeking out exercise or night classes or volunteer community work — if they aren't moonlighting to make ends meet — in order to get back in touch with sides of themselves that have no place in their jobs.

Undeniably, hockey has its own forms of one-dimensionality. The level of physicality and commitment often work against the development of intellectual skills and opportunities for self-development that make a person well rounded. But there is an almost unanimous chorus in interviews with former players about the satisfactions of playing the game as a career. One thing that most contributes to this, and something that players almost always say they miss, is the camaraderie and friendship that come with being a member of a team. At one level, it might be suggested that when players say one of the things they miss most is the friends they made in hockey, this simply represents another instance of the loss of "occupational community" that is a normal problem of retirement. At another level, the statement sometimes carries the sense of leaving a large patriarchal family. Cynics might also be tempted to argue that what is probably missed most are all the times of "fun with the boys" — the afternoons of shooting pool and working out, the nights in bars, the practical jokes and general "acting stupid together." Most of this disappears with the demands of responsible day jobs and the commitments of a more normal family life.

There are also other, more significant factors in this lost sense of fraternal community. When players realize that they can accomplish their own goals more effectively as part of a team, a powerful bonding effect can emerge. In the best circumstances, and most often on winning teams, players learn to support and work for one another, to appreciate each other's contributions and cover each other for their mistakes. When people go through these kinds of experiences together, the friendships that develop (and they will not be with everyone) can be both powerful and durable. There is a certain irony in the fact that despite the rampant individualism that surrounds hockey — despite the cult of the celebrity and the star — it is very often the friendships and the sense of interdependence that former players say they miss the most. This sense of collectivism is not unique to team sports. Men and women whose circumstances have required them to learn to depend on one another (in the military, in labour struggles, and sometimes in political work) have given us their own languages of bonding: solidarity, brotherhood, and sisterhood. Moreover, in many instances hockey players' memories of bonding are not necessarily progressive; for example, they can easily devolve into a tacit celebration of the game as a "male preserve."

Positive memories of the team as a community are undoubtedly amplified because most work today is organized in ways that offer few possibilities for experiencing the level of interdependence found in professional hockey. Whether people work in large organizations or small ones, in the public or private sectors, their everyday jobs rarely produce anything like the special solidarity that so many former players describe. Indeed, increasingly sophisticated productivity measurement systems, designed to make people accountable as *individuals*, usually have precisely the opposite effect. A further problem is that other traditional words of connection are now widely undermined or denied by people's actual experiences. The traditional (and idealized) meanings of "family," for example, are often belied by contemporary life in families struggling to cope with economic and social forces whose effect is to draw family members into increasingly separate lives. The mythical ideals of "community" are difficult to recognize in cities and suburbs where people scarcely know their neighbours and where the ideal meanings of "community" are transparently trivialized by civic boosterism. Michael Ignatieff makes a great deal of sense when he argues, "Words like fraternity, belonging, and community are so soaked with nostalgia and utopianism that they are nearly useless as guides to the real possibilities of solidarity in modern society."[26]

In these circumstances the experience of being on a team may be the most readily available and enjoyable experience of mutual dependence for many people in today's world. And even if that experience is not universally positive for every player — for example, the players that ride the bench, the ones caught up in team jealousies or conflicts, the ones who never quite fit in — professional team sports are one of a handful of occupations in which the possibility of community seems to exist beyond the realms of myth and promotional rhetoric. It is ironic that these moments of solidarity and interdependence are confused by myths of the "team" that are contoured by managerial interests. This confusion is by no means restricted to hockey. Indeed, the metaphor of the team, complete with its mythic promise of community, now provides much of our popular language for articulating experiences of working and living together: phrases like "teamwork," "team player," and "team spirit" have become popular clichés. Yet as they enter our everyday language these concepts become devalued (much like those cited by Ignatieff), precisely when the words that name them are routinely appropriated to name experiences in which the actually lived relations of membership and of working together are quite different.

In contradistinction to the real points of interpersonal connection that hockey has often created, there is a long tradition in the NHL of self-serving managerial rhetoric about "the team." Many players experience a sense of fraternal community in the game — something occasionally conveyed to fans in mythic form — but this sense of community is not something that automatically extends to "the team as a whole," including management. In the final analysis the myth of community and social interdependence expressed in the discourse of the team-as-community is ideological. The myth is ideological not because it is completely false, but because it is only partially true. Yet players and fans are continually urged to mistake the part for the whole, to confuse really existing points of connection and interdependence between players — and symbolic glimpses of idealized productive relations — with the structure and culture of the team as a profit-making enterprise. During their years in the NHL many players have unconsciously internalized this mythic discourse. In retirement they have often felt the need to deconstruct it.

Chapter Seven

The Game Beyond the Pros

The NHL represents the pinnacle of the sport in Canada, but for those many Canadian boys (and for growing numbers of girls) who see hockey players as inspiring role models, the road to the NHL begins in organized minor hockey. Like the NHL, minor hockey has its own "in-group" ways of thinking and being, its own values and traditions that most "hockey men" understand and share. Minor hockey also has its own specialized means of recruitment and acculturation through which aspiring members are initiated into these values and traditions at the same time as they learn playing skills.

At the local, community level, the hockey subculture reaches out to touch the lives of many Canadians who know the world of professional hockey only from a distance. Since the early part of the twentieth century Canadian communities have been home to a wide variety of recreational leagues, church leagues, and industrial leagues. This diversity continues today, with leagues and teams organized for men and women of almost every age and level of ability. Over the last decade there has been an especially notable growth in hockey leagues for both women and "old-timers." Although much of this recreational activity goes on outside the purview of the Canadian Amateur Hockey Association, the CAHA also organizes teams and leagues for men and women that range across a variety of age divisions and ability levels.

Nonetheless, for over forty years the CAHA's major emphasis has been to organize and regulate competitive hockey for aspiring young professionals. More than 450,000 boys between the ages of eight and nineteen were registered as players with the Canadian Amateur Hockey Association in 1992-93. There were also over 12,000 girls.[1] Registered players are often "all stars" in the sense that they've been selected to a local or district team out of a larger pool of youngsters who play in "house leagues" at the younger age levels. After the age of eight, players work their way up a divisional ladder beginning with atom (up to age eleven) and followed by peewee (to age thirteen). The best players up to the age of fifteen are placed in the highly competitive bantam division, where they are sorted into two or three tiers (often referred to as A or AB, B, and C levels) based on their abilities.[2] At this point opportunities to play purely recreational hockey progressively diminish. From the bantam through the midget (age sixteen) divisions and beyond, minor hockey tends to be little more than a feeder system for junior hockey and the NHL.

Minor-hockey organizations continue to be very important in the social life of most Canadian communities, from country towns to our largest cities. Not only do they provide a highly popular recreational opportunity to the young people who play; but they also become a consuming life interest for the host of parents and other volunteers whose efforts as coaches and organizers make minor hockey happen. They are also a focal point of community spirit. Optimists and Lions clubs, church groups and neighbourhood businesses: all these groups get involved in the sponsorship and operation of minor hockey, and they do so in the belief that they are contributing to making their communities better places for growing up.

Benefits and Criticisms of Minor Hockey

It is no accident that the organization of children's hockey today is strongest in the suburbs that grew up around our cities in the postwar boom. Despite all the criticisms of the adult organization of children's play (and, indeed, the criticisms of suburban life) that have become familiar in recent years, these child-oriented communities have embodied an important aspect of the Canadian dream for several generations of parents. The chance to combine opportunities for urban employment with raising children in affordable single-family dwellings — com-

plete with safe streets and new schools, pools, and arenas offering organized recreation for the kids — made suburbs attractive places to live.
Organized minor hockey was part of the attraction, and in the scattered suburbs of the country the municipal arena was often one of the
first public facilities built. Minor hockey got parents involved in community life. It was part of what made the suburbs feel like communities.

Clearly, the organization of children's hockey offers various benefits to the participants and to the game itself. The most important of
these is the provision of regular access to facilities and coaching. Odes
to pick-up shinny often fail to mention that access to ice is no longer
readily available in many cities and suburbs and that play on the outdoor rinks that do survive in city parks is typically dominated by "the
big guys," while smaller and younger players are left to fend for themselves on the fringes of the main action. Organized hockey offers younger
children the chance to play with others their own age, where they get
to carry the puck too rather than being extras in the older boys' game.
It also offers at least a small amount of coaching in the basic skills of
the game and an introduction to the tactics of competitive hockey.

Volunteer coaches undoubtedly display tremendous variations in
hockey knowledge, teaching ability, and motivations. A few seem to
do little more than yell at the kids and officials; but thousands of other
coaches make minor hockey a happy experience for the youngsters
who play for them. These coaches know enough about hockey to give
pointers on skating, shooting, teamwork, and positional play. They also
know that at this level their greatest contribution can be simply to
develop a love of the game amongst their players. They enjoy and support their young charges in the disappointments as well as the triumphs. Indeed, one of the major benefits of organized hockey for children
who are fortunate enough to play for good coaches is the time they
spend with adults who obviously share their enthusiasm for the game.
Young people learn that they can have relationships with adults who
are not parents and not teachers. They also experience new relationships with teammates, and for many kids a sports team is likely to be
the first group outside their family that they have really *belonged* to.
Almost certainly it will be the first time they have any experience of
being part of, and contributing to, something larger than themselves
or their families.

Finally, organized minor hockey, especially at the all-star level, offers
a taste of the perks of the hockey life. Children get a chance to enjoy
the glamour of team uniforms, arenas with spectators, and travel. Even
the status that attaches to hockey jackets serves as a pointer to the

respect accorded to good hockey players among their peers. More substantially, the big tournaments that are the focal point of many teams' seasons can provide learning experiences: of fundraising, of travel, of billeting with other families, of being part of a team in an exciting event. For the best players, the tournaments represent "the dream" of a future professional career. As immediate and tangible goals to aim at and work towards each season, tournaments help to keep the dream alive and real.

Still, minor hockey has been the subject of controversy for over two decades. Critics argue that in the structures of organized competitive children's sports, the agendas of adult coaches and the aspirations of parents transform and distort the young players' experience. Games that should be fun become competitive "tests of character" and occasions of great tension. Kids learn that they are no longer playing for fun but for more important things: for championships, for trips, for scouts' attention, and parental approval. The spectacle of ambitious parents urging their children to skate faster and hit harder and then volubly criticizing their mistakes has long been all too common around minor hockey. Moreover, parental pressure is compounded by coaches who feel their teams must win so they will be recognized as successful coaches. In the most competitive divisions that attitude can lead to them playing the best players while the rest of the team spends most of the game on the bench. Furthermore, the prevalence of a win-at-all-costs attitude includes a tendency for coaches to overly value size, toughness, and hyper-aggressiveness over other qualities. In these circumstances, the fun is taken out of the game for all but the most successful players; and many teenagers give up hockey for more enjoyable recreational experiences.

Another increasingly significant issue is the cost of it all. Outfitting a ten-year-old with the equipment required for participation in organized hockey can cost upwards of $500, which is only the beginning. Every hockey parent knows that children outgrow skates almost every season and that each broken stick costs ten dollars or more to replace. Other equipment lasts longer, and parents can try to hold costs down by purchasing used items. Some leagues, indeed, have instituted equipment swaps and the use of standard sweater designs in efforts to contain the costs of hockey. Yet hockey still commits parents to expenditures that become hard to say "no" to. There are recurring costs associated with registration, ice time, and travel; and all of them are multiplied when more than one child in a family wants to play.

In these circumstances, increasing numbers of families have to tell their children, however reluctantly, that they can't put them into minor hockey. Obviously, the cost factor hits hardest at poorer families. Hockey has been the traditional sport of male working-class Canadians, and this tradition still runs deep, especially in rural areas and small towns. However, in contrast to the postwar boom period when Canadian workers were affluent enough to buy suburban homes and finance their children's hockey dreams, today the situation of many families is different. Many Canadian children now grow up in families in which one or both parents have been affected by layoffs, where part-time or casual wages have taken the place of more secure industrial jobs, where a parent working nights means there is no one to drive the children to a distant rink; or perhaps there is only one parent. Any or all of these factors, in conjunction with the rising costs, make it harder for working-class parents to put their kids in hockey. It becomes more realistic to encourage participation in games like basketball or volleyball, where equipment costs are low and the development leagues remain within the framework of the school system.

There is a further and different kind of problem associated with minor hockey as well: the effects of overly intensive organization and coaching. Despite the positive aspects of formal coaching and instruction, competitive pressures can make hockey seem too much like an obligation and not enough like play. And while some young kids thrive in highly structured settings, others are either intimidated or simply bored by them. We are also persuaded by Ken Dryden's argument that very early organization and coaching can also, ironically, mean less actual hockey; on game days (often two or sometimes three times a week), a player usually rests up, travels to and from the game, dresses and undresses, all for ten or fifteen minutes of playing time. As Dryden notes, "Every day that a twelve-year-old plays only ten minutes, he doesn't play two hours on a backyard rink or longer on school or playground rinks during weekends and holidays."[3]

This also means less time for young players to develop their skills in environments where adults are absent and there is little at risk, and kids are free to make mistakes. Only when the fear of failure is absent can young players enjoy trying things they have never tried before. And only in trying out new moves, trying several things that don't work in order to find one that does, and trying things they could never risk pulling off in a "real" game are skills developed. Becoming comfortable and confident with new skills requires practice and experimentation in a succession of different situations until those skills become second nature, your own moves, what psychologist John Shotter calls "personal powers."[4] Dryden argues convincingly that without enough time like this in *unorganized play*, players' capacities to improvise in skating, passing, and especially stickhandling are likely to be limited. Players may be able to repeat what they've been taught and able to do what is required in predictable situations, but their game will be predictable. Without those extra learned skills that supply the material out of which players can truly express themselves, they are unable to "invent the game" when the predictable things don't work. This is the difference, Dryden concludes, between the products of organized minor hockey, who are "good," and those of the street, the corner rink, and the river, who (albeit less frequently) may be "special."

Hockey in Canada has long been sustained by myths of apple-cheeked boys learning their "special" skills on rinks and frozen ponds across the country. But the reality of hockey today is much different. For the most part hockey has become an indoor and suburban game. In 1964 the smaller mining communities of northern Ontario and Quebec, places like Timmins and Kirkland Lake and Rouyn, were by themselves producing more than 20 per cent of active NHL players. By 1989 the number of NHL players from those areas had dwindled to a handful. Meanwhile the proportion from southern Ontario and British Columbia's Lower Mainland, where rivers never freeze, had risen to almost half of the Canadian-born players in the league.[5] Given that most Canadians now live in cities and suburbs, these tendencies are hardly surprising. But even in small towns people have learned to rely on adult organization of their children's free time, and to believe in its benefits. The reach of urban lifestyles into small-town Canada and the understandable desire of small-town parents to see that their children get all the opportunities available to urban youngsters have together led to a standardization of childhood. In this context, organized hockey is now the more traditional alternative (and there remain fewer alternatives in country towns) to newer indoor sports, or to the entertainment available through the VCR, cable television, or the satellite dish. Moreover, the combined effects of province-wide competitions from an early age, the presence of professional scouts at these competitions, and even the reach of coaching certification programs minimize the differences between suburban players and their rural counterparts. Organized competitive hockey starts earlier everywhere, with pro-type teams and prototype professional players setting the standards to which everyone has to adapt.

Debating the Future of Minor Hockey

Adapt or get out: the thing that has forced a debate among minor-hockey people today, leading some officials to publicly raise questions about what they are doing, is minor hockey's significant decline in participation. Minor-hockey officials first became aware of falling participation rates in the 1970s, and the issue was addressed in a number of government reports and commissions. Still, participation rates continued to fall during the 1980s. In Quebec a study by Francois Bilodeau of Laval University noted a drop in Quebec minor-hockey registrations of 24 per cent over the five-year period between the 1983-84 season and 1987-88. During the same time the total Canadian male population for these groups fell by only 6 per cent. When the figures were broken down by age an even more alarming picture emerged. Of the players who had registered as ten- and eleven-year-olds in 1983-84, fully 56 per cent had dropped out by ages fourteen and fifteen.[6] Similarly, in Alberta, officials in the Edmonton Minor Hockey Association (EMHA) expressed concern that their 27th annual Minor Hockey Week tournament attracted only 396 teams in 1990. At first glance this may seem a substantial number, but it is less impressive when divided among age groups and classes, and it is well down from the roughly 900 that once took part.[7]

These changes are subject to a variety of interpretations, and those who want to can point out quite correctly that factors external to hockey are involved: pressures on kids to grow up faster, a much greater choice of other activities, immense peer pressures to consume the latest consumer trends in fashion and music, and the part-time jobs in retail and fast-food outlets that high-school students take to pay for all of the above. Some people suggest that the most powerful explanation is a demographic one: the men who represent the current growth in old-timers' hockey are the same postwar "baby boomer" generation who made minor hockey mushroom thirty years ago, while today's teenage generation is statistically smaller. All of these explanations can be trotted out to support a contention that the game itself is not at fault. There are other people associated with hockey, though, who are concerned enough to make enquiries at the grassroots. For instance, in the late 1980s the Edmonton Minor Hockey Association circulated more than eight thousand questionnaires among parents, coaches, officials, and players, following up on a survey conducted in April 1989 by the provincial association. A spokesperson for the association noted, "We're trying to find out if we're doing it wrong. We want to know what the people want ... and how we can help get kids back into hockey."[8] Respondents to both studies identified costs as a major concern among parents, followed by body contact, poor coaching, and the length of the season.

In Quebec the Therien task force was initiated outside minor hockey and, perhaps as a result, its preliminary findings met with defensiveness from minor-hockey officials. The task force — including several prominent former NHL players — toured the province for seven months in 1988, hearing the views of more than 3,200 people who had some contact with the sport. The concerns raised by these people overlap to some extent with those of the Alberta study: costs, the number of games and tournaments, the pressures that too many coaches and parents put on kids to win, and the behaviour that these pressures produce in the players. The most provocative suggestion was that standards and expectations that might be quite appropriate for teenage players were too much for eight- and ten-year-olds. This led to the controversial proposal that the structures of competitive organized hockey — inter-community league play and tournaments for "all stars" — be dismantled for children under the age of twelve. If the task force recommendations were acted on, no new registrations would be accepted in hockey's novice and atom divisions, and by the time players currently registered in those categories reached peewee age, elite competitions for younger players would be phased out. Children would learn hockey by playing shinny, playing in house leagues without competitive "all-star" subdivisions, and playing in school physical education programs. In the school system, in theory at least, the emphasis on winning that characterizes so much of minor hockey would be subordinated to sounder educational objectives, including a concern for the less talented player.

Predictably, some minor-hockey officials were outraged. For example, Alex Legaré, president in 1989 of the Quebec International Peewee Tournament, worried not only about the future of this now traditional event but also about the future of francophone players in a game where their prowess is legendary: "By taking away the competitive level you are asking them (the talented boys) to be as weak as the weakest on the team. In Quebec we won't have serious hockey until after the age of 12. It's too late. Competition is part of life."[9] Other critics of the Therien task force ignored the substantive issues and focused instead on the perceived self-interest of groups outside the minor hockey establishment. They argued, for instance, that former pros and physical educators were proposing unprecedented roles for themselves in children's hockey. Indeed, this concern that minor hockey is being "taken away" from the volunteers who have always been its foot soldiers is being heard in other parts of the country.

Nonetheless, the Féderation québécoise de hockey sur glace (FQHG) moved to implement some of the ideas raised in the Therien hearings and to offer families choices in the sporting experiences they want for their children. A new program, Hockey 2000, was established in 1988, and by 1990 it encompassed eighteen municipal hockey associations and more than one thousand players between the ages of nine and eleven. In Hockey 2000 the competitive aspects of league play are diminished by equal ice-time requirements in which lines are changed every five minutes and by "co-operation games," in which sides are picked from the players of both teams in an effort to create evenly matched games. Some municipalities offer parents a choice of traditional competitive hockey, co-operation leagues, and family hockey, in which the co-operative system is taken a step further by encouraging parents, sisters, and brothers to play together. This idea of making hockey something shared across the generations was also central to the establishment of Fun Team Alberta, a program championed by former Edmonton Oiler Randy Gregg.

Critics suggested that such initiatives would only institutionalize what many fathers have been doing informally, on outdoor rinks, for years. However, Marc Beaudin of the FQHG responded that by giving co-operation hockey and family hockey *official* support, and by giving them space and appropriate time in arenas, the Féderation was helping to legitimize an approach that used to be regarded as less "important" than the organized competitive hockey that once monopolized minor-league play. Beaudin also said that Quebec would explore the possibilities of adapting the ideas of Hockey 2000 to other sports.[10] In Edmonton, the EMHA responded to the parental concerns articulated in their survey by instituting more opportunities for non-contact hockey and for tiering that allows groups of friends to play together. The experiment with non-contact hockey proved problematic, not least because of the expectations of the kids themselves. However, the EMHA also introduced a program called Fair Play '91, which offered incentives and awards to teams that played penalty-free games. This program, a version of one first tried in Ontario, attracted an enthusiastic response in its first year of operation, right up to the traditionally rough midget category. Officials reported fewer incidences of fighting, substantially fewer disciplinary cases, and more games that were finishing on time.

At the national level there has also been a recognition that minor hockey needs to change. In 1990 one of the CAHA's vice-presidents, Bob Nicholson, publicly indicated support for new initiatives, especially ones offering structured options so that the choice for families is no longer simply one of highly competitive hockey or no CAHA-organized hockey at all. Nicholson and CAHA president Murray Costello had both long supported structural changes, better coaching education programs, and ways to emphasize fair play. Costello has taken the position that some form of competitive game is necessary to sustain interest, even among youngsters: a steady diet of practices and teaching sessions can be too much like school. At the same time, he agrees with critics who argue that eighty to ninety games a year is too much for eight- and nine-year-olds. He also agrees that the emphasis some coaches place on winning means that too many kids spend too much time on the bench, while those on the ice are subjected to more pressure than they are old enough to handle. The CAHA's current recommendation for an appropriate ratio of practice time to game time is three to one, and it has developed instructional materials intended to help minor coaches make practices more fun. CAHA officials admit that most teams play more often than they practise and that some boys compete so often that they hardly practise at all, but they argue that the CAHA actively promotes coach education and certification, which is intended to lead to more enlightened approaches to the game.

Not everyone within the CAHA necessarily accepts the idea that minor hockey needs to be reformed. Some minor-hockey traditionalists argue that the association's dependence on volunteer goodwill and commitment necessitates conservativism, that the CAHA can't get too far ahead of grassroots opinion. Bruce Hood, former NHL referee and a member of the federal government's Advisory Committee on Fair Play, acknowledges that it is precisely the competitions, rivalries, and ambitions that surround them that are what really matter to a significant number of volunteers. This argument has sometimes been used to discourage reform initiatives in minor hockey on the grounds that reform is not what the game's traditional volunteers really want.

In many instances this assessment is undoubtedly correct. Canadian hockey is a subculture, in which the NHL represents the pinnacle of success and in which NHL-style customs and values remain the ones that really "count." Certainly, the inspiration of the NHL counts for much more than the values and goals of recreational reformers, physical educators, and even legislators. When hockey organizers have tenaciously defended the value of early competition, or when they've fought rearguard court actions to exclude girls from minor hockey, or when Don Cherry and others have disparaged Europeans and anyone else who would change how the game is played in Canada, they have shaken a symbolic fist at social pressures threatening the dominant meanings and values of "The Game" as they know and love it.

What is also under threat, in the eyes of those who resist change, is what many of them believe is the manifest function of minor hockey: the identification and grooming of future professionals. Thus, when coaches keep their stars on the ice too long, teach intimidation as a tactic, and emphasize winning, they are simply (in their own eyes and those of hockey traditionalists) training Canada's best young players in the realities of the pro game. This training involves work on skills, although it is often directed primarily at defensive skills because many professional hockey people consider offensive skills to be innate. The training also involves what sociologists Harry Webb and Edmund Vaz have called "the professionalization of attitudes," so that good young players learn to take the tactics of the professional game for granted and to defend those tactics as simply part of the game.[11] This has to do with one of the fundamental divisions in the debate about organized minor hockey: between those for whom kids' hockey is primarily about fun and personal development, about the majority of kids who will never pursue pro hockey careers; and those for whom minor hockey is understood as a development system for the professional game. For this latter group, the production of "made in Canada" NHLers remains an important and even a patriotic task.

This divide becomes most acute in bantam and midget hockey, when players are between the ages of fourteen and sixteen. Elite play at these levels is actively scouted, so it is here that aspirations for professional careers get sorted out. Bantam-division boys seen as "promising" are identified as prospective midget drafts and invited to junior camps. This scouting is widely understood as a major step towards realizing "the dream." Conversely, boys who find themselves on the bench in key situations or who cannot score or intimidate in this company simply do not get noticed, and they find their opportunities for further competitive hockey drying up. The stakes are large, therefore, for everyone who aspires to progress in this system, and the pressures to show well are correspondingly big-league.[12] It isn't surprising to find that the drop-out rate accelerates rapidly in these age groups. But even those who survive and succeed face some big choices.

Aiming for the NHL: Junior and College Hockey

The most important choice for the surviving young players is whether to pursue the traditional route into professional hockey, through the major junior leagues. These leagues include the Western Hockey League (WHL, with eight teams from the prairie provinces, two from British Columbia, and four in Washington and Oregon), the Ontario Hockey League (OHL, with fifteen teams), and the Quebec Major Junior Hockey League (QMJHL, with eleven teams). The alternative is to play Tier II junior hockey in the hope of attracting a scholarship offer from a major U.S. university. The choice is critical because major junior (Tier I) hockey is considered to be a professional sport by the National Collegiate Athletic Association (NCAA), and playing even one game makes a player ineligible for university competition. At the same time, graduates of

U.S. college programs have only recently made it to the NHL in any numbers. Most players still have to weigh the dream of a pro career against the surer benefits of a college education.

Junior hockey is a longstanding part of the Canadian hockey sub-culture. At one time it was the only route into the NHL; and in the days when NHL teams brought their future stars up through their own farm systems, Leaf and Blackhawks fans could watch in anticipation as future rivals like Frank Mahovlich and Bobby Hull developed. Junior hockey was big business in Montreal and Toronto, because games between the Junior Canadiens and Marlboros mobilized much of the fan rivalry that attached to the parent clubs. Sunday afternoon doubleheaders at Maple Leaf Gardens, with the Marlboros and St. Michael's College Majors as hosts, often drew crowds of close to ten thousand. Junior hockey was especially important to young fans who seldom got to NHL games. The Blackhawks, Bruins, Rangers, and Canadiens sponsored teams in St. Catharines, Niagara Falls, Guelph, and Peterborough, and support-ers of junior teams often became active supporters of the parent clubs. The Memorial Cup junior championship was an important national event.

The advent of the World Hockey Association (WHA) in the early 1970s and the subsequent expansion of the NHL changed much of the meaning of junior hockey for fans, as well as its economics. The prospect of losing players to the WHA — players whose early development the NHL had paid for — marked the beginning of the NHL clubs' with-drawal from direct sponsorship of junior teams. Then, because expan-sion franchises were clearly unable to compete with the established farm systems of the original teams, the NHL's need to seek competi-tive parity required a fundamental restructuring of the development leagues. The corollary of the annual junior draft was the withdrawal of NHL clubs from direct sponsorship and management of junior teams — why develop a player an opponent is almost certain to get? — and a shift to independent (usually local) ownership. This change took money out of junior hockey, even though junior teams are reimbursed for each of their drafted players. More importantly, though, the shift undercut one of the bases of fan identification with junior teams and junior players, their association with a favoured pro team. Junior hockey has had to rely more heavily, as a result, on the strength of commu-nity identifications and the drafting of "winners" from the midget ranks. In this context, junior teams have been prone to look more for imme-diate results than to draft prospects who might not be fully mature physically and would have to be brought along slowly.

Furthermore, while community identification around junior hockey can work in small cities — for example, Medicine Hat and Kamloops in the West and Peterborough and Oshawa in Ontario, cities where good management produces regular contenders that make for easy mobilization of civic pride — it hasn't worked in the major cities, where NHL teams (as well as other "big-league" entertainment) have become the focus of public attention. Junior hockey has disappeared in all Canadian cities that have NHL teams and has struggled in other large centres (Hamilton, Victoria) that have metropolitan entertainment patterns and choices. Attendance is not helped either when struggling NHL clubs bring the best drawing cards into the professional ranks at age eighteen. Significantly — and perhaps ironically — junior hockey has thrived in the U.S. Northwest, not just in the relatively rural Tri-City area of the Washington interior, but in Seattle and Portland, where the Thunderbirds and Winter Hawks draw good crowds in arenas where NBA teams are headline attractions.

While junior hockey in Canada is not what it used to be, it still offers exciting prospects to young players set on a hockey career. On and off the ice, both in the kind of hockey played and in the culture that surrounds it, major junior hockey is the closest thing there is to the NHL. It is therefore widely seen as the best possible preparation for a professional career. For players who do well in junior, team life has some aspects of a dream already come true. Players can enjoy a high profile in a community where junior hockey is the biggest show in town. They will be the object of the attention of everyone from groupies and autograph seekers to the media. They can taste what being a local hero is like and may also find that home-town friends and acquaintances treat them with a new deference. This can produce mixed reactions, as evidenced by comments from one junior player: "The last few days at home, I have found when shopping or running errands that people I once knew treat me now as John Tanner the goalie, rather than John. It's like there is a new found respect for me that I believe is silly; why would things be different just because I play hockey? On the other hand, I don't mind it — it makes me feel a little important."[13]

At the same time there are also real and potential downsides in the major junior system, the most endemic of which involves education.[14] Since U.S. universities started recruiting significant numbers of good Canadian players, junior hockey has tried to convince boys and their families that it, too, cares about education and that it is possible to combine junior hockey with progress in schooling. The claim is true in principle, and today most teams do make some effort to see that boys stay registered in high school and that they attend regularly when they are not on road trips. But the intensity of commitment to hockey works against an emphasis on education, and there are significant differences in how much teams actively help players combine the two.

For older players who graduate from high school it is easier to combine hockey and postsecondary schooling in the East. The road trips seldom last more than four days and half the franchises in the OHL are in university towns. The Western league, in contrast, has much longer road trips that can make any level of school, even high school, difficult to keep up with. Not only are players away from school, but there are also the peer pressures to participate in "team fun." In these circumstances, several contemporary WHL juniors suggest that only extraordinarily disciplined individuals can make true progress in their schooling. One former Portland player interviewed in the course of our research suggested: "You're away from home so that your parents aren't involved in your education any more, the management is always saying hockey comes first, and the guys want you to go out and have a good time. It's easy to just go along with it, and think you can go back to school later, if you have to." The unstated hope is that he won't have to go back to school. Yet the numbers game makes it clear that most juniors do not go on to successful NHL careers. They have to swallow their disappointment and get some other qualifications, and they have to do so at an age when their contemporaries are often getting started in careers.

The attraction of the Tier II–U.S. university path is that the player covers himself against just this prospect, while also continuing to develop in the game. Indeed, the hockey rather than the education is sometimes emphasized by Canadian boys who have chosen this route. Thus, Rod Brind'Amour, a first-round draft choice who successfully made the jump from Michigan State University to the NHL, described U.S. college hockey as better preparation for the pro game than he had really expected: "The players are faster, bigger, stronger, older."[15] Major hockey schools also play in first-class facilities, in front of sellout crowds (6,225 at Michigan State) that can provide more atmosphere than, for example, a midweek game at the Memorial Centre in Kingston, Ontario.

Brind'Amour and others also emphasize the quality of the coaching. The college head coaches are arguably just as knowledgeable as their major junior counterparts, with Bob Johnson, Ralph Backstrom, and Herb Brooks among those who have moved back and forth between college and professional hockey. But also, the structure of college hockey provides the time and resources that make serious coaching possible. A schedule of weekend-only games allows more time for systematic practice than does the seventy-game schedule of junior hockey, while the financial strength of a school such as Michigan State permits the team to have five assistant coaches who specialize in specific aspects of instruction. There is, in short, an attention to skills development that is rare, and indeed difficult, given the circumstances of Canadian junior hockey. Moreover, a scholarship player is in the program for four years, so a coach can afford to take time with his development, a luxury that junior coaches seldom enjoy. What all of this means for the young player is a broad range of opportunities: to improve hockey skills in an exciting and competitive hockey environment; to study and achieve a degree in a scholastic surrounding that is carefully tailored to support that effort; and to develop interests and friends outside the hockey subculture.

College players can get all this without sacrificing their chances of being drafted by an NHL club if they plan to go on to a pro career. The number of players drafted out of U.S. college hockey has risen steadily in recent years; in 1988 forty-eight players were drafted out of U.S. schools, compared with thirty-three from the OHL, thirty from the WHL, and twenty-two from the QMJHL.[16] The combined number of drafted players from Canadian major junior hockey remains considerably higher than from U.S. colleges, but it is clear that NHL teams are taking U.S. college-trained players increasingly seriously. The success of players such as Mike Liut and Dryden, Brind'Amour, Adam Oates, Craig Simpson, and others helps to confirm that college-trained players can go on to illustrious pro careers.

Canadian university hockey has been far less prominent as a training ground for the pros. For a time, the routes to the National Hockey League and through a degree program in a Canadian university were almost mutually exclusive. Canadian university hockey produced dynasty teams under Tom Watt at the University of Toronto and Clare Drake at the University of Alberta, but they often played much of their schedules against less than competitive teams; and rigorous enforcement of the rules against rough play made for a style more akin to international hockey than the NHL. Most Canadian universities have chosen not to offer athletic scholarships, as do U.S. schools; and until fairly recently not many junior players got the grades required for academic eligibility. Thus, although Canadian universities have sent on a series of coaches to the NHL — Mike Keenan, Jean Perron, Dave Chambers, as well as Watt and Drake — university players who have gone on to solid NHL careers, such as Randy Gregg, Gerard Gallant, and Mike Ridley, have been more exceptional.

Some observers believe that all this is changing, and that more Canadian university players are likely to be seen in the National Hockey

League. Expansion will create more jobs and put more pressure on scouts to look for talent outside the traditional pipelines. At the same time, more good junior players are going on to Canadian universities and playing hockey. While not the only factor, these former junior players contribute to what is becoming a more competitive league. Jean Perron, who went on from the University of Moncton to help win a Stanley Cup in Montreal, suggests that the calibre of play at roughly ten schools may now be better than junior hockey. What is most important in the long run, though, is that young players who go through either Canadian or U.S. universities and graduate are preparing themselves for the time when they can't earn a living in hockey.

For most players this time comes immediately after either junior or college hockey. Most of the young elite players who reach junior hockey don't get drafted, and not all of those who are drafted get signed to even minor-league contracts. Then there are those players, typically among the better players in junior or college hockey, who are invited to pro camps, and then sent to American League or International League farm clubs for "seasoning." Some players, like Warren Young, briefly successful with the Pittsburgh Penguins, stick it out in minor professional hockey through their mid-twenties, hoping for the break that will get them a serious trial in the NHL. Some even suggest that hockey in these leagues can be more fun: the sense of camaraderie stronger, the pressure less. But they don't earn big money (typically $35,000 to $40,000 in the early 1990s), and they must quickly face up to the need to prepare for some other line of work. There is also another not insignificant group who play in the NHL for several seasons or parts of seasons, typically as checkers or role players. They make considerably more money than those who never make the NHL, but they tend to get cut loose before long for younger role players who might develop into something more.

Hockey for Girls and Women

One other set of issues needs to be addressed before this chapter on minor hockey and the larger hockey subculture can be complete: the struggle over access to minor hockey for girls, the form that access should take, and the resources to be put towards girls' hockey. As we've seen, hockey in Canada developed historically as a male preserve. Above all, the professional game that Canadians have listened to on radio and watched on television has been entirely male, and boys have grown up imagining themselves to be Maurice Richard or Gordie Howe, Bobby Hull or Bobby Orr, Jean Beliveau or Wayne Gretzky. These stars and others have been held up as exemplars of a particularly Canadian kind of masculinity; and minor-hockey arenas have been "fields of dreams" where Canadian boys have tried to emulate their favourite stars. Where boys have chased their dreams, minor hockey and junior hockey have also provided opportunities for generations of Canadian men who remain staunch believers in the value of introducing young males into the codes of masculine behaviour that have been defining features of their own lives.

Much of this symbolism, if not the substance of hockey, is challenged by notions like family hockey and by the prospect of girls playing on boys' teams. In practice it is an issue that comes to the fore primarily between the ages of nine and thirteen, in other words before boys' later development in puberty gives them an advantage in size and upper body strength they will enjoy, statistically, as adult males. Popular notions about men's supposed physical "superiority" obscure the wide ranges of strength, speed, and co-ordination that exist among males and females of any age. High-performance male athletes can still surpass the performances of high-performance women athletes in both strength and speed events, but women have repeatedly shown that good female athletes who have had real opportunities to develop their athletic potential can perform at levels that will surpass most males. The issue then becomes, from one perspective at least, whether talented girls should be able to get the same kinds of opportunities to develop their potential that boys do, including physically demanding training, expert coaching, and challenging competition. Or will sports organizers continually invoke "tradition" or other arguments whose effects are to restrict girls' pursuit of sporting opportunities and skills?

Canadian girls and women have played hockey in one form or another for over a century. Much of this hockey was recreational with little formal organization, but there is evidence of a number of competitive women's teams existing by the time of the First World War. For instance, in 1914 women workers employed by Bell Telephone organized a competitive league in Montreal, with four participating clubs. More notably, a semi-professional women's league operated in Montreal from 1915 to 1917, with teams that sometimes drew two thousand fans. This women's league played full contact hockey with rules based on those of the National Hockey Association, and the sporting press raved about the skills of star players such as Albertine Lapensée and Agnès Vauthier.[17]

You won't find the names of Lapensée or Vauthier in the Hockey Hall of Fame — at least not yet. Organized hockey has been extremely slow to open its doors to women athletes, let alone recognize their accomplishments. Opportunities for women to play competitive hockey between the early twentieth century and the 1960s were scanty and seem to have been most available in wartime when there were few good male players available and rink owners were looking for new ways to fill their arenas. There were also rare openings in wartime for good women players to play on men's teams. Former NDP Member of Parliament Pauline Jewett briefly played hockey on a men's team at Queen's University during the late stages of the Second World War, but she lost her spot on the roster when former Queen's players returned from overseas.

By the late 1950s, postwar affluence and the baby boom had provided the economic and demographic base for a significant boom in minor-hockey teams and clubs. Still, girls who wanted to play competitive hockey had few opportunities. The early postwar organization of minor hockey was overwhelmingly influenced by the fact that the CAHA had committed itself to be a feeder system for the pros. This strengthened even further the perception of hockey as a boys' game. Girls who wanted to play on good teams were forced to adopt creative strategies. Thus, more than thirty years ago, former Sport Canada director Abigail Hoffman made the front pages when it was discovered she had been playing, and apparently quite successfully, for a good pee-wee team in West Toronto. Once it was discovered that "Ab" was a girl, she was prohibited from further play.

By the 1970s there were considerably more opportunities for girl hockey players than in the time of Abby Hoffman's youth. Nonetheless, older attitudes about the inappropriateness of boys and girls playing on the same team remained strong. In 1976 Gail Cummings, a girl from Huntsville, Ontario, was prohibited by the Ontario Minor Hockey Association (OMHA) from playing on the town's team (which she had legitimately made) in provincial atom playdowns. Although an Ontario Human Rights Commission Board of Inquiry dismissed the OMHA arguments that mixed hockey was physically dangerous to girls and that boys too could be harmed, either by the experience of losing to girls or by learning to play "softer" out of deference to girls, this decision was overturned on appeal. The Court of Appeals judgment didn't address these issues directly; rather, it focused on whether or not minor hockey was a "public service" — an important point because the Ontario Human Rights Code requires that public services be available to all, without regard for gender or race. The Court considered that hockey was available to Gail — she had indeed been playing house-league hockey on a mixed local team, and there was a girls' team in the town, albeit for older girls (ages thirteen to seventeen). It accepted the argument that the OMHA was a private voluntary organization whose reason for being was, legitimately, the provision of hockey opportunities for boys.

This question of whether the official organizations of minor hockey are private or public organizations has been pivotal in subsequent decisions. In 1977 a Board of Inquiry in Nova Scotia ruled that the Yarmouth Minor Hockey Association had infringed the rights of eleven-year-old Tina Forbes by denying her access to its house league because she was a girl. Here there were no alternative hockey opportunities for girls. This judgment emphasized that minor-hockey associations were providing what were portrayed and widely perceived as community services, especially when they routinely used public facilities and solicited public money to operate their programs. This reasoning was also supported in a 1978 Quebec decision, a ruling that went further by also addressing the argument that the existence of girls' teams constituted a legally satisfactory alternative. In this case the judge took the view that it was the responsibility of the association to demonstrate that an *equal calibre* of training and competitive opportunities was available within girls' leagues. In the absence of these opportunities it was discrimination against talented girls if they were barred on the basis of their sex from teams they had made on merit.[18]

Since that decision, more girls and women in Quebec have had opportunities to develop their skills by playing with boys and men. The best known of them, Manon Rheaume, played goal on a Quebec junior A team, was then drafted by the Tampa Bay Lightning before the 1992-93 season, and ultimately given a minor-league contract. Manon Rheaume earned new respect and enthusiasm for the abilities of women players, not least because she acquitted herself credibly by stopping seven of nine shots during a single period in a Tampa Bay preseason game — although her appearance was an admitted publicity stunt by the Lightning's management. Since that time she has become both a role model for women hockey players and a minor celebrity. However, she has also suffered through more than her share of snide commentary about the true level of her playing ability. And in the kind of sexist turnaround that so frequently frames women's athletic performances, she appears to have received as much notoriety for her physical attractiveness, and her refusal to pose nude for *Playboy*, as for her hockey skills.

Perhaps the best-known court case in the 1980s (1986-87) on the question of mixed play involved Justine Blaney and the Ontario Hockey Association. The case is of particular interest because the Charter of Rights and Freedoms was used to strike down a subsection of the Ontario Human Rights Code that had specifically excluded sex discrimination in sports from the code's anti-discrimination protections. Moreover, in an era and a part of the country (Metro Toronto) where other competitive opportunities existed for Blaney — in girl's hockey leagues and in the related game, ringette — the Ontario Court of Appeal had to address directly the validity of claims that such opportunities constituted equality. In Blaney's own testimony, it was precisely the stronger competition available in the boys' leagues that had made her want to try out for the Etobicoke Canucks. Boys' hockey also allows bodychecking and slapshots, which for Blaney added "more fun to the game."

Interestingly, the OHA was supported, at both the Divisional Court and the Court of Appeal, by the Ontario Women's Hockey Association, which took the position that subsection 19(2), which permitted sports organizations to discriminate on the basis of sex, was a necessary protection against men wanting to play on women's teams. For several years women's hockey had been growing in popularity in Canada, and the OWHA was fighting hard for access to rinks and coaching. It feared that whatever gains had been made might be jeopardized if men had access to women's programs. Justice Dubin was not persuaded that this would happen on any scale. The substance of the men's position — and the OHA, together with the OMHA and the Metro Toronto Hockey League, spent more than $100,000 fighting the case — was that separate leagues were warranted by differences in strength and physique and by the confrontational nature of the game. In a restatement of the arguments made a decade before in the Cummings case, the OHA said that its "main concern" was for the safety of female players — although it was also suggested that boys and indeed the game itself would be the losers if players had to hold back or play "softer."

These were precisely the arguments that the court rejected. However, the appeals process took so long that Blaney herself lost interest, leaving the case to be pursued by women's advocacy groups. Nonetheless, it is clear that negative attitudes about girls and women playing hockey have slowly begun to change. The old arguments about women's physical vulnerability and abilities, the old sexist stereotypes, seem increasingly hollow as the years pass and as the skills of female players increase and receive more exposure. In addition to the recent interest in Manon Rheaume, television coverage of the 1990 World Women's Hockey Championship in Ottawa provided unprecedented exposure for women's hockey and demonstrated levels of skill and physical contact that surprised some of hockey's most ardent traditionalists.

The debates around hockey for girls and women have simply been one small indicator of a much broader set of re-evaluations and struggles in recent years over the nature, direction, and control of hockey in this country. These developments have introduced new possibilities and ideas into a subculture that has been highly insular and parochial for decades. The struggle against this insularity and parochialism has become increasingly centred on the degree to which minor hockey should model itself as a feeder system of the NHL — or whether it should instead take up alternative models. There is a good deal at stake in these struggles, because they represent a challenge to the very definition and meaning of hockey in this country. There is also considerable room for optimism in evaluating these struggles — the recent expansion and popularity of girls' hockey, of old-timers' leagues, and of experiments with less competitive hockey are examples — but it is also apparent that the old ideas and the old ways of doing things are extremely persistent. This is particularly clear in the intensity of the responses to anyone who challenges hockey's longstanding status as a preserve of robust, even aggressive, masculinity — which in turn raises important questions about the sources of aggression and violence in Canadian hockey.

Chapter Eight

Violence, Fighting, and Masculinity

Hockey has a level of physical confrontation beyond that of most other sports. Like football, but unlike racing sports such as track or swimming, racquet games, or even baseball, hockey is a continuous physical contest in which the use of force to neutralize speed and skill is a matter of course. For many fans it is precisely this physical confrontation that makes hockey appealing. The thump of a hard bodycheck that catches an opponent at high speed, the toughness of the scramble along the boards and the hitting and hacking in front of the net, and the more direct confrontation of fighting, when the hockey itself is put aside for a one-on-one punching match — all these elements bring crowds to their feet.

Yet controversy over the place of violence in hockey has also been present since the beginnings of the modern game. Many people both outside and within the hockey subculture remain highly critical of how much violent behaviour the game permits and even encourages. The criticisms are raised publicly every time there is an incident that goes beyond the game's traditional levels of tolerance for violent conflict:

for example, stick-swinging incidents like the one that led to Dino Ciccarelli being fined by Ontario courts; the bench-clearing brawl between the Canadian and Soviet teams in the 1987 World Junior Championships; Bobby Clarke's now-legendary injury of Russian star Valery Kharlamov in the 1972 Canada Cup series; Dale Hunter's blindside crosscheck of Pierre Turgeon after the whistle in the 1993 NHL playoffs. The routine incidence of fighting and the (albeit diminishing) employment of "goons" in the NHL — as well as the fact that the NHL model in turn produces frequent fighting in junior and minor hockey — spark continued debate.

Nonetheless, many people in and around the game view fighting and intimidation not only as good tactics but also as essential dimensions of both the hockey culture and the Canadian tradition. All professional hockey players, and especially those developed in Canada, have come up through a system in which physical toughness is not only respected but also required. Many players draw the attention of scouts and managers precisely through their toughness — their willingness to dish it out and to take it. Even finesse players have to prove they can cope with direct aggression — a facility that becomes part of their image of themselves, of what it takes to be a hockey player. It is indicative of the "professionalization" of players' attitudes that most Canadian pros have long taken for granted the legitimacy of intimidation tactics and the necessity of using those tactics even outside the rules. If the players largely accept this tenet, the die-hard fans who worship the game's traditions make it a matter of faith.

The belief in the inevitability and necessity of violence outside the rules in hockey is typically expressed through two lines of argument. The first claims that because physical confrontation within the rules — such as bodychecking and unavoidable collisions — is a necessary and legitimate part of the game, fistfighting becomes a safety valve that helps to preclude more dangerous attacks with sticks. The second line of argument is compatible with the safety-valve theory but adds a moral dimension; physical toughness, including the willingness to fight, is simply a mark of character. People who endorse this position — Don Cherry and columnist Earl McCrae of *The Ottawa Citizen* come immediately to mind — accuse players who don't fight of being gutless and label critics of fighting as bleeding-hearts. As a reader of *The Hockey News* put it in response to an editorial debate about coverage of fighting: "If you don't like fighting in hockey maybe you could cover lawn bowling or something similar, so you won't get offended."[1] This type of argument has always played well in hockey's core market of die-hard fans — a market well primed for macho myth-making and the celebration of fighting skills. Nearly every year journalistic entrepreneurs tap this market with compilations of lists of hockey's toughest guys, greatest fights, or most penalized enforcers. There is also a significant market for videotapes of "the best" hockey fights and the hardest bodychecks.

Theories of Violence in Sport

There are two competing schools of thought about human aggression, and about the effects of exposure to violent behaviour. The first of these, *the catharsis hypothesis*, is highly compatible with hockey's in-house explanations of why violent acts occur. The catharsis hypothesis suggests that fighting in sports provides controlled and symbolic outlets for aggression that might otherwise manifest itself in more serious forms. For players, sport is supposed to reduce or siphon off natural aggressive energies. In hockey fighting is defended as a necessary outlet for the frustrations of a high-speed confrontational game. Without this outlet, it is argued, frustration would build up until it erupted in even more violent and dangerous ways. For fans, aggression is not normally provoked in quite the same ways, but the catharsis hypothesis also suggests that even the vicarious release of hostility is healthy. Thus, when crowds urge on their favourite gladiators to "kill" an opponent or "kick him in the head," it is suggested that, rather like the release of steam from a pressure cooker, the release of hostility that is thereby achieved renders more dangerous explosions less likely.[2] The notion of catharsis is grounded in a view of psychic life as fuelled by innate and powerful drives that will find expression somehow, in more or less damaging ways.

Canadian sociologist Michael D. Smith refers to the alternative school of thought as the *violence-begets-violence* thesis. From this perspective, aggressive behaviours are viewed as products of environments that arouse aggressive sentiments, provide role models of aggressive behaviour, and place people in situations where aggression visibly "works" and is rewarded and that sanction and even applaud aggressive behaviour. The widespread approval of aggression in hockey by many parents, peers, and coaches, and by many journalists and fans, is compatible with this theory. In fact, most available evidence supports the view that aggressive environments serve to arouse aggressive responses, even among spectators. Where the catharsis thesis would suggest that exposure to staged violence allows for its harmless release, several inquiries into violence associated with sport — the McMurtry Commission into player violence in Ontario hockey in the 1970s and several inquiries into soccer hooliganism in England are prime examples — have concluded that exposure to violence serves, on the contrary, to fire people up. Smith's own research suggests that incidences of violent behaviour among hockey fans are directly related to incidences of violence on the ice.

In summary, academic researchers investigating the links between sports and violence stress two recurring themes: first, that exposure to violence and to socially acceptable aggressions is likely to lead to more violence rather than less; and second, that there is more evidence to support sociological and cultural explanations of violence than psychological or biological ones. Sociocultural explanations point to the higher incidence of violence in environments of poverty, in very male environments, and in cultures and subcultures where strength is honoured and the use of force widely accepted. Many of these propositions are supported by systematic research. However, when limited to the discourse of social psychology, they are rarely connected to a historical analysis of the society that allows these violence-producing environments to persist. For example, family violence or subcultural violence among young males is often treated as an individual or small-group pathology; that is, as "deviance" rather than as phenomena that are the products of ideologies of masculinity, endemic poverty, or tensions based on racism, ethnicity, or class hatred.

Aspects of each of the two approaches to sport violence co-exist uneasily in an important discussion of the "civilizing process" developed by the German social theorist Norbert Elias.[3] Elias proceeded from Freudian assumptions (similar to those of catharsis theories) — his foundational idea was that human nature is composed of aggressive drives — but he argues that the civilizing process is constituted precisely by the containment and sublimation of aggression within rule-bound and stylized social contexts. Up until at least the late medieval period, European life was filled with a ferocious violence that pitted small chiefdoms, clans, families, cliques, and classes against one another. But as social life became more highly differentiated under the pressure of competition for scarce resources, institutional life became increasingly complex and individuals became dependant on more and more other people. These increasing social dependencies meant that people were forced to attune their conduct to others in stable and more "mannered" ways. In Elias's words: "The web of actions grows so complex and so extensive, the effort to behave 'correctly' within it becomes so great, that beside the individual's conscious self-control an absolute, blindly functioning apparatus of self-control is firmly established.[4] As this occurred, violence between individuals began to decrease. Meanwhile the modern state began to acquire a monopoly over the use of physical force, and violence became more instrumental, more strategic, than expressive.

The British sociologist Eric Dunning and a number of his colleagues have taken up these ideas and applied them to the issue of sports violence. According to Dunning, modern sport on the whole can be viewed as a notable marker of relatively civilized modern societies. Indeed, the making of modern sport in the nineteenth century occurred only in those societies where more direct forms of fighting were being increasingly and actively discouraged, and where rules and manners (rather than force) were beginning to govern social relations in a growing number of areas of life. The expansion of degrees of regulation and self-control in sport promoted by middle-class reformers since the nineteenth century means that sports have become *less* rather than more violent over time. By the same token modern sport has itself been a constitutive element in the broader control of aggressive drives within civilizing institutions (such as schools and youth clubs). Most violence in sport has now become rationalized, incorporated into the rules in a tightly regulated manner. In modern sport violent outbreaks outside the rules are therefore most likely to be found in sports whose structures, cultures, and forms of social bonding have a weakly differentiated and anachronistic character. In this context, to use Elias's words, the "blindly functioning apparatus of self-control" that is part of sport's alleged insertion into the broader civilizing process is underdeveloped.

There is a lot to be said for this argument, but there are important limitations to the approach as a whole. First, although the best work in this tradition is frequently provocative and intriguing, it tends to underplay the active historical relationship that exists between economic life and culture. Neither Elias nor Dunning have much to say about the specificity of Western capitalism as a context for theorizing about violence in sport. Second, the very idea of a civilizing process is prone to slip into what one critic has called a "generalized evolutionism."[5] The contributions of Elias and Dunning can be read as a highly sophisticated variant of the theory of modernization discussed in our earlier chapters. Differing forms of social bonding (Dunning notes differences between what he calls "segmental" and "functional" bonding) reflecting varying degrees of integration in the social division of labour become tacitly equivalent to the ideas of "premodern" and "modern" social and cultural formations.

More importantly, the implicit assumption that the "civilizing process" is characteristic of modern social and cultural order runs the risk of deflecting attention away from the *endemic* conflicts of interest and power struggles that are a continuing part of the production of that order. Some forms of violence simply cannot be explained adequately in terms of their low integration into the abstract apparatuses of control supposedly characteristic of complex, highly differentiated societies. In many sports, including the popular team games of football and basketball, not to mention boxing or wrestling (where controlled fighting is the essence of the sport), rules and unruliness have *always* existed in a precarious tension. Part of the ongoing appeal, for some fans, is precisely when unruliness triumphs, however temporarily.

Nonetheless, Dunning has suggested in a convincing way some possible effects of sport in the evolution of gender relations.[6] First, he suggests that the power of men in any society is reinforced to the extent that important institutions in that society sanction and indeed celebrate the use of force. Conversely, the power of men is weakened whenever rules against the use of force are exercised to an extent that force becomes widely seen as taboo. Second, he suggests that the power of men is strengthened to the extent that men have their own institutions ("male preserves") that are honoured in the public sphere; and that male power in society is weakened when these institutions are integrated. Together these proposals point to connections between hockey traditionalists' defence of "a man's game" (the defence of rough play and the defence of the game against such heretical ideas as mixed play between boys and girls can be seen as two sides of the same coin) and the defensive feelings of many Canadian men about the contemporary erosion of traditional male privileges. As a prelude to developing this analysis more fully, though, we want to reconnect our earlier observations of the work world of the pro game and the aspirations that surround minor hockey to the approach to physical play that for many years has constituted the unofficial position of the NHL.

The NHL Theory of Violence and the Hockey Subculture

The early years of modern hockey featured plenty of violence outside the official rules of the game. The passions that became centred around teams that suddenly began to represent their communities led to frequent violent outbreaks. Playing to primarily male crowds in mining towns and small industrial cities, the early pro game willingly accommodated these violent tendencies and, indeed, began to institutionalize them. As the years went by the promoters of pro hockey sought to control violence outside the rules only to the extent necessary to avoid widespread public disapproval and to ensure the existence of reasonably orderly audiences. Other than that, the tolerant attitude to violence outside the rules has been rooted in the belief that the occasional fistfight has been good for business. In this context, and in an earlier time when people were less inclined than now to think critically about the legitimacy of combat sports like boxing, or about such things as a parent's right to hit a child or a teacher's right to employ corporal punishment, hockey actively traded on the popular enjoyment of an aggressive masculine physicality. The interesting thing is how this enjoyment has hung on at the core of the hockey subculture even as other attitudes in Canadian society have changed around it.

Several trends in the pro game since the end of the Second World War have particular relevance for understanding attitudes to violence within the hockey subculture. Ken Dryden makes an acute observation in *The Game* that even before NHL expansion in the 1960s, the generation of young men growing up in an era of greater prosperity and better dietary awareness produced bigger and stronger players. At the same time, rule changes designed to increase the speed of the game, together with the advent of the slap shot, contributed to altering the relative importance of strength and skill in the creation of scoring chances. This was not an absolute shift, because there is still a central role for the skilled offensive player who can put away chances in the offensive zone. But between the early 1960s and the 1980s, the task of setting up these chances became less likely to depend on the fine and quick skills of the puckhandler and playmaker and more likely to result from the strengths of wingers who could win the tough races down the boards and the physical struggles in the corners. Pro hockey increasingly became more a game of speed and strength and less one of finesse and delicate skills. The corollary of this is that hockey also became what Dryden calls an "adrenalin game," one in which adrenalin not only often makes the difference between the winners and losers of physical struggles, but also reinforces hair-trigger tempers.

These tendencies towards speed and strength, and then aggression, were further reinforced in the late 1960s by the needs of expansion teams to put a competitive product on display. Forced at first to ice teams made up largely of journeyman players, the early expansion clubs had to try to neutralize the leading skill players on the established teams by emphasizing intensity, size, and defensive tactics. The most successful of the expansion teams in the 1960s, the St. Louis Blues, played this kind of disciplined defensive hockey, and they became respectable, although never exciting. The Philadelphia Flyers of the Fred Shero/Bobby Clarke era took defensive hockey a step further, by refining the use of force into a consistent and well-advertised strategy. Dryden suggests that the Flyers took deliberate advantage of the NHL's reluctance to have referees call too many penalties and built a team around size, strength, and aggression, a team tailor-made for the adrenalin game. They won two Stanley Cups, too; so that for a time in the 1970s the Broad Street Bullies, the first postwar expansion team to win the cup, became a model for teams lacking many players with extraordinary skills.

In the years following the Flyers' successes, teams built only around size, strength, and aggressiveness proved to be vulnerable against teams with a new balance of size, strength, and aggressiveness plus skill and sheer speed. Dynasties like the Dryden-era Canadiens, the Islanders of the Mike Bossy period, and especially the Edmonton Oilers of Gretzky, Coffey, and Kurri demonstrated that skill still mattered and that it was possible to win with a modified version of firewagon hockey. Through the 1980s the excitement generated by fast and offensively minded stars and the obvious promotional benefits that these stars brought to the league began to reduce employment opportunities in the NHL for "goons" and "enforcers." The steady infusion of skilled European players, especially by the end of the 1980s, reduced these opportunities even further. At the same time, heavier penalties against the instigators of fights, against "the third man in," and, more recently, against stickwork have played an important part in regulating the amount of violence outside the rules. Yet while size, strength, and aggressiveness may no longer be enough to achieve success in pro hockey, they remain necessary as part of the formula found by winning teams. The teams that beat the Flyers had to be tough enough to stand up to them; and today it is simply accepted that every successful team still needs its quota of tough guys, or else its skill players will be relentlessly attacked. Small teams tend to be losing teams; and despite new rules to regulate and contain fighting, NHL hockey continues to be characterized by routine aggression and by higher levels of violent play outside the rules than either international hockey or university hockey allows.

This routine aggression and violent play have long been justified through an unofficial NHL theory of violence. The theory combines two arguments. First, the violent nature of the game — high speed, frequent collisions, the incidence of accidental and deliberate infractions — and the inevitability, therefore, that anger will erupt dictate the use of fighting as a safety valve permitting aggressive feelings to be discharged before they lead to more dangerous forms of aggression (such as stick-swinging attacks). This, as many commentators have pointed out, is a straightforward application of catharsis theory. Coaches and managers continue to reiterate this argument, although perhaps not quite as loudly as in days gone by, despite the accumulating evidence to the contrary; despite evidence that anger can be contained if the penalties against it are sufficiently severe (as in football, for example, or in soccer and university hockey); and despite repeated evidence that some players go looking for opponents and retaliate in responses that are often coolly calculated rather than hot-tempered or spur of the moment.

The other argument consistently made by supporters of this traditional NHL position is that fans want the players, and not the referees, to decide the outcome of games, and that when the referees call "too many penalties" it interrupts the flow of the game. These arguments recently came to the fore once again in response to referees' attempts to enforce new rules on boarding and high-sticking in the early part of the 1992-93 season. No fan likes to see games continually interrupted by penalties. However, there is also the important counterargument that allowing infractions to go unpunished can influence the outcome of a game just as much as penalties can. This is clearly understood in both professional football and basketball, where defensive infractions draw penalties even in the closing seconds of championship games. In hockey, the traditional laissez-faire policy can produce significant, but unacknowledged, consequences as players continually push the limits of what they can get away with. In its practice of tacitly supporting minimal intervention, hockey's establishment influences results just as surely as it would by calling for a more vigorous enforcement of the official rules of play.

Attitudes towards minimal intervention mixed with the safety valve theory of violence have simply become part of the folklore of hockey in North America, repeated until even non-physical players like Mats Naslund and Jimmy Carson will say: "It (fighting) has been there so long. I accept it as part of the game."[7] Indeed, in most instances controlled aggressiveness and an ability to "look after yourself" have long been an important part of players' subcultural codes of honour and respect. These codes of honour and respect were investigated in a fascinating study conducted by a U.S. sociologist, Robert Faulkner, in the 1970s. Faulkner drew on the work of Erving Goffman and others on the "presentation of self" and on the reproduction of norms within occupational subcultures to suggest that hockey players have to negotiate a "space" for themselves on the ice or they will be constantly roughed up. Thus, former Oiler captain (and later New York Ranger) Mark Messier responded to suggestions that he is widely feared by saying, "Everybody has to have a little respect in order to get the room they want."[8] To win space *and* respect the player must show both opponents and teammates that he will not be pushed around. The new player, especially, has to demonstrate at the very least that he can't be put off his own game, and preferably that he can and will retaliate. As Faulkner notes: "Intimidation and insult in the form of the deft fore-arm or elbow, butt of the stick, and fist is a recommended procedure for finding out what others are about, what lines of action can be taken against them and what troubles can be anticipated."[9]

The player, like Messier or the legendary Gordie Howe, who can make opponents hurt for such transgressions will be accorded a certain space, while those unable or unwilling to do this will be attacked with enthusiasm. Faulkner's evidence suggests, indeed, that players saw physical encounters as character tests, tests of what someone was made of, and that players who would not stand up for themselves or not support teammates were rarely respected or liked. In Faulkner's study, very few players, even those with reputations as enforcers, spoke as if they enjoyed violence, but most of them did see testing behaviour as a routine part of their workplace, and they saw a willingness to look after themselves (so that teammates didn't have to) and to support mates in times of trouble as part of their code of honour. Social researchers have found much of this to be true as well in other lines of work that pit men against others, for instance in police work.

Clearly, at the top levels of hockey there are a significant number of players — including Steve Yzerman, Pavel Bure, and, of course, Wayne Gretzky — who are not fighters and enjoy the systematic protection of teammates. Even they have to be tough enough not to be put off their own game by aggression; and in these circumstances it is not surprising that even among the skill players there has been widespread acceptance of intimidation as part of the game. At the very least there is an appreciation of its tactical value. A former Boston star, Derek Sanderson, noted: "We practised violence because we know it won hockey games. The other teams were afraid of us. Which meant we had the puck most of the time."[10] Violence tolerated until it became customary in hockey has ultimately led to violence as a tactic in hockey, which has placed significant demands on everyone who wants to play the game. The same testing behaviours and rites of passage found in the NHL are also common in junior hockey, frequently in an even more amplified way. For example, Robert Olver has described how Saskatoon Blades rookie Rob Lelacheur was goaded by some of his teammates to use his size more aggressively, to "play angry." It wasn't part of Lelacheur's natural temperament; but when he did start to hit first and hit hard, his mates let him know they were proud of him. Lelacheur knew, in turn, that he had taken an important step towards being one of the team and one of the guys: now he belonged.[11] This, of course, is only a single instance. Numerous commentators have noted how the use of force in throwing skill players off their game — the instrumental use of aggression in other words — is taught right down into minor hockey.[12]

Not all players necessarily like this state of affairs. Bobby Orr, whose career was undoubtedly shortened by the attentions of less talented opponents who took shots at his oft-injured knees, once reportedly said, "I didn't want to fight, but if they see you backing up in this league, it's no good."[13] Skill players typically wage a constant struggle against attacks intended to neutralize their speed, their moves, their touch in front of the net. For the most part, the ones who make it to the NHL and thrive are those, like Orr and Gretzky, who have learned to play with intimidation. Some of them speak out later, from a position of success and authority. Such statements are a challenge to "traditionalists" in the hockey subculture, indeed to the whole experience of the player who has come up through major junior hockey and into the pro ranks.

In the last few years, the monolithic certainty of hockey folklore in the areas of violence and fighting has begun to show some rather large cracks. The NHL president in 1992, Gil Stein, was prone to muse publicly about the fact that it might well be time to take fighting out of the game, although when the league confronted the issue before the 1992-93 season its authorities couldn't bring themselves to do it. Furthermore, even players who accept fighting are increasingly questioning the notion that a ban on fighting would necessarily lead to more stick infractions. This notion has been a truism among supporters of the status quo; but a *Hockey News* survey in 1989 was surprised to find that nine of twenty all-stars surveyed disagreed. Mario Lemieux, Paul Reinhart, and Scott Stevens, for example, all pointed to other major games (specifically football and basketball), and to hockey in other jurisdictions, where things are different. Where the rules are enforced with penalties severe enough to hurt the team, they said, players simply learn to contain their tempers. In Lemieux's view, "If the right people care enough about it, it will happen."[14]

The belief that violence sells and that eliminating fighting would undercut the game's appeal as spectacle has been the official thinking among the NHL's most influential governors and officers for so long that it seems hard to imagine things being any other way. Indeed, Alan Eagleson recalls that when the players' association recommended a ban on fighting in 1975, "It was categorically rejected by the rules committee."[15] Today, this article of received wisdom is being increasingly questioned, even by some owners. It has also been publicly challenged by a number of the game's foremost stars, most notably Wayne Gretzky, who began to speak out against fighting early in 1989. For Gretzky, the old debates about whether fighting is necessary as a safety valve are simply beside the point. Economics and, more particularly, the growth of the game in the United States are the key issues to Gretzky now, and his position directly challenges much of the received wisdom that has surrounded the game.

Selling Hockey: What Appeals to Whom?

It is noteworthy that Gretzky freely acknowledges that his perspective on these issues has changed as a result of his move to California, to a culture where the taken-for-granted truths of the hockey subculture mean little: "We always talk about the people who come to the games to see the fighting. And I was one of the ones who believed that.... I wonder if they've ever done an analysis on how many people *don't* come just because of fighting."[16] In Edmonton, a city where hockey is king and the major columnists and sportscasters are themselves part of the hockey subculture, Gretzky would have had little contact with those who would question the NHL theory of violence. In Los Angeles he became all too aware of the game's image in the mainstream U.S. media as a kind of wrestling on ice. He was embarrassed at network announcers' jokes along the lines of "I went to the fights the other night and a hockey game broke out." He also heard the comments of people who had never given hockey a chance precisely *because* of its image as an atavistic game — an image reinforced by movies like *Slapshot* and *Youngblood* (with Rob Lowe as the skilled player who has to learn to fight). Yet when these same people did come to a game they were impressed with hockey's speed and skill.

There are many people within the game, as well as in the Canadian hockey press, whose response to this kind of thinking is that "the U.S. media blows it out of proportion."[17] The survey of star players undertaken by the *Hockey News* confirms that many of them believe the media are more concerned about violence than the general public is, and that hockey just gets an unfair press. To Gretzky, though, the fact remains that hockey *has* a poor image in the United States and that this image undercuts the game's potential for growth in this biggest and most affluent market. Gretzky isn't talking here about the committed hockey fan, about those who have filled rinks at close to capacity for years in Boston and Chicago and Philadelphia. He is talking about a *different* audience, some of whom have drifted away from the game because of the extent to which force can dominate skill, and most of whom will never have been part of the hockey subculture. He is

talking, ultimately, about the larger audiences for general sports entertainment who could fill rinks in non-traditional centres and, even more
important, could make hockey on television worth more to the U.S.
networks and cable companies. For it is in television where the real
money is to be found in professional sport. Network and cable contracts and the prospect of pay-per-view promise the greatest returns
to owners, and it is only this level of television revenue that will bring
hockey players' salaries up to something like the levels now enjoyed
by athletes in other major pro sports.

The lines can be drawn this way. NHL hockey has an established
and loyal core audience in Canada and parts of the northeastern states.
Most of these fans love hockey and will probably watch it regardless
of whether violence increases or is contained. Some of them love the
fights and respond with outrage to calls to abolish them. The opinion
voiced in the pages of *The Hockey News* from a fan in Vernon, British
Columbia, is a typical example: "Nothing gets the fans more excited
than when a scuffle breaks out." Yet the television audience for hockey
has not grown in the United States, the way it has for baseball, football, and especially basketball, a sport that was once close to hockey
in its TV revenues but is now far ahead. Other fans, connected enough
to hockey to write to *The Hockey News* in praise of an antifighting column, support what Gretzky and Lemieux say about the game's basic
appeal. A fan from Notre Dame, Indiana, writes: "By abolishing fighting, the NHL will sport a new image and flaunt a better product. A
product featuring skilled, crafty players playing the game as it should
be played." Another fan from Brooklyn, New York, echoes the same
sentiments: "True hockey fans are not interested in hockey violence.
The NHL must ban fighting and stick fouls if this wonderful sport is to
be treated as a major player on the U.S. sports scene."[18]

It is tempting to say that there is an element of macho nationalism
in the Canadian hockey subculture's defence of its own values and
practices as "normal" while deriding others as "sissies." This chauvinism takes its most overt form in Don Cherry's now-familiar attacks
on Swedes and other Europeans as lacking the courage and character
of "our" boys. The same sentiments are also present in the preferences
for aggressive hockey expressed by others more circumspect than Cherry.
Cherry has become something of a caricature of himself in recent years,
but his popularity suggests that a not insignificant number of Canadian
fans love to hear this public persona who gives voice to their own feelings and prejudices. There is a widely shared pride in "our" boys' hardness and bravado, as if this was part of a preferred Canadian self-image:

a symbolic reminder, not unlike skiing's Crazy Canucks, of the tough and courageous traditions of a northern frontier nation.

Is it in fact Canadians, then, who prefer their hockey violent rather than the Americans we have often found it convenient to blame? Earlier we noted Peter Gzowski's argument in *The Game of Our Lives* that the escalation of bullying tactics and illegal physical intimidation in the 1970s was greatly influenced by the number of new U.S. markets that pro hockey was trying to conquer through league expansion. Because most potential U.S. fans lacked a detailed knowledge of the game, hockey's promoters sought to reach them by self-consciously marketing violence and fighting. The obvious implication was that U.S. fans were more likely to be drawn to violent spectacle than were Canadian fans. Yet perhaps we need to re-evaluate this argument. Do Gretzky's experiences in the United States point to a different conclusion?

Certainly, Americans are not known for their distaste for other forms of violent entertainment. Indeed, there is considerable tolerance for pushing and fighting in baseball and the NBA. Boxing still has a substantial following, and the enthusiasm for NFL machismo goes without saying. Moreover, players who have recalled their time playing in U.S. cities in minor pro hockey sometimes note that they felt pressure from team managements "to play rough for the fans." Indeed, one former player jokingly told us that being "sent down" to play in the International Hockey League in the 1970s was similar to "being sent to Vietnam." Interestingly, *The Aggressive Hockey Report*, a small publication that systematically catalogues NHL and minor-league fights, and then provides rankings of the fighters, originates in Brooklyn, New York. Similarly, an overview of the responses to occasional columns on fighting in *The Hockey News* suggests that both Canadians and Americans exhibit the gamut of responses to violent hockey.

It seems that nationality itself matters less than the depth of a person's identification with the "traditions" of the hockey subculture, or conversely a willingness to take an unsentimental view of its dominant values and practices (and clearly there are insiders, from Dryden to Gretzky, who are prepared to do this). The California fans who have changed Gretzky's perspective, and the many other hockey fans of long standing in both Canada and the northern United States whose personal involvement with the game has been with school hockey or recreational hockey, are not fully part of the NHL's subculture and are not threatened by the prospect of change. Thus, *Globe and Mail* columnist Al Strachan argues that one of the fundamental differences between the Wayne Gretzky and Don Cherry positions is that Cherry speaks for the old Canadian hockey tradition — the hard-core hockey fan, so to speak — while Gretzky wants the game to reach out to a broader audience, and to grow, especially in the United States where, Strachan claims, "Fighting is not an accepted part of any sport."[19]

Again, this seems to be an overly generous assessment of the tastes and attitudes of U.S. fans. But it does seem true to say that Americans more than Canadians are offended by how fighting has become institutionalized as an expected part of hockey. A U.S. fan might enjoy an occasional NBA scuffle yet flatter him or herself into believing that the scuffle is "not basketball," that it is a mere aberration outside the rules. But hockey actually seems to celebrate fighting outside the rules as a normal part of the game. There isn't even any pretence that fighting is morally or ethically inappropriate, and that is what seems to bother large numbers of potential U.S. spectators. There is some irony, given Canadians' views of the United States as a violent society, that violence-ridden Americans may well require more lip service to be paid to moral regulation in professional sport than "polite" Canadians do.

Class and the Gender Order
There are also class differences in attitudes to violence. Rough hockey celebrates a hard man's approach to life, which has a long tradition in the history of Western popular cultures and is particularly understood and appreciated among working-class fans, whether in Canada or elsewhere. Social historians in Britain, for example, have argued that significantly different values regarding the use of force, and indeed different ideals about strength and the body, developed in the varying circumstances of working-class and bourgeois life. Notably, Richard Holt has drawn out the distinction that developed between the middle-class ideal of "manliness" — an ideal embodied precisely in sportsmanship, in being a good loser, and in respect for the rules — and the working-class fan's celebration of a maleness with harder edges, more committed to winning, and that didn't mind giving an opponent "some clog" if this helped get the job done.[20] The celebration of unruliness and violence in sports is a good example of the populist pleasure that can be taken in the temporary breakdown of an order whose definitions of good guys and bad guys many people cannot buy. The divisions we find between supporters of fighting and those whose pleasure in games celebrates the triumph of skill in a rule-bound context loosely correspond to differences in the cultures of social classes.

The rush of excitement in a sports crowd when fighting suddenly emerges out of more rule-bound forms of combat is by no means confined to working-class fans. It is more to the point to talk about gender here, or the intersections of class and gender, than about class itself. Hockey has come to occupy the place it holds in Canadian culture in part because it provides a public platform for celebrating a very traditional masculine ideal. For that reason there are important connections between struggles about violence in and around hockey, and larger struggles over changes in what Australian sociologist Robert Connell calls the gender order: "a historically constructed pattern of power relations between men and women."[21]

Connell uses the term "gender order" to sensitize people to the connections between different social institutions. Personal relationships between men and women, and personal feelings about masculinity and femininity, do not exist independently of the practices and meanings that are dominant in the society: in the labour market, schools, media, and popular cultures. This includes the ways that men and women are represented in our most popular sports, as well as the lifestyle advertising that today associates a variety of physical pursuits and the sociability that surrounds them with widely desired social identities. Representations of masculine and feminine identities and ways of being male and female that are normally rewarded tend to be mutually reinforcing; and together they help to constitute a *structure of relations* between women and men. It is this structure that Connell calls the gender order; change in any one part of it (like sport) will have its effects in other institutions and in private relationships as well.

The gender order — like the system of class relations in Canada — is also a structure of *power and privilege* that systematically favours men over women. Like the system of class relations, the gender order is not a monolithic structure so much as a powerful set of limits and pressures. We can see aspects of these in the varied factors that, even today, favour men in the labour market and mean that "women's jobs" are typically less well paid than men's. We can see them in the patterns of domestic life that mean not only that men tend to pursue careers while women interrupt theirs but also that men are much more likely to have leisure "careers," in sport or in other community activities or associations. In either case, the male partner's progress has often required his female partner to "mind the home front" while he is out training or attending competitions.[22] Finally, we can see these limits and pressures in our culture's celebration not just of maleness, but of maleness defined in a very specific way. The idealized vision of masculinity in Canada obviously involves far more than physical strength and toughness, but the priority given to these values in sports and the particular attention we lavish on the traditional games that showcase these qualities testify to their continuing importance in the culture.

The gender order (again, like class structure) is also a social and historical product, rather than a natural order. Even though gendered divisions of labour had their origins in biology (in the demands of early motherhood, and in the upper body strength required in combat and some kinds of manual labour), contemporary society privileges men in ways that have no continuing relation to biological necessity. The gender order of Western societies has been changing, arguably, ever since the increasing importance of intellectual and technical knowledge in production processes made physical strength less valuable, and since the extension of rules and laws into successive areas of life has penalized (though not eliminated) the use of force. Yet such change as *has* been achieved has always faced systematic male resistance, as well as entrenched ideas about masculine and feminine "roles." Sport is only one area where women have made dramatic progress by overcoming not only official practices of exclusion but also popular stereotypes. In sport as elsewhere, though, things have only changed as a result of considerable effort: economic pressures and incentives, political campaigns and court challenges, and the cumulative work of many women and some men whose examples have challenged received ideas.

It is against just this background of contested changes in the gender order of contemporary societies — mediated by a widespread transformation in the class structures of Canadian communities — that the attempted reformation of hockey, and resistance to it within the hockey subculture, are best understood. Because women have always been excluded from hockey's institutional structures, even though women have been playing hockey-like games for almost as long as men have, organized hockey developed as a distinctly masculine subculture, a game played (at the organized level) almost exclusively by men and boys, and a game whose dominant practices and values have been those of a very specific model of aggressive masculinity. At its best this model of masculinity defines the real man as a decent person of few words, but with a powerful sense of his own abilities and the toughness and physical competence to handle any difficulties that might arise; a man that people respect and look up to but don't dare cross; a man who generally respects the rules that govern social life, but knows how to work outside them if necessary. In the United States from the 1940s to the late 1960s this image of masculinity was stereotypically expressed by the kinds of movie roles usually occupied by John Wayne. For generations of Canadian boys a slightly meaner version of that same image was represented by skilled but tough hockey players, the archetype of them being Gordie Howe.

This image doesn't exhaust the range of sources for the construction of masculine identities in sport. There are other archetypal images of masculine prowess in Western cultures that stress sheer power, aggressiveness, and emotional volatility in addition to the morally balanced ideal of decent but uncompromisingly tough masculine competence. Maurice Richard's explosive competitiveness — an unwillingness to be denied that at times seemed to verge on mania — was a model of aggressive masculinity that thrilled young Canadian males both in and outside of Quebec. But there is also a tradition in Western culture that celebrates masculine power for no other reason other than its ability to dominate anything that gets in its way. This has ensured a following for athletes whose masculine styles are based solely on a combination of aggressiveness and destructive power — for instance, former heavyweight boxing champion Mike Tyson. Certainly, there is an immense difference between the masculine styles of Mike Tyson and Gordie Howe. The line between toughness and brutality in the "ideal" definition of masculinity has always been notoriously difficult to draw.

Hockey's status as a man's game in Canada has been partly due to the fact that the game continues to be one of the few areas of life where hardness and overt physical intimidation are still allowed to count — places where men who love to hit can still enjoy doing so. Such opportunities assume considerable importance in a changing world where traditional places and times for men's exclusive association are disappearing, and where many rural and working-class males, in particular, feel a loss of control because of the transformations in the workplace. The infusion of women into traditionally male jobs, the devaluation of physical work in an emerging service-oriented society, the dominance of an urban culture with its privileged classes of managers, professionals, and bureaucrats — all contribute to this perceived loss of control.

Faced with this feeling of loss, many men are desperate to hang onto whatever "traditions" they can. The Canadian sports historian Bruce Kidd has noted that hockey arenas have long acted like "men's cultural centres" in cities and towns across the country.[23] Even minor hockey has been a traditional site — and a site until recently unaffected by changes in the gender order — for the initiation of boys into the realm of masculinity. The proposals to take the fighting out of hockey do not really threaten the game itself, despite what is often said in public forums. The ultimate threat, the threat that produces a recalcitrance to change, is the perceived threat to the maleness of the game, and beyond this to the place of traditional masculinity in a changing economic, cultural, and gender order.

Making Boys into Men

Sport in Western societies has traditionally been used, as the saying goes, to "make boys into men." Sport was a central focus of the character-building program of the boys' public schools in England from the Victorian period onwards, and many of the same beliefs about the effectiveness of sport in promoting a particular model of masculinity have long been present in the leading boys' private schools in Canada.[24] In the English schools it was not hockey but soccer and rugby that were the centrepieces of this program; and even in Canada, the importance of class and Britishness to the particular ideal of manliness these schools sought to produce meant that English games were given preference over the native ones played by boys of other classes. In hockey the overt Britishness may have been rejected, but the emphasis on "manliness" remained, even in the amateur game.

In amateurism the display of masculine competence was linked to a more self-consciously modern model of masculinity, in which the expression of strength and force was ritualized and disciplined into recognized forms of competitive achievement. We wouldn't want to identify the attempt to constitute sport in this way as part of a quasi-evolutionary "civilizing process" in the manner favoured by Elias and his followers; rather, it was the result of a more open set of struggles — struggles that the moral entrepreneurs responsible for organizing sport in the nineteenth and early twentieth centuries did not always win. In the programs of the British public and Canadian private schools, and in the early culture of the amateur code, sporting prowess and physical and moral accomplishment were meant to be combined in a model of masculine superiority appropriate to a world in which authority had increasingly to be earned, at the same time that the overt use of force was becoming socially unacceptable. Even Pierre de Coubertin's dedicated promotion of the modern Olympics was very much tied to his belief that young French men of his class were becoming effete.[25] Yet all of this effort was included within the broader attempt to remake often "uncivilized" and unorganized sporting recreations into a supposedly higher, more socially improving form of culture.

The problem was that neither the folk sports of the past nor the longstanding conceptions of often rough masculine competence that went along with many of them were quite as malleable as nineteenth-century moral entrepreneurs had hoped. The Victorian quest for a highly regulated, respectable form of sporting enterprise was shot through with contradictions. Indeed, as soon as teams began to represent their communities the ideal of masculine honour was quickly bonded to the need to win and dominate the opposition. Incidents of domination became the stuff of reputation and legends, and tough guys became widely celebrated in fan gossip and in the sporting news. Almost certainly these tough guys helped sell the game as an entertainment commodity to primarily male (rather than family) audiences. As professional franchises moved to bigger cities, and with the formation of the NHL and its eventual dominance of the entire subcultural world of the game, hockey's traditions of violent play simply became another part of the game's "common sense."

Violent play in the late nineteenth and early twentieth centuries was by no means restricted to hockey. Tolerance for unruliness and occasional violence has long been a part of "popular" entertainment traditions in Europe and North America. At the same time, there has been a steady domestication of these traditions in all areas of North American popular culture over the past two hundred years. The celebration of unruly pleasures and disorderly entertainments, often with the overtones of a rebelliously aggressive masculinity, still exists as a notable element of North American popular culture; but it has been largely contained by the combined demands of twentieth-century work life and nearly two centuries of moral entrepreneurship and state regulation. Yet hockey's own version of this containment of the rough and the unruly has been unique. Rather than legislating rough and unruly practices out of existence, or domesticating them completely through rigidly enforced rules — as the promoters of nineteenth-century amateurism tried to do — hockey institutionalized them through a complex system of subcultural codes and the game's own internal divisions of labour.

The irony is that these codes and divisions of labour ultimately subordinated hockey's traditions of popular pleasure and potentially rebellious masculinity to a paternalistic conservatism. In this paternalistic system, respect and rewards came to be built around an obsession with toughness and mateship set in organizational settings that required high levels of deference to formal authority and to tradition. Rebellious only in response to the criticisms of outsiders, and to a world where bleeding hearts seem to be gaining a larger and larger voice, this paternalistic conservatism still recycles its own internally consistent moral system and self-justifying theories. In Canada, hockey's traditionalists still tend towards an unswerving devotion to the efficacy of this system, its customs, and theories, and Don Cherry is their unelected spokesman. But even people in the game who are highly critical — for instance, of hockey's inability to offer sufficient moral differentiation between clean players and goons, or even between the Mike Tyson and Gordie Howe variants of physical aggressiveness — nonetheless hang on to the belief that hockey as it is continues to offer important lessons for young boys.

Indeed, far beyond hockey there is a widespread belief in the value of contact sports for making boys into men, and this belief dies hard. The broader cultural resilience of this view not only explains much of the resistance to suggestions that fighting be totally banned from hockey, but also underwrites a lot of the resistance to other changes that might threaten hockey's traditional role as a training ground for masculinity. It is in this sense that we can understand the fear expressed by some minor-hockey officials about allowing girls to play on boy's teams — a fear that boys might learn to "play softer" while adult men will have a harder time reproducing the old codes of masculine honour and superiority. There are indeed real grounds for these fears from the perspective of the maintenance of old-fashioned styles of masculinity. When boys and girls alike can see with their own eyes that pain thresholds and physical and moral courage are not necessarily gendered qualities at all, but aspects of individuals that are widely distributed among both sexes, the ideologies central to an older generation of men's beliefs about themselves and about gender relations stand to be severely challenged. The association of masculinity with strength and courage — the very association that underwrites the historically tenacious ideology of male superiority — is challenged at its very roots when women are seen to perform the same feats and demonstrate the same qualities.

A corollary issue is that the increasing presence of girls and women in areas of life that were formerly all male really does reduce the spaces in our culture where "men can be men" and male solidarity can be rehearsed. Here we are talking not so much about the game itself but about the camaraderie of all-male company, in which sexist humour and the language of sexual bantering are part of belonging, and indeed markers of masculine status.[26] Such talk is not eliminated by the integration of children's hockey, or by mixed play in recreational leagues for adults, needless to say, but the contexts in which it is socially legitimate — and indeed an expectation — are further diminished. In mixed company it is harder to sustain the juvenile and sexist initiation practices common in many male preserves.

Gender relations involve not just relations between men and women but also hierarchies among men and different ways of being male. There are clearly many ways of being male. For example, the non-contact sports (running, swimming, racquet games) offer ways for adolescent males to stake a claim to a masculinity that is more tied to competitive achievement than aggression, more tied to skill than force.[27] Yet pride of place in the eyes of many men still goes to the games that seem to most clearly differentiate men from women — games featuring force, aggressiveness, and the opportunity to dominate an opponent physically. It is precisely this capacity to dominate that is at the core of many men's traditional ideals of masculinity, and hence at the core of a hegemonic masculinity that remains dominant so long as its exemplars are celebrated as heroes in our culture. In the continuing connections between masculinity and domination the ideology of male superiority is reaffirmed. The celebration of violence in sport, like the celebration of the tough guys who are its champions, is a way of publicly reiterating the apparent common sense of this hegemonic masculinity — something that registers viscerally to a great many men even as it is being contested all around them.

Masculinity is a socially constructed set of meanings, values, and practices. It is something boys *work at* and try to stake their own claim to, rather than something they grow into simply by virtue of being male. Sport and other ways of demonstrating bodily prowess are particularly important among adolescent males, for whom other sources of adult male identity (fatherhood, family authority, earning power, and career) are not yet readily available. Masculine identity is pursued as an urgent task by most boys, and sports, especially sports involving strength and aggression, are among the surest ways of staking a claim to masculine status.

There is nothing inherently wrong with the fact that hockey provides a site where boys construct their masculine identities. Indeed, a great deal of what is learned in team play — for example, lessons about mutual help, friendships, or working as part of a group — is extremely important and remembered fondly by former players. The problem lies with the particular model of masculine identity that the hockey subculture has promoted in the past. This problem extends to how common-sense views about the legitimacy and necessity for violence and the quintessentially masculine character of the game have worked to inoculate the subculture against progressive ideas. At stake is a defence of traditions that have brought together a number of identities — nation, class, gender — in a highly conservative and paternalistic manner. Analysis of violence in hockey inescapably leads us to consider the state of gender relations both within and outside the hockey subculture. Like other aspects of "common-sense" understandings of the game, hockey's masculine traditions have a mythic and ideological character. In hockey the existing gender order is made to appear "natural," rather than something that has been socially and historically constructed and thereby open to change.

PART III

HOCKEY AND THE REMAKING
OF COMMUNITY

Chapter Nine

Communities, Civic Boosterism, and Fans

Cultural symbols like flags and anthems, as well as games and their associated traditions, play an important role in representing communities and nations to the outside world. They also point to the role of popular culture in the making and remaking of identifications that constitute our sense of community or nationhood. However, increasingly popular culture has become the site of multiple and borrowed symbols of identification, which have the effect of complicating the seemingly more stable meaning systems we've known in the past. Symbols like the maple leaf have appeared on T-shirts, beer labels, and cereal boxes so often that their original meanings have become blurred. As modern marketers have deployed signifiers of community and nation for the promotion of particular brands and products, social identities have become ever more closely connected to consumer choices. The high-school sports jacket of the 1950s and 1960s that proudly displayed the emblem of the school team is as likely to carry the emblem of Roots or Club Monaco today. The sense of identity that comes from choosing fashions or musical styles in an increasingly global teen culture rivals, and sometimes surpasses, young people's identifications with their geographical homes.

Moreover, these homes themselves have changed markedly over the past forty years. The mining and mill towns, fishing villages, and farm communities of the 1950s were exposed to a more urbanized and standardized "North American" popular culture through national magazines, CBC radio, television, and increased use of the automobile. Since the 1950s this trend has intensified and cultural influences have become even more global because of cable and satellite television, improved highways and telecommunications, and the reach of international "franchised" retailers and restaurants. At the same time, many industrial and agrarian communities have experienced continuing economic difficulties and depopulation. Even the largest provincial cities have been substantially affected, especially since the recessions of 1973-75 and 1981-82. The long postwar boom from 1945 to the early 1970s was built upon a configuration of political and economic power that has shifted considerably over the past twenty years. The early twentieth-century practices of "scientific management," standardized mass production, mass marketing, and mass consumption — in addition to the Keynesian welfare state — have been challenged by the gradual development of more flexible labour processes, the simultaneous fragmentation and internationalization of markets and audiences, rapidly changing consumer tastes and preferences, and a revival of neoconservativism in government financial policy.[1] These changes in the character of international capitalism have meant hard times for many locally owned businesses in the manufacturing and retail sectors in Canada; and the failure of many local businesses and the conversion of others to national and internationally owned franchises have transformed the economies and the appearance of many small and medium-sized Canadian communities.

All of this change has significant implications for hockey's role as a source of community identification. Historically hockey has had a special relationship to the experience of life in Canadian communities and, indeed, to the very idea of community in Canada. Canadians have experienced the game both as a community practice and as a commercial product — variously connected to the local community, to broader "communities" of loyal fans who follow professional teams, and, finally, to an imagined national community. The local game has been the stuff of community volunteer work, sociability, pride, and entertainment. The professional game has provided a common source of entertainment and national conversation, an opportunity to share a common passion as well as to rehearse old rivalries. When Calgarians anticipate a visit from the rival Oilers, when Toronto fans desperately hope that the Leafs will beat the Canadiens, when the Nordiques carry the pride of Quebec City into Montreal, Canadians become involved with one another in a particularly dramatic way. Furthermore, come playoff time, when East plays West, or when Canadian teams play U.S. teams, most of the country watches. And even though sides are taken and historic rivalries relived, the games provide country-wide points of interest and a tableau of common memories.

Yet even though hockey continues to provide occasions when shared interests and identities appear to transcend, temporarily, the economic, political, and cultural struggles that divide the country — something that helps create a sense of being *Canadian* — we have to ask whether the game continues to have the same relationship to Canadian communities and identities that it once had.

Leisure, Popular Culture, and the Idea of Community

The word "community" expresses an ideal in Western social thought, evoking a widely honoured way of life. But its use also often evokes a nostalgia for social practices and relationships that are increasingly hard to find in today's mobile, highly urbanized societies. Over twenty-five years ago the U.S. sociologist Robert Nisbet argued that "community" was the most basic unit of human society.[2] It was the level at which "society" was really experienced; and its use as an analytic term pointed to the social units in which shared identifications (that is, as "us") grew out of interpersonal experience. "Community" was perhaps the largest social group — larger, certainly, than circles of kinship and friendship, but smaller than city or nation — in which individuals could feel they had a "place." To be a member of a community did not necessarily mean that everyone liked each other. It did point to varied and overlapping involvements that produced a sense of identification and group membership.

The sense of "place" attached to the idea of community has often been understood simply in geographical terms, a specific residential location. This is the word's most common connotation in sport: rooting for the home team. But if this was all the concept of community meant, it wouldn't be very important. By contrast, the most influential discussions of community in Western social thought have focused attention on the historical and social processes that construct and transform people's identifications with others, both locally and more broadly. More specifically, the discussions have drawn attention to changes in the bases of social solidarity that have accompanied urbanization, industrialization, and the advent of societies with mobile populations less firmly rooted in place than in pre-industrial times. The making of modern industrial societies shattered the connections between places of residence and common experiences of work, commerce, and leisure, which had long characterized both town and country.

Once more it is important to remember that these modern industrial societies had capitalist economies geared to the production of commodities in conditions of wage labour and market exchange — a point occasionally underplayed in classical writing on the changing nature of community. Indeed, few things have been more significant in the transformation of community since the early nineteenth century than the reorganization of human settlements around the changing demands of the capitalist labour process. For example, it was the advent of wage work and industrial production in the nineteenth-century Canadian city that led to the formation of working-class communities with distinctive conditions of life and a sense of mutual interest.[3] Likewise, it was capital-driven resource extraction and the need for a male labour force to work in mines and mills in isolated areas that together created "company towns" across the Canadian north.

Accounts of the resource towns and rural areas of Canada have typically emphasized patterns of local self-sufficiency and interdependence: local labour markets, local shopping, local institutions of leisure (baseball teams and annual fairs) and mutual aid (fire departments).[4] However, the continuing rationalization of production and commerce into larger economic units and networks has worked to undermine the viability of these communities. This process started as far back as the last century, but it has accelerated with the economic reorganization of the past two decades. For example, in rural Saskatchewan today, highly mechanized and capital-intensive farming requires fewer people, with the result that the market-town businesses that serviced the needs of farm families have been steadily losing their customer base. In addition, the piecemeal reduction of public services due to the fiscal crisis of federal and provincial governments — for instance, the cutting back of postal services and rail lines — has contributed to a growing sense of isolation and desperation. Added to all this is the increasing removal from local control of decisions affecting rural production and services. The prosperity of rural life has become more and more influenced by GATT decisions, free trade, and European and U.S. farm subsidies — matters that are all decided a long way from the Saskatchewan countryside. You can paint a somewhat similar picture of mine and mill towns across the country. Indeed, the mining towns of northeastern Ontario that used to provide a steady flow of players to the Toronto Maple Leafs are in decline because of similar national and international pressures.

It is important to evaluate the pressures that are remaking small-town life in Canada without romanticizing the past. There is a tendency in contemporary Western culture to represent city life as rootless and self-centred in contrast with a sepia-coloured vision of rural togetherness. This view is evident when people tacitly express the notion that small-town Canada is somehow the *real* Canada when in fact it is really only the *simpler* Canada of childhood memories. This discourse of the "real" Canada — the Canada of wide-open spaces, far-flung communities, inherent rural decency, and togetherness — clearly resonates with real memories, but there are aspects of the historical experience of urban and rural life alike that it distorts.

In the urban case, the longstanding association of the idea of real communities with rural or small-town life can lead us to overlook the existence of tightly knit urban neighbourhoods. Overlapping networks of kinship, friendship, and mutual aid, patterns of local shopping and street life, and the routine use of the neighbourhood as a site for leisure (in cafes and pubs, parks and community centres) have all contributed to a sense of community in Canadian cities that is as close and personal as the rural counterpart. Throughout the 1980s the exploding property markets of larger Canadian cities, the gentrification of urban neighbourhoods, and the rationalization of the retail industry into chains and malls began to restructure the texture of urban and suburban life. Still, even though urban neighbourhoods have changed, this doesn't mean that many city dwellers are not actively involved with "communities."

Equally, we shouldn't gloss over the social constraint and the homogeneity that have been the traditional price of "belonging" in the small town. Undoubtedly, there is a genuinely personal quality to many social interactions in rural and small-town life — interactions that are typically more impersonal in cities — and people in small towns frequently note the willingness of their neighbours to be friendly and supportive. Yet it is also true that this sociability and friendliness are not always so readily extended to people who are strangers or "different." It is not only probable that visible minorities will be even more "foreign" in small towns than they are in urban centres; but it is also probable that the sometimes suffocating Kinsmen/Rotary norms of familism and small business will dominate the life of small towns more thoroughly than is the case in larger and more heterogeneous centres.[5] The result is that even local people who think differently, act differently, or experiment with different lifestyles can find themselves the objects of gossip and ostracism. The pressures towards conformity are one reason why some young people leave small communities for cities. They also go in search of job opportunities and to escape the sense of boredom that sometimes pervades life in small towns. They want something beyond the bar, the mall, the baseball diamond, and the rink; and they are attracted by the excitement of urban life. At least some of them are also looking for a greater openness of mind and spirit, for people who think like they do and care about the same things.[6]

In recent years, though, long-established contrasts between city and country life have been complicated by changes in communications technologies and in the economics of retailing and entertainment. In small towns, eating at McDonald's, watching MuchMusic or YTV, or following major-league sport on TSN all open up a greater possibility of identifying with geographically dispersed "consumer communities" than ever before. Meanwhile, many Canadian cities have tried to make up for declines in their traditional economic bases in manufacturing or distribution by encouraging retail and entertainment complexes and promoting themselves as centres of culture and consumption. In *Home Game*, Ken Dryden and Roy MacGregor note how people now travel routinely from Prince Albert, Saskatchewan, and other rural communities not just to watch hockey in Saskatoon's new "big-league" arena but also for "shopping in Saskatoon's bigger and better stores, eating in its more numerous and varied restaurants, using all of its bigger city's amenities."[7]

To some extent this pattern has always existed. But it has increasingly become a pattern that has put significant pressures on the recreational and entertainment practices that developed in small communities after the Second World War. The effects are clear in numerous formerly hockey-mad communities. As Dryden and MacGregor point out, in most of Saskatchewan hockey is now simply one competitor in an entertainment market that encompasses Nintendo, Benetton, Nike, and Asian and European restaurants, as well as rock videos and U.S. college basketball on cable TV. The effects of these globalized leisure markets and of communications technologies that have made the private home into a diversified entertainment centre have been twofold. They've propelled more visitors from small towns to pursue their leisure in regional cities; and they've featured a gradual withdrawal of people's time and commitment from the local leisure practices — whether minor hockey or crib tournaments — in which "community" has historically been grounded.

Hockey and Community in Small-Town Canada

In the days before satellite dishes and paved highways were common in rural areas, hockey emerged as a centrally important communal activity in Canada. Churches and women's institutes were important focal points of community life too, but sports often cut across occupational, religious, and ethnic divisions and offered fun and entertainment for most of the community. For well over a century, baseball tournaments were regular features of rural fairs and generated great interest as teams of local men (and women) competed against neighbouring areas or touring teams. Nonetheless, the place of baseball in rural community life was always limited by the short summer and, in farming communities, by the rhythms of agricultural work. Hockey was different in several important respects. On the Prairies the long winter was the slack period for farm work and thus a season when people had more time for socializing and leisure activities. Euchre, crib, and bingo were popular in pre-television days, but men and boys played hours and hours of hockey on ponds, rivers, and outdoor rinks. Watching hockey was limited by the cold and the lack of spectator facilities. Communities that could afford it enclosed their natural ice rinks; yet even under these conditions games were cold for spectators, as well as dependent on weather. As Ken Dryden observes, for Prairie boys of the vintage of Max Bentley or the young Gordie Howe, there was much less *organized* hockey than later became the norm.

The hockey culture that came to characterize the rural Prairies after the war couldn't fully develop until relative affluence and wartime construction techniques brought indoor arenas within the reach of smaller towns and villages. Better rural roads and increased ownership of pleasure vehicles also played their part by making an evening's travel to other communities more feasible. Together these developments meant that winter sports played indoors — curling as well as hockey — became the focal points of a gregarious intracommunity and intercommunity culture that, for the generation of Canadians who grew up between the 1940s and the 1960s, represented the friendliness and togetherness of small-town Canada. Small towns all over the country built "memorial" arenas, and along with bonspiels community hockey (at all age levels) became synonymous with small-town Canadian life.

In the 1990s, these postwar rinks, and even a later generation of "centennial" arenas, are becoming old and sometimes uninsurable. They need to be replaced, but with costs now running into the millions of dollars, new buildings are almost impossible for a hinterland town or village with an eroded municipal tax base. Yet without the arena one of the major centres of community life disappears. There is less "to do," and this makes it harder to attract the teachers and medical personnel who provide other contributions to the viability of rural communities. Without the arena, moreover, it also becomes more difficult to keep people "at home" on the weekends; they'd rather travel to the nearest big city. It is not surprising, then, that Dryden and MacGregor found that men they interviewed in Radisson, Saskatchewan, feared the loss of their arena as the beginning of the end for their village and way of life. As Dryden and McGregor conclude, "The arena that was a symbol of community development is becoming a symbol of community transformation and dissolution."[8]

It is worth underscoring the importance of hockey in the traditional life of small-town Canada. Even though many towns and villages only got indoor arenas in the postwar boom, there was a long tradition of competitive senior hockey in larger centres such as Trail and Penticton in British Columbia or Whitby and Belleville in Ontario. In the 1950s and 1960s all of these towns produced world championship teams with semi-professional players. While senior hockey has since withered away in most parts of Canada, junior hockey still thrives — and still matters — in places like Kamloops, Medicine Hat, and Swift Current in the West, or Peterborough, Belleville, and Kitchener in Ontario. Moreover, senior hockey continues to hang on in parts of Saskatchewan and Atlantic Canada that remain relatively isolated from urban entertainment. Having the best team in the area still means something in places such as Kindersley, Saskatchewan, which has a population of about five thousand and is half a day's drive from the nearest big city. Senior teams like the Kindersley Clippers still play skilled hockey, and the players and fans who keep the senior game alive represent a powerful tradition in Canadian sport and community life. It is partly because of this tradition that saving the arena takes on such symbolic significance and has become a focus for urgent fundraising campaigns in many small communities.

There is much to honour in this tradition of community hockey. It is necessary, nonetheless, to understand the limits to hopes that community hockey can help preserve the small-town way of life. First, we shouldn't lose sight of the economic forces and the political decisions that are restructuring the face of rural Canada. Community hockey thrived in Canada when residents still looked primarily to their own communities for entertainment, shopping, and socializing. Today senior hockey is struggling in rural Saskatchewan because drought and debt combine to squeeze farm-belt incomes and because cable TV and satellite technology now bring much more NHL hockey, as well as other "major-league" entertainment, into local living rooms. In other areas, as mines and mills have closed or laid off workers in resource-extraction communities, families have moved away and the businesses that remain have struggled. These tendencies have made it increasingly difficult to raise money for any kind of community recreational activity.

It is difficult, but sometimes possible, for communities to resist the effects of closures by trying to reconstitute essential services themselves. A recent study of a rural community in transition conducted by sociologists Philip Hansen and Alicja Muszynski describes a Saskatchewan village that, over ten years, lost its rail line, its grain elevators, its co-op services (including grocery store, lumber yard, and garage), and a farm implement dealer whose franchisor switched to a dealer in a larger town nearby.[9] Not unlike the people of Radisson who Dryden and MacGregor describe in *Home Game*, the village people and surrounding farmers were determined to do whatever they could to save their community — so much so that local families now operate the garage, the grocery, and the lumber yard, while a young electrician has started up a new business. The village, as a result, continues as a viable service centre for surrounding farms.

Hansen and Muszynski indicate that economic survival is not by itself a sufficient condition (though it is certainly a necessary one) for the survival of a rural community. Community survival also requires a collective sense of identification and public spirit, which in turn requires the survival of other kinds of organizations and associations that can regularly renew social relationships. Recognizing this, people in the community were raising money for a curling and bowling facility that would serve as a multipurpose community centre. Indeed, Hansen and Muszynski note the popular sentiment that it "is the strength of these institutions of common life, and not just the strength of the local business community, which accounts for the survival of the village against the forces arrayed against it." Popular cultural practices, as well as the organizations and associations that promote them, have long helped to cultivate community attachments. Without curling, bowling, hockey, and the local cafe, many people believe that "the community, if it existed at all, would be very different and it is doubtful if local businesses would survive for very long."[10] One rural reeve cited in Hansen and Muszynski's study highlighted the plight of hockey as part of a set of connected processes of disintegration, noting a "decline in the number of committees dealing with local issues and the inability of the village to ice a youth hockey team, just ten years after a local squad had won a provincial championship." This was seen to be "part of a larger process in which people constructed ties to other areas, and no longer concentrated on building a local community."[11]

The villagers in this study also realized that community spirit and good leisure facilities were not enough by themselves to keep their community viable. These things make a place "lively," and they provide reasons for families to stay and attractions for young professionals or business people to move in. However, rural towns and villages still need a critical mass of commercial services, and they also need the public services that are necessary to both business and community life. The most important public services are the school and the post office, and many villages see the potential loss of either of these as a continuing threat to their survival. Such threatened losses underline the vulnerability of peripheral communities across the country to political and economic decisions made elsewhere, exemplified in recent years by the federal government's decision to "rationalize" post and rail services in rural Canada. Here, we are brought face to face with the "limits of leisure" in accomplishing community renewal. Hockey has long been an important rallying point for community spirit across rural Canada; but when the economic viability of life in, say, rural Saskatchewan or northern Ontario is undermined, it is unrealistic to expect leisure practices, organizations, and associations to make more than a symbolic difference.

This brings us to a further concern — the issue of gender relations. We've already noted how hockey rinks in Canadian communities have tended to serve as men's cultural centres and as arenas for the rehearsal of a limited range of masculine styles. The issue is simply that a public recreation facility other than an arena — perhaps a curling and bowling complex, or a small community centre — might provide more options for women, as well as for other potential user groups. It is worth comparing hockey in this respect with curling, which has the same winter season (when agricultural communities have more time for socializing) and the same need for covered and quality ice surfaces. An Alberta historian, Paul Voisey, argues that curling, and not hockey or baseball, quietly became the most characteristic sport of prairie culture in this century. It did so for two reasons. First, curling was an ideal game for socializing: "None rivalled curling as a forum for idle chatter. Frequent lulls between throws provided ample opportunity for eight people to discuss strategy or gossip."[12] Second, curling could be played by men and women, either together or separately, and indeed by middle-aged and older persons of either sex. Curling thus offered *participation* opportunities for women, and especially adult women, that hockey has provided only recently and grudgingly. The culture that has surrounded curling has always been mixed.

In contrast, hockey rinks around the country have always been steeped in a male ambience. An Esso commercial shown during the television series that was the basis of Dryden and MacGregor's *Home Game* featured a woman talking about the hockey arena as a centre for the whole community, women as well as men. For generations of hockey moms and, now, for increasing numbers of young women players, there is a measure of truth to this statement. However, Dryden and MacGregor themselves make a point about the very male atmosphere of the old Saskatoon arena, and in many arenas across the country this masculine identification has stubbornly persisted. Moreover, this masculine camaraderie is often also bound up with dynamics that have to do with the experience of social class. In communities where the mill managers (of Abitibi, or Cominco, for instance) and the doctors and lawyers are apt to live in "houses on the hill" and where they and their families dominate many of the public activities of the town (including those associated with the school), the hockey arena often served as a home away from home for working-class men and their sons. The arena was a place where working men and working-class masculinity were honoured, where miners and machinists and men who worked in Loblaws could establish their own sense of community. It was a place where the values and standards of working men remained simply "common sense," where men could talk together in their own language, free temporarily of the conventions and different kinds of words that professionals use in other places to diminish working-class people or put them down. Small wonder, then, that for many local "hockey men" the potential loss of the rink, or even its transformation into a more general-purpose social centre, has become an important and emotional issue.

Yet where the hockey arena has been the only major public facility in a community, the entertainment choices for women have been extremely limited. Sometimes there have been only two options: you either go out to hockey or stay home. It is not that women living in small towns and rural areas don't enjoy going out to watch their men and children play hockey; many do. At the same time, though, women from northern Ontario to interior British Columbia have pointed to the lack of *other* recreational facilities as an endemic problem of small-town life: "With few exceptions there are no bookstores, no good libraries in these towns.... There is never more than one movie theatre, and it alternately shows Walt Disney and smut. There are always several bars. There is always a hockey arena."[13] Rural women have also pointed out that men who will leave no stone unturned to provide for hockey routinely say the community "can't afford" facilities that would offer more opportunities (and especially opportunities to participate) to women. To the many women who have become frustrated by these attitudes, the claim that the hockey rink is the rightful heart of the Canadian small town is a symbol of everything that is wrong with the traditional gender order that has long structured life in rural Canada. Thus, one recent commentator, a cousin of the San Jose Sharks' Pat Falloon ("The Pride of Foxwarren"), takes Toronto author Stuart McLean to task for his uncritical celebration of the "hockey men" of Foxwarren, Manitoba, in the book *Welcome Home.* She argues that in "wheat and hockey" towns like Foxwarren, hockey has a significant patriarchal character: women and girls inevitably "come second in the whole community to hockey and to keeping the arena alive."[14]

Boosterism, Urban Communities, and Professional Sport

Another important issue is whether the boosterism that is a feature of small-town life has the same meanings as in larger cities. In their discussions of both small-town Saskatchewan and the city of Saskatoon, Dryden and MacGregor positively equate boosterism with community spirit and with a commendable refusal to give up in the face of challenges. Boosterism combines a promoter's professional optimism with a competitiveness that is presented simply as an instinct for survival. "Things come to those who go out and get," and in the competitions for businesses and rail lines, as well as hospitals and schools, that have been part of the history of the West, boosterism has long been regarded as necessary.

The turn of the century was a period when the map of the West that we take for granted today — a map that has well-established centres of population and commerce, and substantial road, rail, and telecommunications networks to service them — was very much open to be drawn. It was, as Dryden and MacGregor suggest, a country that attracted dreamers and promoters. It was also contested terrain, in the sense that dreams (and investments) could quickly turn to dust if not enough people could be persuaded to share in them by settling in your community rather than somewhere else. The presence of more settlers in a locale might make a trader set up a store or a doctor establish a medical practice. In turn, the presence of businesses and services that attracted farmers to do their business at one crossroads rather than another served to attract other businesses and more settlers to the area.

Certainly, it was not just business activity that mattered. It was also the presence of "community life," both because this did make a difference to the happiness of settler or labourer families and because it reinforced the image of a vital (and hence probably growing) community. There was, to use a sporting metaphor, everything to play for, and local boosters reached for anything that would distinguish their tiny community from countless others like it. Thus, it became common practice for business people and others who had an interest in promoting their communities (including, interestingly, United Farmers locals in the Prairies) to support a variety of community associations and organizations. One of the most popular vehicles for spreading a town's reputation proved to be sports teams, especially the ones that beat their neighbours' teams at fairs and regional competitions. And, as we've noted in earlier chapters, it became established practice very early on for sponsors to pay expense money and recruit "ringers" who might make the local team a winner.

Dryden and MacGregor emphasize the continuities between the history of small-town boosterism on the Prairies and the campaign waged by promoters to bring NHL hockey to Saskatoon (or, one might add, by extension, to bring the Olympics to Calgary or Toronto). In our view, however, this emphasis on what is common obscures a number of more significant differences. The small-town hockey arena today is largely a participatory recreation facility. Such facilities are usually simple and inexpensive in design, because providing a spectator "experience" is not a major part of the objective. The arenas are primarily community meeting places where local people gather to participate and socialize. And even in small communities with semi-professional teams, the teams and facilities have tended not to be run with profit-making as their central purpose.

Conversely, "major-league" professional hockey teams have been part of an expansive world of commercial entertainments that help to constitute "modern" urban culture in the twentieth century. Civic "builders" from Montreal to Vancouver saw successful pro hockey teams and large arenas as assets that could attract continent-wide media attention to their cities and advertise them as dynamic, modern places, with local economies that invite investment. Urban professional sports teams were promoted, to use Carl Betke's phrase, as part of a broader "corporate-civic" project.[15] Betke's own analysis of this corporate civic project focuses on the case of Edmonton beginning in the first decade of the twentieth century. In Edmonton city politicians were sometimes even partners in specific sports promotions. More typical, though, was the networking of local business and political leaders on the board of the Edmonton Exhibition Association, a voluntary association whose purpose was to bring events and "attractions" to the city. The construction in 1913 of the enclosed Edmonton Stock Pavilion, which would provide an attractive venue for a variety of indoor events, was of great significance. The Pavilion was the pride and joy of local boosters. It had an arena floor "larger than that of Madison Square Garden in New York" and could seat six thousand spectators "as comfortably as in a modern theatre" for events as various as circuses, jumping and horse shows, theatrical productions, and hockey.[16]

A more widely known counterpart to the Edmonton Exhibition Association was the Calgary Exhibition and Stampede. The Stampede didn't grow out of a traditional rodeo, as is often supposed. It was inaugurated in 1912 by civic promoters who hoped that an event whose size and prize money and "Wild West" imagery *surpassed* those of other established rodeos would attract attention and business to the city. Over time the Stampede Park facilities came to include a racetrack, an exhibition floor for trade shows and conventions, and a hockey arena. The Stampede itself and the other events that take place through the year in Stampede Park have always been part of a strategy to showcase Calgary as an attractive location for investment and tourism.[17] Given this history it is not surprising that the Stampede board was an important promoter of the city's commitment to the new Saddledome, a key to Calgary's Olympic bid as well as to the NHL moving a franchise to the city.

There is nothing unusual about these stories. The coalitions of business, political, and media leaders in Edmonton and Calgary have all been duplicated with minor variations in Vancouver, Toronto, and Montreal. However, it is worth noting the extent to which civic and *commercial* ambitions have combined in facilities ranging from the Edmonton Pavilion to the more recent construction of Olympic Stadium in Montreal, the Olympic Saddledome in Calgary, the SkyDome in Toronto, and B.C. Place in Vancouver. These commercial entertainment facilities have been built first and foremost to accommodate spectators, and often in a style that is itself intended to be part of the attraction. The promoters of professional sports have pushed for these grand facilities because they know their competition is with other forms of entertainment as much as it is with other teams. Thus, the facility, the hot dogs, and the crowd atmosphere are all part of the stadium "event" that is marketed to prospective fans. At the same time, in their size and often in their design features, these facilities are also intended to be civic monuments. Olympic stadium, the SkyDome, and the Saddledome were designed to give a distinctive stamp to the cities that built them. Distinctive architecture is combined with a grand spectatorial capacity to make a statement about the city's apparent entrepreneurial drive and boldness of vision. Such facilities are rarely appropriate for high levels of public participation, nor are they usually very cost effective.[18]

Nonetheless, largely because of the apparently "natural" connections between public entertainments and the promotion of "community," there is a long history of popular support for the civic provision of land for professional sports venues. Any opposition has seldom received the same kind of coverage in the local media as do the supporting views of local business leaders, politicians, and sport figures. Opponents of such projects have been repeatedly cast as carpers and naysayers, or as members of special interest groups who don't have the overall "community's needs" in mind. As a result their arguments have seldom received serious coverage.

One argument worth noting here is the suggestion that boosterism may well have quite different effects in big cities than in small towns. In smaller centres where cheap land has allowed widespread property ownership, growth-oriented "community" projects may well benefit a significant majority of community members. In larger centres, the ambitious projects of boosters have often absorbed civic resources, while much-needed public services remain underfunded. Meanwhile the "attractions" that such projects add to the life of the city often prove too expensive for the city's least affluent citizens.[19]

The promotion of spectator sport in large cities has sometimes brought together in common projects and aspirations people who would otherwise be strangers. Civic boosters in these cities have been able, certainly, to tap into this sense of collective identification. They have established a strong cultural link between popular desires to have high-profile sporting teams represent the city and a narrower set of corporate and/or civic interests. Popular expressions of pride and desires for entertaining spectacle have coincided with the financial interests of local business and the sometimes self-aggrandizing aspirations of local politicians. The irony is that the fortunes of professional teams featuring players from outside the community — and owned by private citizens or companies for the purpose of making a profit — gradually come to be seen as civic resources, as an integral part of the life of urban communities. So, even though the Canadiens are owned by Molson's, the Oilers by Peter Pocklington, or the Canucks by the Griffiths family, people in Montreal, Edmonton, and Vancouver still feel that the teams belong to them. These attachments to professional sports teams have been relatively easy to mobilize in support of land deals, zoning concessions, and public subsidies that clearly benefit private interests.

Communities, Popular Culture, and the Pleasures of Fandom

We don't mean to suggest that the widespread support for professional sport as a form of urban spectacle in Canada has *only* worked on behalf of narrow corporate or class interests. Since the early part of this century the sense of rivalry and the rooting for the home team that developed around professional sports have offered more than the experience of belonging to a particular city or community. It also afforded a sense of membership in a wider community of interest, as well as an entrée into the international world. It was, in part, through the construction of popular identifications with the progress of local representatives in national and continental competitions that many people who had been local or at most provincial in their horizons began to follow events in the world beyond. And if membership in the "wide world of sport" didn't necessarily turn sports fans into cosmopolitans, knowledge of results, techniques, and standards developed elsewhere at least gave some fans a broader frame of reference they could use to view local performances.

This kind of comparative knowledge has always been one of the pleasures of being a sports fan. It is also part of what it means to feel like you belong to broader imagined "communities" of enthusiasts and like-minded consumers. In the case of hockey the knowledge that has come from accumulated experiences of playing and watching the game at different levels has settled so deeply in the Canadian social memory that the very act of consuming the game has had a tendency to make people feel "Canadian." In this regard hockey's integration into consumer culture from the late nineteenth century to the present day has opened up important forms of communal experience and identity. For example, the consumers of commodities associated with hockey — sticks, sweaters, pads, playing cards, hockey books, as well as professional games — share names, legends, and histories that correspond with specific teams and brand-name products. Through their acts of consumption and the accompanying display of goods, players and fans from Victoria to St. John's have been able to feel a sense of having something in common. This sense of commonality has fixed itself in the Canadian collective memory to the point where it has helped to build a national popular culture.

We've already noted how this version of a national popular culture has never been quite what many advocates of a Canadian "national culture" had in mind. For one thing, it is a national popular culture that became consolidated as much through commercial as non-commercial activity. English-Canadian cultural leaders in the late nineteenth century tended to believe that Canadian culture could best be fashioned through widespread acceptance of the British ideal of the "amateur." By the 1940s that commitment to amateurism in the arts and in "cultural" organizations had broadened to include recognition of the importance of professional artists, authors, and other cultural producers. But the idea remained that an indigenous national culture was best pursued through public initiatives designed to make connections between "nation" and the idea of self-improvement. While organizers of amateur sport have sometimes suggested that sport has a place alongside more traditional cultural initiatives, this argument has never impressed many Canadian intellectuals. They have usually seen commercial sport as being even worse than amateur sport, and hockey's obvious success in helping to define a national popular culture partially explains the lingering resentment that people with highbrow inclinations frequently have for the game. "What kind of country," someone inevitably writes at playoff time, "postpones the national news for a hockey game?"

The note of condescension in this question has never played well in communities such as Trail, Timmins, Whitby, or Chicoutimi. Part of hockey's significance as a form of commercial spectacle is precisely the degree to which it has allowed Canadians to express themselves *outside* of the "socially improving" activities promoted by intellectual and political elites. Yet at the same time hockey has also contributed to a vision of Canadian culture that is resolutely masculine and white. Moreover, when it comes to defining the nature and meaning of hockey's place in Canadian culture, the prominence of the professional game has given an edge to commentators whose views of the "good of the game" have been virtually synonymous with the marketing ambitions of advertisers, media professionals, team owners, and corporate and civic boosters. Strangely, the continentalist nature of the hockey business created an immensely ironic situation where the doings of, say, the Detroit Red Wings, Pittsburgh Penguins, or Boston Bruins came to be seen as major "Canadian" events, the subject of much national interest and conversation.

The paradoxes and ironies in all this testify to the complexity of hockey's relationship both to different forms of identity in Canada and to different collective interests. Like all sports, hockey has the capacity to dramatize *both* imagined unities and social differences — a capacity that has always been an important element in the common pleasures of fandom. Professional sport, at its best, allows fans to watch athletes who are the best in the world at what they do. Their skills, courage, and flair are something that people can readily appreciate, and the almost superhuman character of a Mario Lemieux rush or a Michael Jordan dunk can leave fans cheering in awe. It is clear that these players are performing under the most intense competitive conditions, and knowing how difficult it is to produce under pressure, fans thrill to the athletes who rise to the occasion when it matters most. Such athletes become larger-than-life folk heroes, exemplars of skills and apparent personal qualities that most people can only dream about.

At another level of appeal, the cycles of the fan's year — the training camps, the early part of the season, the struggles for playoff positions, and finally the playoffs themselves — provide a familiar punctuation to everyday life. These rhythms have a seeming permanence that comes from their loose approximation of the seasons; but in a sport like hockey each season also seems to correspond to a particular stage in a serial narrative that builds towards an annual climax and conclusion. Moreover, with each new sports season there is the prospect of renewal — new hope, for example, that the Leafs or the Canucks will finally have a successful season. In addition, the repetitive rhythms of sporting seasons lend themselves to a familiarity of characters and plots, not unlike those of favourite melodramas. For many fans it is precisely the familiarity of the characters and the ways they respond that has helped to make *Hockey Night in Canada* a Saturday-night family ritual.

Fandom also draws upon a sense of fantasy. Many Canadian men remember childhood fantasies of the sort described so lovingly by Peter Gzowski in *The Game of Our Lives*: a small boy taking shots on an outdoor rink, feeling the cold and listening to the sound of skates on ice and the puck against the boards, suddenly transported to Maple Leaf Gardens and hearing the crowd explode and the voice of Foster Hewitt announce, "He shoots, he scores!" Or, as Roch Carrier writes in *The Hockey Sweater*, a boy getting up and wanting to be Maurice Richard; wearing Maurice Richard's number, skating like Maurice Richard, even combing his hair like Maurice Richard. Such fantasies have been a vital source of heroes in Canadian popular culture, and they have been part of the material out of which generations of Canadian boys in small communities and big cities alike have imagined themselves and constructed their identities.

Many would suggest that for adults hero-identification is properly a passing phase and that adolescent dreams ought to yield to a realism induced by jobs and families. There are, of course, some adult men who live most of their weeks in sport-related fantasies and never cope well with everyday life. But many adult fans who lead perfectly normal lives find that sports speak to their dreams and fantasies in positive ways. We agree with the U.S. historian Elliot Gorn that "for most of us, whose work lives are reduced to dull routine," sport represents a life of passion and possibility, in which self-expression and total commitment still matter. In a largely rationalized world, "We go to the ballpark not just to watch craftsmen, but to be infused with passions, to love and hate, to be moved by all we see."[20] The abiding involvements of many adult fans with the dramas and the heroes of popular culture can be understood as ways of responding to needs that point to "the gap between lived experiences and human hopes, in a world with too many broken promises and too many unrealized dreams."[21] The problem is that civic boosters, team owners, and other corporate interests have exploited precisely this same set of needs in their efforts to sell projects that often only deliver more broken promises and unrealized dreams.

The fantasies that sport promotes among many adult fans are rooted in images from the past. Visiting arenas and ballparks, even watching sports on television or listening to the radio, can bring back visions of warmly remembered places and times, friends and families. In this remembering, people feel reconnected with parts of their lives that they may have lost touch with. These experiences of memory and connection may be especially important in understanding the appeal of sports among the mobile middle classes. The sports world, through the continuing involvements it offers with the teams, heroes, and memories of childhood, can provide threads of continuity (however apparently trivial) in lives otherwise lived in separate chapters: in different jobs, with different partners and sets of friends, in different cities. At another more collective level, team traditions like that of Les Canadiens or stirring comebacks like Team Canada's victory in the 1972 Challenge Series with the last-minute heroics of Paul Henderson's winning goal all become part of a collective popular memory which, in turn, can become the currency of identification among strangers.

But while sport can bring people together it can also divide them: for the darker side of fantasy in the life of the committed fan is fanaticism. Fans often distinguish between "us" and "them" in ways that are fiercely partisan and intolerant. The often passionate attachment that hockey fans feel for their local teams, or for their favourite pro team, can lead to shouting matches as well as occasional fights in parking lots and bars — a facet of the sporting experience that relates to our earlier discussion of amateurism. At least part of the goal of early amateur organizers in sport was to introduce an element of self-control into the playing and watching of sports that would in turn limit the passions invested in team games. In the emerging ethos of middle-class sports consumption, the result was supposed to matter less than the fact that spectators had witnessed a "good game," and there was to be a sense of pride in applauding good (and fair) play by both sides. By contrast, working-class fans, or fans in clearly defined ethnic communities or in rival small towns, often felt a keener sense of "us" versus "them." As a result of these differences, two distinct types of enjoyment developed in the consumption of sporting spectacle: the connoisseur's critical appraisal of skill and tactics contrasted with the die-hard fan's sometimes fanatical emotional (and financial) investment in the result.

In Canada today the class origins of these different spectatorial practices often seem little more than a distant memory; even though the French sociologist Pierre Bourdieu reminds us that the attitude of dispassionate connoisseurship in sports spectating is still regarded as "better" in the hierarchy of cultural distinctions associated with "taste" in Western societies.[22] What also needs to be recognized is that even the most partisan fan's way of watching is not undiscriminating. Cultural studies researchers have argued that throughout contemporary popular cultures discriminations and choices in cultural consumption are frequently made according to criteria of social relevance rather than abstract notions of quality. In sport this means that when people identify themselves as Bruins fans or Canadiens fans, or when they root for the underdog, they are "choosing sides" in ways that say something about their own social identifications. For example, even though the traditions of flair and style versus tough "lunch pail" hockey that the Canadiens and Bruins historically represented have become altered in the makeup of the present-day teams, the connotations live on and help to construct popular identifications. Similarly, when people identified with the Flyers in the 1970s, or with a Bob Probert or (in a different way) a Ron Duguay, they were celebrating various kinds of unruliness and expressing another kind of social identification.

Through such identifications, fans "live" a side of themselves that may occasionally be expressed in more concrete and politically significant ways, but which for most people is normally repressed in the context of their rule-bound lives. Moreover, when people display their consumer choices with sweaters, caps, and jackets they participate in identifications among like-minded people. Through such choices they advertise their social allegiances and often experience a sense of community and a sense of collective fun that is quite different from the experience of the connoisseur. Fans become participants in the show, and, in the words of the British cultural theorist John Fiske, their "participation brings with it the pleasures of revelry and festivity, of self expression, and the expression and experience of solidarity with others."[23]

We should be wary of implying that these different ways of watching sport are mutually exclusive. Certainly, one of the features of any truly popular form is its capacity to mean different things to different people, to lend itself to many different readings and fantasies. This is arguably one explanation of sport's widespread appeal, as well as of what some would call its triviality. It may also be that watching sport involves "a kind of unspoken dialogue between the rational assessment of the strengths and tactics of each side, and a fierce loyalty to one of the two teams."[24] Some of the most committed fans are also among the most knowledgeable. What is almost certainly true is that this loyalty, and the sense of involvement that comes with it, together add another whole dimension, a feeling of community, to the appreciation of the connoisseur. It is through this involvement that the fan becomes a participant and a member of ... something.

But what exactly is this something? What kinds of communities are communities of fans? Undoubtedly, professional sports teams have become important focal points of civic attention and pride in many North American cities, and it is clear that some pro teams — like the Toronto Blue Jays or the Los Angeles Raiders — develop a national and even continental following. Yet there is a clear difference between these communities of sporting enthusiasts and the idea of "community" as a group of people united by their common fate and by the need to make their community a humane and decent place to live and work. Spectators at professional sports contests, like those at other professional entertainments, know one another only accidentally. They are consumers of a collective entertainment experience, temporarily united by common passions and memories centred around a shared product preference, but not necessarily by anything else. To say this is not to deny the potential power of these experiences. It is only that "communities" formed around acts of consumption or product loyalties (whether to the Toronto Maple Leafs or Ford trucks) are not political communities in any meaningful sense of the word. If we confuse these different meanings of community on a continual basis, or if political communities are effectively remade into communities of consumption and lifestyle, then surely we lose something important about the meaning and practice of public life.

This is not to downplay the ways in which large public events in contemporary popular culture offer experiences of being part of something larger than oneself. Opportunities to gather in arenas and theatres and to be part of large and heterogeneous crowds in which our own excitement is amplified by the passions of those around us are among the quintessential stimulations of contemporary popular cultures. In a less immediate way, to watch events such as the Stanley Cup, the World Series, and the Olympics on television is to be made to feel part of happenings that become national and international news. We are addressed as members of national and international audiences, indeed of national and international culture. This phenomenon throws into relief, yet again, the historical transformation of sports audiences over the last century.

From its very beginnings professional sport has traded on the idea of civic representativeness. But it soon transmuted the fan's role from that of citizen or local club member to that of loyal customer. Like other established merchants, the owners of pro sports franchises tried to position their teams as members of their home communities. They encouraged citizens to think of the team as theirs and to support it out of a loyalty based in place and in common civic membership. This discourse frequently had its share of hypocrisy and promotional rhetoric, but in the very early years of professional sport, owners and promoters tended to be local businessmen with close ties to their home community. These community attachments were particularly strong in early professional hockey, and this deeply reinforced the idea that pro teams were assets belonging to the community as a whole. However, early pro hockey also saw the beginnings of a tendency for teams to be viewed simply as mobile assets that could be arbitrarily moved in response to shifting market conditions. The Patricks' willingness to relocate financially troubled franchises in the PCHA was an early indicator of this tendency — a tendency strengthened during the late 1920s when the NHL emerged as hockey's equivalent to a "nationally branded product."

After the 1920s some NHL owners continued to have deeply felt beliefs about their teams' attachments to their communities — Conn Smythe is arguably the best example — and the stability of the six-team NHL after 1942 contributed immensely to the sense that, somehow, the cities themselves owned the teams. However, since the NHL's initial postwar expansion in 1967, and in the contemporary context of additional expansion and free agency, the rhetoric of civic loyalty in hockey now seems almost completely promotional (although some teams continue to invoke it very effectively). As this has occurred, and in the context of the increasing instability in consumption practices more generally, the traditionally stable identity of fans as "loyal customers" has also eroded. Hockey audiences today continue to contain such loyal customers, but increasingly they are made up of less dependable consumers whose product preferences can never be guaranteed.

The now familiar construction and display of personal identities on the basis of consumer preferences, and the apparent naturalness of the notion that people have common "interests" with those who share their preferences, are the cumulative effects of nearly a century of sustained promotional endeavour (from lifestyle advertising to cross-marketing). Modern marketing, and beyond it capitalism itself, promote brand-name products at one level and more general kinds of products (from professional sport to adventure tourism) at another. But the most general accomplishment has been to construct the modern identity: consumer. This way of thinking about ourselves — an identity which is naturalized by constant appeals to our interest as consumers — as well as facile talk about "consumer sovereignty" began to emerge as part of a postwar era that included new levels of disposable income for most people, the consequent development of the larger family home as a well-equipped leisure centre, and increased social and geographic mobility. One notable effect of this was what Raymond Williams has called "mobile privatisation," a more individual or family-centred "lifestyle" that included a gradual (and often unintended) withdrawal from older habits of community entertainment.[25] Because these consumer lifestyles were so heavily dependent upon media and marketing imagery they developed an ephemeral character that rendered them highly volatile and subject to rapid change, particularly over the last two decades.

We want to follow Raymond Williams and suggest that today's ephemeral consumer identities are "radically reduced" identities, insofar as the act of pursuing our interests *first and foremost as consumers* may actively undermine the livelihood of the communities we live in and whose vitality we depend on in other parts of our lives. Another corollary of learning to identify ourselves primarily as consumers is that we come to be persuaded that our lives are most effectively enhanced by more consumer choices, in other words by the expansion of the market alone rather than through political activity or voluntary community activity. This trend seems to translate, for many people, into an almost supernatural worship of the market and, coincidentally, into a belief that the best and most attractive communities are the ones that offer the most dynamic entrepreneurial environments as well as access to "world class" entertainment and shopping.

Chapter Ten

Hockey and the New Politics Of Accumulation

Commercial hockey in Canada has been transformed, albeit unevenly, by the entertainment industry's growth away from live audiences as the principal source of revenue to television and other sources of auxiliary income as key components of commercial viability. This tendency is not exclusive to hockey. On the contrary, every major North American professional sport has become dependent upon revenues from sources beyond the live gate. The escalating pressures to increase money spent on team and league promotion and to sustain multimillion-dollar salaries and expensive playing facilities have led to an aggressive pursuit of subsidiary revenues. The money comes primarily from larger television audiences that can be sold to advertisers, but it also comes from cross-ownership (such as Labatt's ownership interests in the Blue Jays and TSN), corporate sponsorship, and merchandising. Since the mid-1970s, technological innovations in mass communication and pressures to liberalize international trade have created new opportunities to pursue these subsidiary revenues and audiences throughout North America and around the world. The result is that North American professional sports today are beginning to position themselves in an increasingly global sports entertainment market. It is a market where Canadians now have more access to more U.S. sports than ever before, while Canadian and U.S. fans alike are also more exposed to European sporting events and personalities.

Paralleling these developments has been a loosely related set of international dynamics involving urban growth and decline. We now live in a world that has produced heightened competition between cities for major-league franchises and international sporting events, and a near-global economy in which capital has secured unprecedented mobility across political boundaries. In hockey several Canadian cities have found their hard-won major-league status to be somewhat precarious. For example, in Quebec and Winnipeg, local leaders have recently gone to considerable lengths to keep the Nordiques and the Jets in town. In Edmonton in early 1993, the Oilers' owner Peter Pocklington was threatening to take the team to Hamilton unless he got a new arena or access to all revenues generated by the publicly funded Northlands Coliseum. The point is that it is simply through the negotiation of the financial interests of team owners (that is, in maximizing the profitability of their franchises) and the co-ordination of these interests with the growth strategies of local political and business elites that new arenas are built or not, and that teams come to and threaten to leave cities like Edmonton, Winnipeg, or Quebec.

Indeed, the pursuit of major-league franchises and "world class" events today is now best understood as part of a larger project in which corporate and civic elites struggle to establish and maintain their cities' status in a transnational economic and cultural hierarchy of cities. In this project, economic growth is the ultimate objective, but major-league franchises and international events are also widely understood as badges of a city's stature, a symbolic sign of "arrival" from which other forms of growth will (presumably) follow. But, surely, we need to ask whose interests are best served by a city's pursuit of "world class" status? What is at stake in the struggle to define what being world class really means? Who is positively and negatively affected by the pursuit of world class status, particularly in the area of commercial sporting entertainment?

Capital Accumulation and Franchise Placement in the Hockey Business

To explore these questions we need to review the current dynamics of capital accumulation (in other words, the dynamics of making money), both in sports entertainment and in urban development, and consider how they intersect. In the first case, we've already argued that the availability of professional sport, as well as of other kinds of professional entertainment, quickly became one of the characteristic features of modern urban life. It was part of what made, and still makes, cities exciting and attractive places with "lots to do." To enhance the profitability and stability of local professional teams, urban elites have frequently offered public subsidies to sports entrepreneurs, typically in the form of free civic land for an arena or stadium, construction of necessary facilities with public funds, zoning concessions, and often negligible rents for using public facilities. If such subsidies have needed any justification — and they usually don't because of the popularity of local pro teams — the justifications offered have typically been of the boosterist sort, emphasizing the business and enhanced reputation that a professional team can bring to the city.

Over the past two decades professional sporting entertainments came to be seen not only in terms of how much money they bring in directly from ticket sales, but also in terms of how much additional consumer activity can be generated around them (for instance, through advertising, tourism, and merchandising). These criteria were to have decisive effects, both with respect to which sports were able to produce successful subsidiary consumer activity and with respect to the increasing importance of star athletes who could draw crowds. The saleability of star quality underwrote the development of a system of publicity in which the presence of stars and then superstars came to be increasingly hyped. Along with this came a process of valorization (that is, making valuable) and revaluation of urban lands. The construction of arenas and ballparks became an integral part of "property development" in which land became commodified and land values came to be determined by exchange values (that is, how much the land could be sold for) rather than use values.

Of course, the two types of value aren't unconnected, but once land is designated as commercial its value becomes a function of how much money can be made from and around it. The great sports palaces of early twentieth-century North America — the Forum, Maple Leaf Gardens, Madison Square Gardens, the Olympia — were, along with movie theatres and concert halls, part of the creation of modern downtowns in which the presence of "world famous" entertainments, shopping, and restaurants all drew people into the city core. Each contributed potential business to the other, and together they helped constitute the spatial and commercial patterns of city life. They also supported huge increases in the value of downtown real estate, increases often based as much, if not more, on the values attributed to shopping and leisure rather than to office buildings and factories.

These relationships between the money to be made in entertainment and leisure and the values placed on downtown and, later, suburban real estate have never been static. Rather, they've changed continually — sometimes slowly, sometimes dramatically — as a result of particular economic developments (for example, in hockey, the growing infusion of television money or the rise and fall of the World Hockey Association in the 1970s), political pressures (anti-trust legislation in the United States, pressure from Canadian politicians in the late 1960s to include Vancouver in the NHL), or technological innovations (radio and successive television-related technologies). For that reason it is best to think of *critical stages*, both in the capitalization of hockey and in the commodification of space in Canada, rather than a smooth or linear process. Moreover, just as the economic value of urban space can often fluctuate wildly, different local economies have been able to support professional sports at some times, but not necessarily for ever.

In earlier chapters we drew a broad outline of the movement of pro hockey teams from small towns to big cities that was characteristic of the first thirty years of this century. The history of professional hockey in Manitoba provides a useful example. After being home to pioneering professional teams in the first decade of the twentieth century Manitoba was left behind when the structure of North American professional hockey became crystallized in the big-city media markets of the East in the late 1920s. Manitoba was neither populous enough to be able to offer top hockey players the kind of money available in eastern Canada or the United States nor close enough to other centres of population to be easily included in the big-league circuits. Thus its best players, just like Pat Falloon eighty years later, would not remain at home. Many Manitobans wanted major-league professional hockey in the 1920s, but they would have to wait another fifty years before a favourable conjuncture of political, economic, technological, and cultural factors would make pro hockey available again.[1]

Similarly, the professional leagues that first emerged in Alberta, Saskatchewan, British Columbia, and the northwestern United States — the Western Canadian Hockey League, the Pacific Coast Hockey Association, and, later, the Western Hockey League — had comparatively short existences and disappeared when the NHL expanded into big cities in the eastern and central United States. Commenting on the Edmonton entry in the Western leagues, Carl Betke reminds us that the team had played to packed audiences and was not moved out of any lack of local interest.[2] But the state-of-the-art Edmonton Pavilion, built in 1913, had become unsuitable by 1926. The arena floor might have been larger than the floor of Madison Square Garden, but its six thousand seats were not enough to compete with the Garden or other arenas being built in U.S. cities in the 1920s. In addition Edmonton simply couldn't compete with the financial or promotional connections to other big-time professional sports or world class events that existed in the big cities of eastern North America.

Even in eastern Canada a comparatively small city like Ottawa had found it increasingly difficult to support a profitable professional team by the end of the 1920s. Ottawa had been represented in Stanley Cup competition since 1893, and its teams had won the cup nine times.[3] The original Ottawa Senators were six-time Stanley Cup Champions between 1905 and 1927 and one of early pro hockey's most storied and successful clubs. But the Senators had problems at the gate, which worsened considerably with the advent of the Depression. To avoid having to pay high salaries the team began to trade away its best players. That included star defenceman King Clancy, who was sold for an estimated $35,000 to Toronto.[4] But these cost-cutting measures weren't enough, and in 1932 the Ottawa team ownership made a request to the NHL Board of Governors to suspend operations for a year so it could stop sliding into debt. The NHL approved the request and leased the Ottawa players to other clubs for the season. The Senators returned to play in 1933 and 1934 but finished last in the NHL's Canadian Division, and in a dramatic move in search of profitability the club's directors moved the team to St. Louis. After an unsuccessful season in St. Louis, the NHL bought out the Ottawa interests and dispersed the players around the league.

Together these stories from the early years of pro hockey, in which teams in smaller cities departed in search of larger markets, simply drive home the point that profit-driven hockey teams have never really belonged to their fans. Decisions about the placement and subsequent movement of franchises, the sizes of salaries, and the prices of tickets have always been influenced by the broad political-economic dynamics of contemporary life. In chapter 4, for example, we noted how professional hockey first developed in a political-economic environment that was consolidated around resource extraction, finance, primitive factory organization, low wages, and limited commodification. In that context resource towns were booming, manufacturing was comparatively decentralized, and local popular cultural practices, while often commercial, were only beginning to enter the market in a systematic way. It was a time when local passions, local aspirations, and local identities were readily dramatized in hockey; a time when competing community clubs and competing local businessmen began to pay players and collect money at the gate in order to pursue their communities' interests; a time when amateur teams could still be competitive with professional teams and when small communities could command sufficient resources to challenge teams in larger cities.

After the First World War, Canadian and U.S. capitalism began to consolidate a new configuration that ultimately laid the foundation for the long postwar boom that ran from 1945 to the early 1970s. That configuration brought together factory-based assembly-line techniques and a large, semi-skilled, and predominately male labour force with the creation of national and continental markets for standardized manufactured goods and entertainments. The NHL emerged as hockey's equivalent to other nationally branded products and took firm root in the manufacturing and financial centres that were flourishing during the postwar boom: New York, Detroit, Chicago, Boston, Toronto, and Montreal. In each of these cities the team came to anchor a landmark sports arena built during the 1920s and 1930s. With their paid mortgages, loyal fans, revenues from other events, comparatively low NHL salaries, broadcast rights, and franchise fees, the owners of the NHL's "traditional" six teams were engaged in a profitable venture for much of the postwar era. The result was a stability in franchise locations that has been nothing short of remarkable — a stability that further reinforced the sense that the teams somehow "belong" to their communities.

More recently, in the age of Bruce McNall and Disney chairman Michael Eisner and the Mighty Ducks, there is the sense that nothing can be taken for granted; that no "home community" in hockey has any necessary guarantee that it will retain its team. For one thing, there is simply so much more money at stake now that very little else seems to matter. The $50 million franchise fee required of Ottawa and Tampa in 1991 represented a more than eightfold increase over the $6 million price tag for the new franchises of 1966-67. Meanwhile, players' salaries, at least for established players, have risen just as dramatically.[5] The irony is that many of the same economic forces — pressures as well as opportunities — that produced the expansions and mergers that brought major-league hockey back to Vancouver, Edmonton, Winnipeg, and Quebec in the 1970s now threaten its survival in some of these same cities. In response to these forces teams are now being managed much more like mobile financial assets than at any time since the emergence of relatively stable professional clubs in the NHL during the 1930s.

Recent research on the capitalization and internationalization of many kinds of popular culture since the early 1970s — TV programs and their associated toys and fashions (from Ninja Turtles to the Simpsons), as well as pop music and commercial sport — points to several phenomena that underlie these developments. In one of the most notable studies, the British geographer David Harvey has argued persuasively that the direction and character of capitalist accumulation since the mid-1970s are closely related to new information technologies and communications industries that have magnified the potential profits of commercial entertainment.[6] Cable and satellite technologies, pay-per-view, and global information and promotion systems together create a potential for audiences of unprecedented size, wealth, and distribution. They also typically involve large initial investments: in production technologies, promotion, and superstars; and these in turn require national or multinational advertisers attracted by the prospect of large and affluent audiences.

This is the context, then, in which professional sports entrepreneurs now pursue expansion into new and non-traditional markets. The up side is the new audiences and a potentially dramatic increase in revenues. Yet the corollary is that to remain profitable, professional sports leagues now find they *must* seek new audiences. One key factor in this is that the revenues generated from the sale of conventional network television rights now appear to have reached a plateau and, indeed, seem likely to fall off from the huge contracts signed, for example, by major-league baseball and the NFL during the 1980s. Complicating this is the fact that audiences in the traditional heartlands of every major sport are now being increasingly exposed to new choices in sports entertainment. The NHL is reaching out to new fans in the United States at the same time as more and more Canadians are following the NBA and even U.S. college basketball. A further consequence is that expensive packaging and imagery — what media people call high "production values" — become central to efforts to expand beyond a sport's traditional audiences. In the professional sports-entertainment industry of today, the ever increasing concern is for high "value-added" entertainment products with large investments in personnel and promotion and corresponding costs for consumers.

This means that capital resources (having money to spend) and ultimate market potential (the money to be made) have together become critical both for which sports become (or remain) visible in North America and for which cities become or remain part of the major leagues. This raises particular difficulties for undercapitalized professional sports, such as CFL football. It also raises difficulties for smaller cities, for peripheral cities, and for cities that lack large surrounding television markets: in other words, most Canadian cities. This was highlighted in the mid-1980s in the NHL's refusal to approve the transfer of the St. Louis Blues to Saskatoon. What stood out in that case was that a long tradition as a hockey hotbed didn't count for much in the face of the league's collective interest in strengthening its position in the much larger U.S. sports entertainment market. Saskatoon backer Bill Hunter offered $14.5 million for the team, more than Harry Ornest subsequently paid in the deal that kept the Blues in St. Louis, and he proudly pointed to eighteen thousand pledges for season's tickets. However, in the eyes of U.S. NHL governors, even if Saskatoon could sell out all the seats in its arena, and even if the management was wealthy and the franchise stable, such a move stood to hurt the league in its quest for national stature in the United States and access to a U.S. national television market.[7]

Hockey has long been a regional sport in the United States, limited largely to the northeast seaboard and the industrial centres around the Great Lakes. In this context the NHL has never really been more than a peripheral major league in contrast to major-league baseball, the NFL, and, during the 1980s, the NBA. During the mid-1960s most NHL teams were playing to near capacity crowds and expenses were increasing. Even with complete control over its labour market, growing intra-league competition, the prospects of intervention by the courts, and the growing use of player agents were putting upward pressure on the NHL's characteristically low salaries. While this had yet to substantially threaten the league's comfortable profit margins, NHL owners were faced with the problem of finding new ways to increase revenues. Given the unlikelihood of dramatic increases in television broadcast fees from local U.S. stations and the CBC, and the unwillingness of Canadian owners to share their television money, the most promising solution was to try to pursue a U.S. national network television contract. The NHL's expansion strategy of the 1960s, which placed franchises in St. Louis, Atlanta, and Oakland — cities that NHL president Clarence Campbell described as having "major-league status" — was intended precisely to break hockey out of its traditional heartland.[8] The league's project was to make hockey a more widespread presence in the U.S. national popular culture — a project that appeared to meet with initial success when the NHL was offered a national network contract with CBS within a year of expansion.

CBS aired NHL hockey nationally in the United States from 1968 to 1972 and NBC carried NHL games from 1973 to 1975, at which time the league lost its national network contract because of uneven ratings.

Meanwhile, competition with the fledgling World Hockey Association led to a dramatic increase in salaries and to subsequent expansions — expansions designed in part to protect future television markets from the possibilities of WHA growth and to continue the NHL's strategy of moving from the margins to the mainstream of major-league professional sport in the United States. Counting both the WHA and NHL there were over thirty major-league professional hockey teams by 1976, many of them exceptionally marginal economic ventures. Between 1977 and 1979 many of the weaker franchises folded, and the NHL absorbed WHA teams from Hartford, Quebec, Winnipeg, and Edmonton in time for the 1979-80 season. However, the return of professional teams to smaller Canadian cities was a setback for the NHL's expansion agenda of the 1960s and 1970s, and so too was the Atlanta Flames' subsequent relocation to Calgary. While Edmonton and Calgary in particular proved to be strong franchises through the 1980s, placing NHL franchises in regional Canadian cities was not something that many U.S. owners wanted to repeat. Thus, Bill Hunter's bid to move the St. Louis Blues to Saskatoon — a city even smaller and less known to U.S. fans than Calgary, Edmonton, or Winnipeg — had little chance of garnering significant support around the league. Indeed, in the calculation of potential television audiences, the entire Saskatchewan market counted for almost nothing (since it watched CBC already), while the loss of the midwest and midsouth was potentially important.

Somewhat similar thinking can be seen in the 1991 expansion decisions. When the NHL lost its national television contract in the mid-1970s it began to negotiate with cable operators in selected markets (primarily Buffalo and New York). Hockey was an attractive way for new cable operators to sell their services, and more and more NHL games began to be carried on cable through the 1980s. Then, with the advent of national cable program services such as the USA Network and ESPN, the NHL was able to cobble together a combination of strong regional coverage and selected national exposure. Revenues grew as well, although they fell far short of the kind of massive network contracts negotiated by other professional sports during the 1980s. With the advent of pay-per-view technology and increased cable services, the possibilities of new revenues again seemed bright, but only if the league could gain a significant toehold in the largest markets for specialty-television services. In this regard the NHL now feels compelled to follow the general movement of the U.S. population south into sunbelt cities in Arizona, California, Florida, and Texas — all regions featuring growing audiences of affluent, specialty-television subscribers. Florida is particularly central in this strategy because it features one of the largest and fastest growing television markets in the United States. The presence of large numbers of Canadian "snowbirds" in the live audience is only a bonus.

Yet the fact that Ottawa was also awarded a franchise in 1991 appears to run contrary to these trends. The Senators' bid had going for it the owners' apparently deep pockets, the national capital's greater "name recognition" among Americans than other Canadian cities (such as Hamilton or Saskatoon), and its airline connections with many U.S. cities. It also worked to Ottawa's advantage that the league's $50 million franchise fee and the requirements for a suitable arena had deterred once promising bids from more "desirable" locations, including Miami and Seattle. Nonetheless the NHL remains committed to placing franchises in the U.S. South and West, and there is even talk about staging occasional games in Europe and marketing television rights and merchandise to European hockey fans.

In this context the unexpected announcement of two additional new franchises in December 1992 should not be surprising. The franchises, awarded to the Disney Corporation in Anaheim and to Wayne Huizinga, the owner of Blockbuster Video, in Miami, continue the league's planned expansion into the affluent television markets of the American sunbelt, and the franchise fees will provide a badly needed infusion of cash into the league. In addition the league will benefit economically and promotionally from its connections to two highly visible corporations with unmatched expertise in the global media and entertainment industries. This is particularly true in the case of the Disney Corporation, which brings unprecedented visibility, marketing expertise, and international connections to professional hockey. With Disney on board, and with a new league commissioner schooled in the highly successful marketing techniques of the NBA, the NHL hopes to finally develop a truly national presence for hockey in the United States and a strengthening international profile for the league.

Given these developments, it is highly likely that with the addition of Ottawa Canada now has the most NHL teams it is ever likely to get. Indeed, by the normal criteria of assessing market potential, which factor in not only the metropolitan populations but also the size of the hinterland population that watches a city's television stations, only Toronto and Montreal are truly "major-league" size. Even Vancouver, by these criteria, ranks somewhere around Portland and Memphis. Obviously, markets are more than abstractions, and the willingness of audiences in any region to actually buy a particular entertainment product matters too. This is why western Canadian cities that are not "major league" by conventional marketing standards have, in fact, been able to support major-league hockey at the gate (but only Triple A base-ball).

But with average annual team salaries in the NHL jumping to over $10 million, the irony is that the very successes of teams in western Canadian cities can potentially threaten their economic survival. Undoubtedly, this threat has been most public in Edmonton, precisely because the Oilers' fabulous success on the ice increased the bargaining power of players such as Mark Messier, Esa Tikkanen, and Glenn Anderson on the free agent market. As the salaries of average players also rise, and with the NHLPA pushing for free agency, Edmonton's unwillingness to retain star players will probably become a more general problem. Canadian franchises will be unable to survive on gate receipts alone, or even on their share of Canadian television revenues. They will need substantial auxiliary incomes from insignia sales, corporate boxes, additional media tie-ins, and especially their own television contracts, at levels that are difficult to generate in small markets. The Oilers, Jets, or Nordiques may be forced to choose between letting some of their top players go and surviving with less expensive teams unlikely to win championships, or moving to a larger market in the United States.

While a franchise and the capital invested in it are mobile, a local community is not. Fans of the Oilers or the Nordiques will be able to cheer for their old favourites if they are sold to San Diego or Phoenix or relocated to a larger Canadian market like Hamilton-Niagara, just as fans of the old Brooklyn Dodgers could follow their team's fortunes in Los Angeles. They will be disabused, though, of any illusions they might have harboured that their team "belonged" to them. Teams move in search of larger markets and greater profitability, and they trade actively on the discourse of community in their new location, urging the locals to get behind what is now "their" team. In professional sport the word "franchise" is increasingly revealed as having the same meaning as in the travel or fast-food industries: the right to offer a nationally recognized product, in this case NHL hockey, in a protected market area. We can see clearly, also, the interest of the franchisor, in this case the league as a cartel, in placing franchises in markets most likely to enhance its general revenue potential.

Another point has to do with the health of small-market franchises and, paradoxically, with the likely ill health of the league if these franchises can't remain competitive. Inasmuch as even a limited form of free agency gives players like Messier the opportunity to cash in on their stardom, it has also given the biggest market franchises, notably the New York Rangers and the Los Angeles Kings, the opportunity to try to buy a Stanley Cup by offering players such as Gretzky, Messier, Adam Graves, and Charlie Huddy more than Edmonton could afford to pay them (which is not the same as saying more than they are "worth"). At one level this simply repeats the familiar dynamics of show business: most stars wind up in New York and Hollywood, where they can make more money than they could if they stayed in Winnipeg or Quebec — a lesson not lost on Eric Lindros. This is why New York and Los Angeles, as international centres of cultural production, have the stars they do.

Yet the structure of professional sport also depends upon some measure of competitive parity. It would quickly become boring if New York and Los Angeles won every season, and the maintenance of national audience attention to a sport depends upon the fact that local audiences in a variety of markets continue to care. In other words, sports leagues can only operate effectively as profit-maximizing ventures if they take steps (often opposed by some recalcitrant owners) to help selected small-market franchises stay competitive. In the past pro sport has attempted to do this through a variety of strategies, including restricting player mobility, penalizing "tampering" in the recruitment of coaches and players, organizing the player draft to favour weaker teams, and different types of revenue sharing.[9]

Civic Boosterism and Capital Accumulation

Whether cities constitute big or small markets for professional sport, all franchise operators have a strong leverage in their dealings with local and regional governments. Local governments have been placed, in the United States and Canada, in the position of competing with one another to attract and keep what are scarce and mobile assets (major-league franchises). They are asked for stadium improvements and luxury boxes, for one-sided deals on concession revenues, for zoning variances, and sometimes for development opportunities in adjacent real estate. All these deals give team owners the right to make more money in a facility usually provided for them at great public expense. Demands like these have recently been made in Edmonton, Winnipeg, and Vancouver, and from the owners' perspective they are entirely reasonable, if only because their teams have increasing salary budgets in small markets, and they are in a business where many of their U.S. competitors enjoy the advantages of sweetheart facility deals as well as greater market size. Indeed, some U.S. economists have suggested that for all the apparent profitability of sports franchises, many U.S. franchises make money on their operations only when the capital costs of their facilities have been borne by the public.[10] There is no shortage of civic and regional governments willing to spend this kind of money, in an era when governments across the Western world have been cutting back on most other kinds of public spending. This is because local movers and shakers believe that gaining or losing a major-league franchise will be a catalyst to gaining or losing other kinds of businesses, with further effects on urban or suburban property values, urban investment, and job creation.

There is a difference, though, between public spending intended to provide public services, such as subsidized housing and recreational facilities, and public spending intended to attract private investment and stimulate economic growth through offering tax incentives or providing infrastructure — in short, by subsidizing the normal costs of development. Over the course of "economic restructuring" since the mid-1970s, public leaders at almost every level of government have sought to cut back on subsidies to public services. Meanwhile government spending has been diverted into "development" assistance programs designed to attract new investment. Indeed, there is a real sense in which the subsidies offered to sports are not unlike those that have attracted other entrepreneurs to shopping malls and industrial parks. Stadium developments create opportunities to make money in finance, construction, hospitality, tourism, and, ultimately, real estate. Thus, government spending to attract and keep sports franchises needs to be understood as part of larger strategies for local capital accumulation.[11] Moreover, in a climate of intense inter-urban competition, spending on image-making and public relations has often been perceived to be as important as spending on urban infrastructure. The more that cities like Calgary or Vancouver (or Indianapolis or Denver) can appear to be "in the same league" with New York and Los Angeles, the stronger that local leaders believe their chances will be of growing and prospering rather than remaining simply as regional or provincial centres on the margins of the "major leagues" in business, politics, and culture.

This point about the competition between cities — in a context of economic, political, and technological developments that have increased the mobility of capital — requires some additional elaboration. The 1960s and 1970s saw a series of changes in the relative wealth, power, and status of cities and regions across North America: shifts of wealth and people away from once powerful industrial centres into other kinds of economic activity in the West and (in the United States) the South. Since then there have been further increases in the flexibility and mobility of capital, to the point where money can now be moved expeditiously across borders or into other kinds of investment. Among the effects of this is a transformation of the relations between mobile investors and the governments of fixed places that need business activity if they are to survive. Indeed, in this environment growing and declining centres alike find themselves in a ruthless competition, both for specific investments and for relative position. As civic governments have competed for new kinds of investment beyond older industrial investments, they've become more self-consciously "entrepreneurial." These "entrepreneurial cities" now compete to be financial centres, administrative centres, and (most important for our purposes) cultural and entertainment centres.[12]

Several factors contribute to the enhanced importance of culture and entertainment. First, there is simply the enormous economic importance of the "culture industries" today, and beyond this there is the extent to which famous entertainment events and entertainers have become the stuff of daily media fare and hence effective vehicles for getting a city into the news. When civic boosters claim that a sports event or a major-league team will put their city "on the map," they are banking on this aspect of media appeal. Second, an analysis of the redevelopment strategies of a series of older downtowns indicates that projects oriented around high value-added culture and consumption — upmarket shopping and restaurant complexes, as well as concert halls and professional sports facilities — have been important in bringing the affluent middle classes back downtown.[13] Finally, there is the phenomenal growth of tourism in the new urban economy. In North America this urban strategy has also been very much directed at attracting conventions. The boom in hotel construction and convention centres of the 1960s through the 1980s — a key factor in the revalorization of downtown property — created a need for a variety of attractions to draw conventioneers and tourists. Sports stadiums, convention centres, festivals, and upscale retail developments all received public subsidies in a strategy for urban revitalization based around leisure and tourism.

This was the political, economic, and cultural context for the expansion of all the major professional sports in North America after the late 1960s: growth in the West and new possibilities for the industry in television revenues, if more markets could be integrated into "major-league" culture. At the same time civic boosters in newly booming cities were actively pursuing major-league franchises and "world class" events as signs that they had achieved a cultural status to match their new economic stature. Boosters in cities with established franchises sometimes had to fight to keep them — a struggle that has not yet happened in hockey to the same extent as in football. However, we can expect controversy if, or more likely when, well-supported teams in Canadian cities seem on the verge of moving out. In the face of such controversies it could well be political suicide for local politicians to resist the pressure to make major concessions paid for out of the public purse. For instance, in early 1993 there was immense pressure on the mayor of Edmonton to provide substantial subsidies to the Oilers; such a decision would run contrary to her longstanding political identification with a social services agenda rather than subsidies to business.

For Canadian cities on the periphery of the recognized international circuits of cultural production and attention, the attraction of sporting and cultural events has typically meant significant infusions of money from senior levels of government. Indeed, the pursuit of federal and provincial funding for facilities suitable for major-league franchises has often been a subtext in civic bids for international games and events. In the case of Montreal three levels of government were willing to spend public money on Olympic "monuments." The Olympic Stadium was also intended to be a "world class" home for the Expos and, some hoped, for an NFL franchise too. In Edmonton and Calgary the bids for the 1978 Commonwealth Games and 1988 Winter Olympics provided opportunities to get funding from senior levels of government for facilities that would become appropriate venues for the Eskimos and the Flames. In both cities there were also significant commitments of civic lands and civic funding, and they were justified to the public on this basis.

Although sports franchises create opportunities for the local business sector, there is typically a genuine and widely shared belief in the broader civic purposes of such endeavours. Many officials and business leaders "perceive the sport franchise as a cultural resource, one that helps sell civic identity and community involvement," in an age when many other pressures work to undermine these elements.[14] Here our attention is drawn beyond pure economics to the political and ideological agenda that is always a part of boosterism, for it is clear that major-league teams have a history of populist appeal that tenants in industrial parks do not. Part of the explanation is clearly that large numbers of people enjoy professional sport *as consumers*. Even if fans only consume them through the media, teams become part of a city's collective life. The cycles of predictions and postmortems, the trade talk, and the excitement generated around the annual playoff and pennant races all contribute to a continuing "buzz" of sports talk that many people follow avidly and others enjoy as background noise. Television clearly has the lead role here, but the newspaper coverage, the radio stations that carry the games, the talk shows, and the marketing of caps, sweaters, and other team souvenirs all play their part in building and sustaining the community of fans who are the constituency of professional sport. Each of these contributes to the sense of excitement and interest that is generated and amplified in city life as professional sports teams like the Montreal Canadiens and the Toronto Blue Jays pursue successful seasons.

In all of this team sports are particularly effective, not least because the very names of the teams continually restate the apparent common interests of the city and the idea of a specifically civic identity. Hockey's rivalry between Edmonton and Calgary is a good example; but where such "traditional" rivalries don't exist, professional sport has always traded on constructing them. Indeed, media cheerleading for professional teams has typically represented hometown fans as "us," a common identity that presumably includes everyone in the city — business people and wage earners, property developers and low-income residents, and men and women, as well as the imported athletes who are paid to represent "us" and the entrepreneurs who pay them.

The problem is that this common identity tends to gloss over what are real and important differences of interest and power *within* cities. In their assumed role as civic representatives, professional sports teams provide for a public discourse of togetherness that asserts the existence of a "community-as-a whole" with a common interest.[15] Of course, this ideological effect isn't always accomplished. The symbolic meanings of professional sports franchises and professional sporting contests are often interpreted differently by people belonging to different subcommunities in a city. However, in broad measure, the idea that pro sports franchises help to constitute a common urban culture and, along the way, act in the general community interest has achieved more and more credibility over the past century. In the last two decades, in particular, this idea has emerged as an almost uncontested feature of the common sense of our time.

In addition, as our earlier discussion of turn-of-the-century Canadian sport suggests, civic boosters have long sought to create popular identification with the idea of *growth itself* and to suggest that a status attaches to the city as a result of the presence of major-league teams, "world class" events, and giant facilities. In the postwar era this approach has included among other things, NHL teams, professional baseball franchises, domed stadiums, ballet/opera houses, world's fairs, and Olympic Games. The imagery circulated around such teams, events, and civic monuments has typically had a twofold purpose. Although these projects are clearly intended to impress visitors from elsewhere, they have also sought to reconstruct the self-image and aspirations of the home population: from a focus on "normalcy" to a more ambitious and competitive mentality with national and international reference points rather than local. In this sense, major-league teams and "world class" events and monuments have always served large cities as symbols for a public discourse about ambition, growth, and civic greatness.

"Cities and Their Dreams"

But what aspirations and identities are being promoted in the notion of a major-league or world class city? Who really participates and benefits, and how? What would losing the Oilers mean to Edmonton? What would the hockey Blues have meant to Saskatoon, or the 1996 Olympics have meant to Toronto? The most material beneficiaries of these projects are the sports-entertainment and media industries and the hospitality and tourism industries, where business is directly increased by the accumulation of attractions and events. Also benefiting are people with stakes in the local real estate and construction industries, and indeed all of those who stand to gain from a general rise in land values.

When we talk about those who care about "world class," though, we are also referring to people for whom attendance at these events becomes part of their lifestyle and their presentation of self. Some of these are the same people as the material beneficiaries. The use of the SkyDome in Toronto highlights the enthusiasm of corporate Canada for luxury boxes as preferred sites for client entertaining and executive leisure, but the more general use of professional sports tickets for business entertaining and favours goes a long way back. A significant proportion of the season's subscriptions in rinks like Maple Leaf Gardens and the Forum has long been taken up by "company tickets." In addition, over a twenty-year period Maple Leaf Gardens added private boxes, which are now fully subscribed at prices ranging from $40,000 to $175,000 per season. Luxury boxes are an integral feature of most new professional sports facilities, and indeed in awarding its most recent franchises the NHL required evidence of income potential from boxes. In 1991, when the Montreal Canadiens announced the planned construction of a new Forum, they indicated that the new facility would include 130 luxury boxes — and that these boxes had already been sold out with completion still five seasons away.

It is worth noting here the lifestyles of the mobile, sometimes transnational, professionals and managers who are part of the new elites of Canadian cities — professionals and managers exemplified in *Globe and Mail* editor William Thorsell's account of people who came to Edmonton during the years when the oil boom had "raised incomes

and aspirations beyond anything Alberta had known."[16] These professionals were attracted to Edmonton by the opportunity to be part of
building an urban metropolis on the northern frontier, with opportunities in the public sector as well as the private. Thorsell describes
them as having come mostly from bigger cities, so they brought with
them urban expectations and urbane tastes. They supported the Oilers
with their patronage, just as they supported Edmonton's vibrant Citadel
Theatre. These kinds of people are not unique to Edmonton, of course;
indeed, place typically matters less to their sense of community than
does access to "world class" culture, which remains an interest wher-
ever they are. For some of them, especially the men, fan involvement
with major-league sport provides familiar pleasures and threads of continuity in their lives. For others, it is not unlike having access to other
nationally and internationally known, high-value-added entertainment
products: to *Phantom of the Opera*, or *Les Mis*, or whatever is commercially hot at a particular time. In either event, these business executives are not "dyed-in-the-wool" hockey fans who would be likely to
turn their support to junior hockey if the NHL franchise moved south.

Clearly there are many hockey fans for whom rubbing shoulders
with the rich and famous is not part of going to a game. There are
many fans at the SkyDome, the Northlands Coliseum, or the Montreal
Forum who share season's tickets with groups of friends and attend six
to ten games a year. There are others, often from out of town, for whom
the chance to see "live" the teams and heroes they follow mostly through
the media is an annual treat. Nonetheless, we want to question the
view widely circulated in the media that the quality of life in Canadian
cities is defined by the presence of such events. Thorsell describes the
rapid exodus from Edmonton in the early 1980s of "the kind of people who had really made a difference" in the city during its years of
growth. When the boom collapsed, and with it Alberta's willingness to
think big, "The city-building adventure that Edmonton offered in the
1970s slipped just across the line into normalcy." The mobile urban
professionals left, in search of opportunities to do important things and
be part of important events elsewhere. Like Thorsell himself, a lot of
them went to Toronto. Their departure, in his view, "meant the loss
of a dream that Edmonton might emerge from provincial status to
become a `national city.'" Thorsell makes analogies with Toronto's luke-
warm support of the bids for the Olympics and a World's Fair, and with
the civic and public opposition to "civic monuments" like the bal-
let/opera house, Harbourfront, and the SkyDome. He argues that monuments and spectacle are important to the life of a big city, and he

worries that as Toronto, too, "deliberately crosses its own line into normalcy," it will no longer provide a good enough context for the ambitions of its best and brightest, and they too will move away.

It is precisely this equation of "a city's dreams," let alone its needs, with the aspirations of its business and professional elites that needs to be questioned. Consider, for example, the case of Vancouver. Only a small fraction of Vancouver's citizens really live their lives in the Vancouver that the Tourist Bureau and Real Estate Board like to promote.[17] This Vancouver consists of happy and prosperous individuals enjoying the city's many and varied "lifestyle" assets: its opportunities for scenic recreation, its cosmopolitan restaurant and night life, its modern venues for "world class" sport and culture. The problem is that this Vancouver has become too expensive for many of the people who actually live in the lower mainland area, except insofar as they get caught up in the excitement generated by local media. Indeed the very developments that contribute to the international status of cities often have negative effects on the quality of everyday life for citizens of modest and lower incomes. The influx of investment that fuels development also produces an increase in property values and rents, which can lead to neighbourhood transformations: higher density land use, gentrification of housing, and parallel changes in the character of the businesses that serve the community.

This brings us back to a final issue, namely the different ways in which relatively affluent and poorer people use a city and its amenities. For the affluent, the people with the means to satisfy both needs and wants in the market, neighbourhood use values and the quality of public services (public transport and recreation facilities) typically make only a marginal difference in their lives. What matters much more are rising residential property values and the presence of a downtown district with smart restaurants and shops and sophisticated entertainment. Able to avail themselves of whatever amenities the downtown environment offers, including "world class" entertainment, they benefit doubly from developments that increase the exchange values of their properties while also adding to the range of their leisure choices.

The less affluent, in contrast, must use the city differently; or, as Vancouver writer Brian Fawcett puts it, they must use a different city. They are more likely to benefit from good public services, and their leisure activity is more likely to make use of strictly local amenities and spaces rather than the expensive downtown amenities upon which "world class" reputations are constructed. Their lives are more likely to be harmed, then, by developments that raise land values and contribute to the transformation of neighbourhoods and by shifts in public spending. When urban governments subsidize spectacular leisure-oriented projects with public funds, unspectacular community services are usually being sacrificed in favour of upmarket developments that keep affluent consumers downtown and provide developers with opportunities for capital accumulation.

This is not to say that such subsidies are unpopular. Subsidized professional sports teams and events like the Olympics *are* popular; as we have noted, they have become part of the collective life of cities. Certainly, in Edmonton the departure of the Oilers would leave a void and a residue of bitterness. Still, most Edmonton fans of average incomes are limited to following their team through the media, or perhaps they attend one or two games a year. This is largely because ticket prices have increasingly restricted the regular live audience for NHL hockey to the more affluent sectors of the population, even in one of the most hockey-conscious cities in Canada. As NHL hockey becomes increasingly capitalized, it will become more and more difficult for smaller cities anywhere, and for people of ordinary means, to support it. Alan Friedman, editor of the Chicago-based *Team Marketing Report*, speculates that major-league professional sport may be in danger of losing a significant part of its traditional fan base, as the "dyed-in-the-wool" fans who used to attend most of "their" team's home games — in other words, the loyal customers — are priced out of the market.[18] If this happens, or if NHL hockey can no longer make enough money in cities like Edmonton or Winnipeg, junior hockey would most likely return to these cities, and hard-core hockey fans would most likely support it enthusiastically, as they have in Saskatoon.

The "Global Consumer" and the Standardization of Cities

With these perhaps gloomy prognostications, we return to the question of how the changing logic of capital accumulation in international capitalism has influenced the development of hockey, and how it will continue to influence its place in Canadian culture. Throughout this chapter, and earlier in the book, we've seen how commercialization and professionalization have reconstructed traditional understandings of the representativeness of sports teams. This reconstruction has taken place along lines that commercial sport could trade on, lines suited to modern capitalism and urban development. We've noted how the search for new and larger audiences meant that professional hockey left western Canada for a long time; and indeed it didn't return until the competition for players from the WHA led the NHL to incorporate demonstrably popular operations in Winnipeg, Edmonton, and Quebec.

Yet the increasing internationalization of the sports entertainment industry has also meant vigorous competition for audiences, involving many new sports, or at least sports not previously promoted to Canadian audiences. As a result of *Wide World of Sport* and *Sportsweekend* and the advent of specialty sports channels on cable TV, more and more Canadians are becoming consumers and fans of PGA golf, WCT tennis, NBA and NCAA basketball, and NFL football. This consumerism is part of a global trend in which Europeans, Japanese, and Australians are also becoming audiences for the same sporting events. Sports marketers frequently suggest that this is a welcome indicator that all of us are becoming more sophisticated in our sporting tastes.

Another perspective would suggest that much that is presented as cultural progress and sophistication also obscures a changing economy of production and distribution, in which more and more production decisions are being made in New York, Los Angeles, Atlanta, London, and Tokyo: and that these decisions are aimed at reaching affluent audiences around the world with the same heavily advertised cultural products and events. On the one hand this activity produces significant audiences and profits in Canada, for events like the Olympics, Andrew Lloyd Webber musicals, and superstar concert tours, as well as the circuits of "world class" sport. On the other hand, local cultural producers — musicians and theatre groups, for example, as well as minor-league sport — and even "national" cultural institutions (of small nations, at least) continue to face difficult choices in their struggles to maintain audiences. This is precisely the context of the Canadian Football League's continuing difficulties, and it is the context in which hockey, more than ever before, has to actively reproduce its place in Canadian culture.

We can lament how readily Canadians have become "followers" and consumers of these increasingly transnational events, and the corresponding withdrawal of interest and resources from our own more Canadian or North American traditions. In any case, sports fans today are increasingly addressed as free-floating consumers rather than as customers with assumed loyalties. Neither individual teams nor whole sports can afford to take "brand loyalties" or even national loyalties for granted, because there are other teams and other sports trying to win over the audiences, which is all part of the more competitive struggle for *product preference*. It is precisely this expansion of consumer choice that modern sports promoters and, indeed, modern capitalism itself, love to celebrate. In the view of marketing guru Theodore Levitt, as well as transnational advertising and public relations firms such as Saatchi & Saatchi, the wave of the future is precisely the development of global markets and, along with them, "world standard" products. The international marketplace is portrayed in this discourse as a modernizing and liberating force that brings more and better choices to everyone than the protectionist politics of nations and of regions would allow. Indeed, the new rhetoric of consumer sovereignty suggests that as people gain better access to global information, they will develop global needs and demand global products, ultimately becoming global citizens.[19] We are all encouraged to think that our lives are made richer in the process. Beyond this, as we suggested at the end of the previous chapter, all of us are encouraged to think of our cities along the model of shopping centres. The best cities are the ones that offer the "world famous" shops and entertainments — whose fame is itself a product of international marketing.

There remain, however, at least two reservations that need to be entered against this celebration of the apparent global marketplace. The first of these builds on a concern about the limitations of consumer identities. What is ultimately being promoted by Saatchi & Saatchi, and by global marketing generally, is a personal sense of "membership" in a global consumer culture, a sense of membership realized primarily through personal consumption patterns and product preferences. Within this global marketing discourse there is an implicit hierarchy of identities. It is implied that one will feel the greatest sense of membership by consuming global brand-name product-lines and "world class" entertainments and by visiting or, better yet, living in "world class" places. The problem with this discourse is that the taste for world class entertainment is essentially the taste for big-budget, high-cost entertainment that effectively excludes a great many people in even the most exciting cities, except insofar as they can follow this entertainment through the media.

What global marketers like to celebrate as a growing convergence of lifestyle interests and tastes around the world can be more accurately represented as an actively cultivated convergence of lifestyle and consumer behaviours among affluent groups in the "developed" world. Indeed, the cultivation of transnational audiences for major-league sports is not much different, in this respect, from the international promotion of golf and ski resorts, or indeed croissants and sushi bars.[20] All of these items constitute real and pleasurable expansions of consumer choice for people who can afford them; and all of them have become familiar and widely appreciated options in the lifestyles and identities of our increasingly cosmopolitan business and professional elites. What is less widely appreciated is "the imposed loss of identity, the almost 'no person' status of those not able to make meaningful market choices or even present themselves as potential buyers."[21] This is not often remarked upon, precisely because in the discourse of consumer sovereignty, the *buying* public is the only public that counts.

The second reservation relates to what the increasing internationalization of consumer opportunities means for standardization of major cities (and many minor ones too), as well as the standardization of sporting and cultural "interests" around the developed world. Although many cities have sought to construct themselves as "world class" centres of culture and consumption and have invested hundreds of millions of dollars trying to construct a distinctive "place identity" that would position them favourably in the competition for tourism and convention business, the distinctiveness and successes of these glitzy developments are often short-lived. Each domed stadium, each architecturally novel hotel or cultural centre, each harbour development is quickly reproduced elsewhere, in what David Harvey calls "serial monotony"; and the effect is that the leisure and consumption districts of major cities around the world — the parts of these cities where money is spent — have lost much of their distinctive national characters.[22] In addition, overinvestment in large-scale shopping malls, harbour developments, and cultural facilities in cities tends to make the values embedded in urban space highly vulnerable to devaluation. This type of land devaluation hit urban centres around the world especially hard at the end of the 1980s, pushing many of even the most innovative developers into bankruptcy.

The language of global consumerism has vigorously celebrated as "progress" the spread of global products, global images and entertainment forms, and global superstars; and in doing so it has traded very skilfully on the idealism of an older kind of internationalist discourse. In that idealistic discourse, cultural exchanges and travel and even pictures and stories of other places were all supposed to make us interested in other people, to help us transcend stereotypes about "the other" and encourage cross-cultural understanding. A cosmopolitan was someone who was knowledgeable about other cultures and interested in engaging with those cultures on their own terms. That internationalist project and cosmopolitan identity represent something fundamentally different from the ideas of global culture in the current conjuncture. This newer sense of global culture is part of a business-led agenda. It idealizes an expensive international culture in which differences are smoothed over and standardized, in which North Americans, Europeans, and Japanese follow the same sports in similar "world class" facilities. The meaning of "world class" relates simply to the standard of facility these upmarket entertainments require and the standard of production that their upmarket audiences are accustomed to. The agenda of "global culture" has nothing to do with cross-cultural understanding and everything to do with the larger profits to be gained by expansion into new and affluent markets. Indeed, as cultural products become directed at international markets rather than at national or regional markets, many of the traditional connections between cultural practices and national identities threaten to be lost in the process — with the connections between hockey and Canadian "national" identity as a prime example.

Chapter Eleven

International Hockey: Patriotism, Profits, and Shifting Identities

If the sense of community generated around professional teams involves an actively mobilized identification with civic "representatives" who have only the most tenuous connection to the particular community, this situation is all the more likely to be found in international competition. Athletes on international teams are celebrated as individuals, but what is also celebrated tacitly is the community or society that produced them. It is implied that we can glimpse aspects of a society's collective qualities in the skill and character of its athletes — which gives rise to the now familiar phenomenon of national, indeed nationalist, pride in the successes of sporting representatives. Canadians have generally not treated sporting defeats as national disgraces in quite the same manner as have, say, Brazilian or Scottish soccer fans. The closest we've come to this level of passionate identification was in the now legendary 1972 Challenge Series with the Soviet Union, and it may well be that Paul Henderson's last-minute goal was the only thing that saved Canadians from a significant bout of national angst.

The roots of international hockey go back far beyond that water-shed series of 1972. International matches were played virtually from the outset of organized hockey in Canada. Travelling hockey teams in the 1880s and 1890s spread the Montreal-style game to universities, towns, and cities in the United States, and this game gradually began to supplant the stick games on ice being played across the northeast. In Europe there is evidence of organized hockey being played in Vienna in the late 1880s; and in 1908 Belgium, Bohemia, France, Great Britain, and Switzerland formed the International Ice Hockey Federation (IIHF). The timing of the organization of the IIHF coincided with a number of important events in Canadian hockey. Most notably, 1908 was a time of growing conflict around the issue of professionalism in hockey. The same year the IIHF was founded, professional teams took over the Stanley Cup and senior amateur teams in Canada began to compete for their own trophy, the Allan Cup. After 1908, and especially with the founding of the Canadian Amateur Hockey Association in 1914, amateur and professional hockey in Canada began to follow qualitatively different lines of development.

One significant difference was that amateur hockey in Canada almost immediately developed loose ties to international amateur organizations. International hockey was quite self-consciously "amateur," and international amateur organizations became closely connected to the Olympic movement. As a result, hockey's first international world championship was held in conjunction with the Antwerp Winter Olympics in 1920. That first championship was won by the Canadian Allan Cup holders, the Winnipeg Falcons — a win that initiated a long string of Canadian victories in international competition. Indeed, until the mid-1950s Canadian teams repeatedly and almost effortlessly won Olympic gold medals and IIHF world championships with a diverse assortment of senior amateur clubs, including the Toronto Granites, the University of Toronto Grads, the Winnipeg Hockey Team, and the Lethbridge Maple Leafs.

During the 1950s all of this began to change. Canadians had become used to the idea that hockey was "our game," and when Canadian teams began to lose in international competition — especially to the Soviet Union — enough popular concern was created that some politicians began to take an interest. In a time of Cold War rhetoric the emergence of the Soviet Union as the dominant power in international hockey gave an added edge to the competition. The Soviet ascendancy made it easier for commentators to frame the challenges in a wider and highly dramatic context — "our" system against theirs, as indeed the Soviets constructed it themselves — and to win sympathy at the political level for arguments that "something should be done." Meanwhile, the effect of Soviet membership in the governing bodies of the International Olympic Committee (IOC) and the IIHF after the Second World War was to legitimize the Soviet system of state-sponsored professionalism, while keeping out Canadian professional athletes who made their careers in a commercial sport system. Many Canadian fans were aggrieved by this double standard and looked forward to the day when the best NHL professionals would reassert what we believed was our rightful supremacy in international hockey.

That opportunity came, as almost every Canadian knows, in the 1972 Canada-Soviet Challenge series; an event that mobilized patriotic interest among Canadians like no other cultural event before or since. Since then, throughout numerous international challenge series, Olympics, and world championships, the intensity and the level of public interest in Canadian teams have dissipated; and today our "national team" typically plays to modest crowds in provincial cities. International hockey pales against the presence of the NHL in Canadian popular culture, except when it involves the best NHL players or when it showcases future NHL stars. Now international hockey for many Canadians is simply not interesting unless it is linked to the big-league world of the NHL. When international hockey does feature big-name players, like in the Canada Cup or Marcel Aubut's "Rendez-Vous '87," it becomes one more "world class" consumer choice in the entertainment marketplace. At the same time the marketing appeal of commercial sport is enhanced when it can use the symbolism of international competition and mobilize nationalistic sentiments in its quest for larger audiences.

We still cheer for "our" boys in the Olympics and world championships, but the identifications currently mobilized around international sport are increasingly difficult to disentangle from the marketing of sports, sportswear, and sports celebrities. When the IOC approached the NBA to send the U.S "Dream Team" to Barcelona, this marked a new stage in the transformation of the national symbolic identifications that once defined international sport. In one promotional stroke, the greater publicity generated for the Olympics, for the sport of basketball, for the NBA and its celebrity stars, as well as for the products they endorsed, stood to benefit all parties to the arrangement. Many hockey people were thinking that if the NBA and the IOC can get together and attract greater audiences for each other, why can't the NHL do it too? Here it seems clear that the motives and meanings that will surround any future Canadian NHL "Dream Team" will be vastly different from the "National Team" assembled for the 1972 Soviet

Challenge series. International hockey in Canada — somewhat like pro hockey before it — has seen a subtle change in the kinds of relationships that fans have with their "home" teams. It is a change from a relationship centred around common membership and patriotic attachment to the more ephemeral consumer relationship created when international hockey simply becomes one more "world class" entertainment product.

Popular Cultures, Nationalism, and the Modern Nation-State

The modern nation-state system is a product of economic, cultural, and political developments that occurred over the course of the eighteenth and nineteenth centuries. In a world where local communities were economically self-sufficient and most people's horizons were bounded by local attachments, national identities had little meaning outside of the circles of aristocrats and merchants who warred and traded in the pursuit of "national" empires. It was the advent of industrial capitalism and the search for wider markets and secure sources of raw materials that gave additional impetus to the imperial quest for control of resources and trade routes, and the emergence of competitive nation-states with boundaries (or hinterlands of control) that encompassed more territory than the city states of the feudal period. The establishment of English rule in Britain and the consolidation of Germany and Italy into nation-states in the nineteenth century were an early part of this process. So too was the division of Africa, Asia, and the Americas into spheres of colonial influence and the subsequent emergence of the United States and Canada as independent new nations.

The emergence of the modern nation-state system meant that internationally recognized boundaries were established around a series of new nations, even though in many cases these boundaries encompassed different peoples who felt little historical or ethnic connection with one another. In some cases, indeed, national boundaries denied the claims to national status of ethnic or linguistic minorities: Scots, Basques, Kurds, and Québécois and First Nations peoples in Canada. In other cases, national boundaries effectively ignored the interests and living patterns of regional societies — in New Brunswick, for example, or in Alberta — that carried on more trading and cultural intercourse with neighbours across a border than with faraway "compatriots" in the same country. Modern nation-states, in other words, were often arbitrary territories that represented settlements among political factions within European and colonial dominant classes. They didn't necessarily produce a felt sense of nationality among ordinary people, whose lives were often still local in their orientation. In this context the political elites of the nineteenth and early twentieth centuries were sensitive to the need for what English historians Eric Hobsbawm and Terrance Ranger have called "the invention of traditions" that would encourage popular rehearsal of a sense of nationhood. Indeed, modern nations such as Canada have tended to be "imagined communities," in which the popular experience of fraternity with fellow nationals who are rarely if ever seen has had to be actively created and ritualized.[1] Flags and anthems, public holidays and festivities, and especially myths of national character — whether toughness, flair, discipline, or passion — have all contributed to the creation of national identifications. What is crucial to the success of such "representational" projects is the linking of national symbols and myths of national character with the lives of ordinary people and with widely shared and popular experiences.

When this linking is accomplished, practices rooted in popular life are effectively articulated with ideas of "the nation" in public discourses that naturalize the habit of identifying with the nation and its "representatives." As we've seen, the active content of Canada's "national popular culture" has been somewhat different from the content of local popular cultures and has also typically differed from the "national culture" envisaged by many intellectuals and professionals. Since the late 1960s the lines between local popular cultures, the "national popular" culture, and elite conceptions of the "national culture" in Canada have blurred markedly. Canadian culture now often has the character of pastiche: a mix and match combination of genres, styles, and practices that come from local popular cultures, the national popular culture, and elite cultures. Accompanying this, culture has become highly self-referencing, frequently to a point where the origins and early preferred meanings of different genres, styles, and practices have become lost from sight.

Still, it is nevertheless possible to delineate significant differences between various fields of cultural practice in Canada: to cite just a few examples, the national popular culture is more likely to include hockey and baseball, Madonna, and the Tragically Hip than experimental video art, ballet, Genevieve Cadieux, and General Idea. We could say that the cultural content of the national popular culture is genuinely popular only to the extent that it involves cultural practices and symbols that people enjoy in very large numbers across the country. These practices could also include, for example, popular television shows, popular music, and widely circulated product symbols. At the same time, cultural practices and symbols enjoyed by "the people" in various regions of Canada are usually only able to take on national connotations when they're given national media exposure and attention and are thereby publicly articulated as "national" pastimes and symbols.

Hockey has found a central place in Canada's national popular culture through many factors, including *Hockey Night in Canada* broadcasts on the CBC; the long history and sheer numbers of community, industrial, and age-graded teams; and the collective memories of nearly a century of hockey folklore, subcultural traditions, and heroes. As part of the Canadian national popular culture hockey has always contained a measure of antipathy to paternalistic invocations of duty and morality. In this sense the game has simply never fit very well with a nationalism in which "Canadian culture" is a code phrase for the promotion of highbrow sensibilities. Hockey has also been rooted in collective traditions that dramatize the importance of community in ways that sometimes run counter to the market-centred individualism that defines so much of contemporary cultural life. Over the last two decades, hockey's origins in local cultures and its deeply rooted associations with the idea of community have often been seen as a central part of its distinctively Canadian heritage. The perceived erosion of these associations in recent years has allowed hockey to be depicted by some nationalist commentators as a dramatic symbol of Canada's absorption into U.S. commerce and mass culture.

As we suggested early in our discussion, this image of an organic Canadian culture gradually becoming swallowed up by American commerce, American media, and American culture is a dangerous half-truth. This is so not only because it tends to romanticize the past, but also because it overlooks the degree to which many of the very "Canadian" traditions that nationalists want to protect are themselves implicated in sustaining relations of power and privilege. Certainly, many of the populist traditions and communal identifications in hockey have been readily articulated with ideological themes that have tacitly supported the dominant culture: the celebration of individualism through the star system; the naturalization of commercialism; the tendency to reproduce "hegemonic masculinity"; and the capacity to blur the lines between "community interests" and the interests of private capital.

The meanings both of actually existing national popular cultures and of imagined national cultures are always a contested terrain. At stake is the struggle to define a "national common sense" not only about such abstractions as democracy and justice, but also about everyday relations between social classes, men and women, work and leisure, asceticism and pleasure. The concepts of people, nation, and culture all have different histories, different meanings, and different possibilities of combination in various nationalist discourses. Yet what is particularly notable when discussing relations between nationalism, populism, and culture in Western societies is the ease with which the national popular culture has been appropriated into discourses that have an inherently conservative character. This has typically occurred when national institutions or national leaders have been able to associate themselves with events of genuine popular interest, in a manner that encourages popular identification with the nation and, more notably, its leadership. For instance, after England's victory in the 1966 World Cup, the English press proclaimed the event as a triumph for traditional English virtues. Similarly, after Brazil's 1970 World Cup win, the military government tried to portray the triumph as a victory "not merely for the country, but for the regime, for its policies, and for its vision of a powerful, disciplined, and technocratic Brazil."[2] Closer to home, Canada's ultimate success in the 1972 Challenge series provided the opportunity for many pundits and politicians to celebrate the result as a triumph not only for "Canadian virtues" but also for capitalist liberal democracy — a point frequently reinforced by the players themselves.

Undoubtedly, sport has lent itself particularly well to the promotion of national identity and pride. International sports competitions have become particularly attractive signifiers for both national unity and international standing precisely because they are competitive, because they involve "us" pulling together against "them." The point is similar to the argument we've made in earlier chapters about the power of sporting representatives to mobilize the idea of a "community as a whole" in the city. Unlike artistic traditions, which do not normally have this competitive subtext and may also be foreign to the lives of many people outside metropolitan elites, traditions of sporting prowess often have deep roots in popular life. Whether we are talking about hockey in Canada or soccer in Scotland or Italy, famous triumphs and great moments in sport become a part of the collective memory. As these events are retold and embellished, "the re-presentation of history so central to the construction of national identity can be effectively achieved."[3] When the rootedness of sport in popular life is combined with the advent of a communications technology that can bring events like the Olympics, the Challenge Cup, or the Stanley Cup into millions of homes, it is little wonder that ordinary people "are much more likely to identify with the elite athletes representing their country than they would with artists or even politicians."[4]

This is a lesson that has not been lost on politicians, in Canada and elsewhere. While team sport participation and gymnastic exercises were promoted as part of the moral agenda of state institutions like the military and public schools in the late nineteenth and early twentieth centuries, most politicians of the era tended to view high-level spectator sport as either socially worthless or simply not relevant to the business of government. But since the Second World War, governments of every political stripe have sought to associate themselves with athletes who have represented their countries successfully. Indeed, in many countries government policy has actively endeavoured to produce such successes. Canadians often associate this with the state-run sports systems that characterized Eastern Europe prior to the breakdown of Soviet dominance there in 1989-90. Certainly, governments in the former Soviet bloc spent significant human and material resources trying to produce sporting successes. They also sought to frame those successes as symbolic statements, not only to the rest of the world but also to their own people, about the virtues of the socialist system that made the achievements possible. This was particularly the case in East Germany, a "nation" that was purely an artifice of Cold War boundaries.

The socialist nations have not been alone in their political and ideological use of sport. For example, in the new nations of the "developing world," governments have never been able to devote many resources to the creation of a high-performance sports system. Nonetheless, when world-level athletes have emerged, scarce resources have often been made available to increase their chances of success. Indeed, men like Kip Keino, Ben Jipcho, and the other Kenyan track stars who burst into world stardom in the late 1960s had a double symbolic significance. At one level they represented, to everyone, the emergence of African nations onto the world stage after the demise of colonialism. At home they were also presented to Kenyans as examples of what the new Kenya could accomplish. The post-colonial leadership was trying to inculcate a sense of *Kenyan* identity in a large country made up of many ethnically different peoples. In this context Olympic successes became ready focal points for attempts to build not only national identity but also a sense of national competence. This latter project has been extended further through the hosting of international games. In Japan, Mexico, and most recently South Korea, international events become part of a discourse of "development" that is addressed to the home population and the outside world alike. In demonstrating that they can stage such events with style and efficiency, aspirant nations proclaim their membership in the dominant world order.

Of course, the Western nations have the longest tradition of making sports events into occasions for the rehearsal of national identity and pride. There is now a large literature on the place of sport in British consciousness and indeed in the continuing separate identities of the English, Scottish, and Welsh "nations." Some of this literature also draws attention to the role of sports in the "diffusion" of British culture and British consciousness in the colonies, especially in dominions like Canada, where settlers of British extraction sought to build British societies in the New World.[5] For its part, the United States, "the first new nation," was also the first country to publish medal tallies in the Olympics, and the U.S. press has not exactly been diffident about using successful athletes to make great claims for the American way of life. Yet there appears to be considerable contradiction built into the discourses and ideological claims that surround international sport. On the one hand there has long been an idealistic discourse emphasizing the potential of sports for promoting cross-cultural understanding and international brotherhood. On the other hand, almost from the beginning international sport has also provided a forum for national self-promotion, and indeed nationalism. British sociologist Alan Tomlinson summarizes this tension aptly when he notes, "It was as if nations wanted to reach out to each other for a handshake, whilst simultaneously puffing out their chests in pompous self-satisfaction."[6]

The organization of sport has remained largely independent of state governments in Western societies for most of this century. Again, this is not to say that the state hasn't been influential in shaping the context within which modern sport has developed. But until comparatively recently there has been little inclination on the part of national governments to intervene directly in the affairs of the organizations that emerged to administer modern sport. For example, in both Britain and the United States the major team sports in popular culture — soccer-football in Britain, baseball and later U.S.-style football in the United States — were established on a commercial basis, roughly along the same lines as hockey. These commercial organizations were independent of any supranational control, even though the Football Association in England grudgingly entered representative teams into the International Football Federation (FIFA) World Cup and European club competitions. U.S. professional sports leagues have simply declared their own champions to be "world champions" without bothering with international competitions. Meanwhile, in both Britain and the United States,

Olympic sports have been traditionally run by voluntary associations whose "official" status has owed less to governments than to their officers' roots in privileged social classes, as well as to their membership in international sporting federations.

The funding of British and U.S. Olympic sports for most of this century came primarily from private and business donations, which has of course reinforced the importance of "old boy" connections. Most often this kind of fundraising was insufficient to do more than cover the cost of travel to events like the Olympic Games. So it isn't surprising that amateur athletes, and indeed most amateur sports, largely disappeared from the public view in between Games, or that the best athletes — and almost all working-class athletes — typically chose to pursue professional team sports. In other words, the professional sports leagues and the bodies that ran amateur sport constituted two distinct worlds. There was little formal dialogue or co-operation between them, and some suspicion. Both sides warily guarded their own spheres of influence from each other and from governments.

Canada has experienced a very similar pattern. We've had the same commercial organization of our most popular team game, hockey. We've also had, until fairly recently, the same "amateur" organization of our representation in Olympic and world championships and the same wariness of government. This has been true in all sports in varying degrees. But hockey in particular has faced a rather unique set of jurisdictional tensions and challenges that made the selection of Canadian teams that could be competitive in international hockey a politically complex and difficult endeavour.

The Federal Government, the National Team, and Hockey Canada

Over the course of the postwar era, several factors emerged that led to an increasingly significant role for Western governments in the production of sporting excellence. The first pressures in this direction were political. They derived from the Cold War and the entry of the Soviet Union and its satellites into the Olympic movement and international sports federations. The socialist countries' manifest determination to pursue sporting success and to use it as an advertisement for their social system threw down a gauntlet of sorts to Western societies. The Soviet challenge to Canada's traditional supremacy in hockey, a challenge that developed from the late 1950s onwards, is only one example of this, though it is the one that concerns us most here.

The model of state-sponsored talent-development systems and state support of high-performance athletics was clearly a profound departure from the traditional International Olympic Committee policies against professionalism and against the mixing of sport and politics. However, athletes from the socialist countries were not being paid directly, unlike Western professionals, and in the political context of the day a ban on East Bloc athletes would have been against all the Olympic rhetoric about internationalism and co-operation. In addition, once the socialist countries were members of the IOC and other international sports federations, they formed a powerful coalition with established sports officials (of whom long-time IIHF president Bunny Aherne was a prime example) whose opposition to allowing North American professionals in their events had a great deal to do with maintaining their own control over international sport. Western countries were left to address their relative disadvantages in their own ways.

It is also important to recognize the effects of the affluence generated in Western nations through the 1960s, and the commitment undertaken in many Western European societies to create unprecedented levels of social infrastructure. In many of the countries of northern and western Europe, publicly funded sports and cultural facilities came to be understood as "citizens' rights," part of the social fabric of an affluent society. In continental Europe, "centres of excellence" and the support of coaching and research, often in association with specialist schools of physical education, came to be familiar. Support for sport was understood as a way a society could make possible for its young people the development of socially valued forms of excellence. At the same time, television and sponsorship were gradually transforming some "amateur" sports into lucrative fields of endeavour on a continent that had always produced paying audiences for international skiing and track and field.

This, then, was the political and economic context in which the Scandinavian countries, the Italians, the French, and especially the West Germans all developed their own state-supported sport systems. They didn't threaten the Soviet and U.S. positions at the top of the Olympic standings, but they did push Britain and the other Commonwealth countries such as Canada, which had maintained the amateur tradition and had not developed government-subsidized "sport systems," well down the medal table. What was becoming increasingly clear was that part-time athletes couldn't win in any sport. The commitment to full-time training and competition (in other words to professionalism, even when it was not acknowledged as such) raised the levels of competition so much that other countries had to develop "sport systems" of their own or fall further behind.[7]

In Canada the first significant development came with the passage of the Fitness and Amateur Sport Act in 1961. This provided for a federal government role in the funding of amateur sport through modest levels of aid to national sport organizations. Part of the rationale for this initiative was couched in terms of concerns about national health and fitness in the face of suburban affluence and the prospect of more sedentary lifestyles. However, it wasn't long before another stated objective began to connect the improvement of Canadian performances in international sport with the general project of national identity. Nonetheless, in the early years of the Fitness and Amateur Sport Directorate (FASD), through the Diefenbaker and Pearson administrations, this objective remained at a level that was low key compared with what was to come. Fitness and Amateur Sport provided a regular budget, which permitted forward planning and development activities between Olympic Games. Regular funding also made possible the beginnings of national offices, with professional administrators and coaches. The corollary of regular funding was that national sport organizations became accountable to government for the first time, which some in the sport community saw as a dangerous departure from the tradition of independence. Still, through most of the 1960s, the FASD left the responsibility for programming and for the success of national teams largely to the sports governing bodies themselves.[8]

Much of this was to change by the end of the decade, partly as a result of growing anglo-Canadian nationalism. The 1960s was a time of resurgent concerns about Canadian identity and unity. A number of factors contributed to this: the beginnings of the Quiet Revolution in Quebec and dramatic increases in immigration from southern Europe together underlined that Canada was no longer the British and French society it once seemed to be. Moreover, anxieties about the increasing presence of American popular culture — American films, popular music, professional sport, and television — had reached even greater heights than in previous decades. Canadians suddenly became deeply concerned about national symbols: we chose a new flag and adopted "Oh Canada" as our national anthem, both after vigorous debate.

Yet in our centennial year, 1967, the NHL's initial expansion failed to include a single Canadian team. Because one of the major goals of expansion was the pursuit of a national television contract in the United States, Vancouver was conspicuously overlooked. Indeed, Vancouver was even denied permission to purchase the failing Oakland Seals in 1968. The NHL's behaviour led to considerable public complaint, in Parliament and elsewhere, about U.S. corporate domination of a game we still thought of as "ours." Numerous calls for the government to "do something" about the game led to the threat to investigate the NHL under the terms of the Combines Act, and the issue also led finally to a national task force on amateur sport. The emergence of hockey as a public issue in the 1960s also owed something to two other related concerns. One was the NHL's virtually complete control over amateur hockey through control of the CAHA, the direct sponsorship of junior teams, and particularly the notorious "C form" contracts that tied teenage boys to a particular NHL team's farm system. The second was Canada's poor showings in international hockey after 1961. Many Canadians were embarrassed and even angry about this; and some knew that in part, at least, the failures stemmed from the refusal of professional teams to loan promising juniors (such as Yvan Cournoyer) to the national team, as well as the NHL's general antagonism towards the national team concept.

In the early 1950s most Canadians simply took Canada's supremacy in international hockey for granted and there was only passing interest in the IIHF World Championships. Moreover, because the CAHA offered to do little more than pay expenses few top-rank senior teams were willing to pass up several weeks of home gates in their own leagues to compete in Europe. Indeed, when the CAHA began to look for a suitable representative to send to the 1954 World Championships in Stockholm they were turned down by every top-rank senior team in the country. The best of the Canadian teams that were willing to go was the East York Lyndhursts, a team that made history of sorts by losing to the Soviet Union. Canadian fans were initially shocked, but we quickly rationalized the loss by reminding ourselves that the Lyndhursts, sponsored by a Toronto car dealer, were simply a moderately good industrial team — a team that had trouble winning its division in the Metro Toronto Hockey League before finishing third in the Ontario senior B playoffs.[9]

This led to more determined efforts to send the Allan Cup Champions overseas — in other words, to send the national champions at the much stronger (and often semi-professional) senior A level. Through the remaining years of the 1950s, the Penticton Vees, the Whitby Dunlops, and the Belleville McFarlands went on from Allan Cup titles to win the world championships for Canada, often bolstered by former NHL players. However, by the early 1960s — despite the success in 1961 of the Trail Smoke Eaters — it had become clear that the small cities that supported senior hockey could no longer provide teams of the calibre necessary to be competitive at world championships. Major-league or professional calibre players now seemed to be required; and the money necessary to assemble and keep good teams simply couldn't be recouped at the gate in cities the size of Whitby and Penticton.

By 1962 all of the Allan Cup winners who had gone on to win world championships for Canada in the late 1950s had folded, as had the Kitchener-Waterloo Dutchmen, the Canadian representatives at the 1956 and 1960 Olympics. There were now calls for some sort of all-star team. But the difficulties of assembling a good senior team and financing it to stay together were already apparent, and proposals to create a team of all-star juniors were non-starters because of the NHL teams' ownership of the best junior players. The problem, of course, was that what Canadians thought of as their national game was owned, at its top levels, by a commercial entertainment organization whose partners, just like all businesses, routinely put their commercial interests before "national" interests. The NHL, which had become widely regarded as "a national institution," was also a business, and for the league's governors business interests came first.

Into this vacuum stepped Father David Bauer with a proposal to assemble a team of good college players and players graduating from junior hockey and base the team at a Canadian university in a major city. The team, as Bauer envisaged it, would attract good players by offering them not just the opportunity to represent their country — a chance they wouldn't get if they turned professional immediately — but also the opportunity to combine international hockey with a good education. In principle, players could go on to professional hockey after representing Canada; and indeed players such as Morris Mott, Brian Conacher, and Rod Seiling did just this. The NHL consistently opposed the national team concept, not least precisely because it did offer good young players an alternative to immediate professional careers. Players of the calibre of Bobby Orr and Serge Savard apparently considered the national team option, and they raised this prospect in their contract talks with Boston and Montreal, respectively, thereby introducing a bargaining power that led, particularly in Orr's case, to uncharacteristically large salaries for the time. NHL teams didn't want outstanding players — whom they saw as the league's own property — playing elsewhere and possibly jeopardizing their professional careers. Nor did the league want good players to have options that gave them a greater measure of bargaining power.

The national team of the 1960s might be considered a success by some standards. It not only offered players an opportunity to combine high-quality hockey with a high-quality education, but also offered an aspiration that was an alternative to the dream of money and celebrity status that went with an NHL career; or at least it created an option in which players could pursue a patriotic dream before turning pro. It also offered a model of idealism — the honour of representing one's country — to the Canadian public. But the team didn't succeed well enough on the ice to really establish itself in any of these ways.[10] The national team came close in the 1968 Winter Olympics, winning a bronze medal, and scored a notable victory in the 1967 Centennial Tournament in Winnipeg. Yet although the team developed a core of solid players, some of whom would go on to NHL careers, it never did attract the star players who could possibly have made the difference between winning and coming a close third. With NHL support, especially a willingness to loan star juniors, the national team might have had greater success. But given its history and the Canadian public's expectations, third and fourth place finishes were not enough to turn around a public perception that something more needed to be done to regain a supremacy Canadians thought they deserved by right.

It was in this context that Pierre Trudeau promised a task force on sport during the 1968 federal election campaign. Trudeau saw sport, and more broadly culture, as highly relevant to the questions of national identity and unity that were political issues of the time, and these issues became noteworthy themes in his campaign. He expressed specific concerns about the Canadian failures, internationally, in "our national sport," and about the NHL's apparent refusal to grant expansion franchises to Canadian cities.[11] The Task Force on Sport for Canadians was established in August 1968. Although its mandate was broad, a substantial section of its final report, delivered in the winter of 1969, was addressed to hockey. The report was critical of a structure in which the NHL's "ownership" of all of Canada's best young players effectively meant that the country couldn't ice a competitive team in international hockey; and it proposed the creation of a new body, Hockey Canada, which would be responsible for Canadian participation in international events. Health Minister John Munro moved to establish Hockey Canada even before the Task Force report was officially presented, and by mid-1969 a board was in place that included representatives from the CAHA, the Canadian Intercollegiate Athletic Union (CIAU), the three Canadian teams in the NHL (under pressure the NHL had finally awarded Vancouver a franchise in 1969), and the NHL Players Association (a role filled by the NHLPA president, Alan Eagleson).

The task itself would require some hardball diplomacy, in which the various stakeholders used all the political and economic leverage at their disposal. It was widely agreed that if Canada was going to beat the Soviets, the national team would have to be augmented by good professional players, and this had to be negotiated not only with the

IIHF but also with the National Hockey League and its member teams. In 1969 Hap Emms, a former general manager of the Boston Bruins, was hired as director of the national team with a mandate to strengthen it for the 1970 world championships, scheduled to be held in Winnipeg. Emms recommended that NHL draft rules be changed to allow the national team access to twenty of the best juniors over the three years leading up to the 1972 Olympics. The players would go back into the draft after a stint with the national team. In addition, Toronto's Stafford Smythe promised three players from the Maple Leafs. But at a meeting involving Hockey Canada, Sport Canada, and the health minister, NHL president Clarence Campbell and league governor David Molson made it clear that the NHL was not prepared to modify its draft to allow top juniors to play international hockey before turning professional. Nor could other owners accept one team (the Leafs) loaning players out. They proposed instead an ad hoc team, assembled for a few weeks for an international tournament, out of players the league would supply. Hockey Canada reluctantly accepted this less-than-complete co-operation; but Emms quit in disgust.

At the same time, to make any version of this plan feasible, Hockey Canada also had to negotiate increased use of professionals with the IIHF. At a meeting in July 1969, Hockey Canada representatives failed to secure unrestricted use of professional players; but a compromise agreement approved the use of nine non-NHL professionals for the 1970 world championship tournament. This agreement didn't last long. Behind-the-scenes lobbying by the Soviets (in some accounts) and IOC president Avery Brundage (in others) persuaded other European nations that their subsequent participation in the 1972 Olympics could be jeopardized by competing against Canadian professionals. An emergency meeting in January 1970 rescinded the previous agreement, and Hockey Canada, after consultation with John Munro, refused to participate under the old rules, thus forfeiting the right to host the tournament. Canada would remain out of international hockey until after the 1972 Olympics.[12]

Team Canada and Beyond

Canada's triumphal return to international hockey in the 1972 Challenge Series with the Soviets involved the top stars of the day, other than the WHA's Bobby Hull, whose exclusion became a controversial demonstration of the NHL's veto power in negotiations surrounding international hockey. In the opinion of many knowledgeable observers, the series offered fans some of the most exciting hockey ever played. Despite the initial shock of the Soviet victories in the first games in Canada, the manner of "our" victory in the deciding match in Moscow led to an orgy of self-congratulation about the triumph of "Canadian virtues" — individualism, flair, and most of all, character — over the "machine-like" Soviet "system." Even though some people outside the hockey community were critical of the behaviour of some of the players and of Hockey Canada's Alan Eagleson, most Canadians felt confirmed in finding that our image of ourselves as the best hockey country in the world could be sustained.

Yet although the 1972 Challenge Series seemed to reconfirm Canada's hockey supremacy, it also pointed up important areas of the game — skating, stickhandling, and especially passing — where the skills of Canadian players had fallen behind the skills of Europeans. There has been continued resistance in parts of the Canadian hockey subculture to the notion that there is anything to learn from Europeans, or that we should adapt our game at all. But over the course of the 1970s and 1980s Canadian hockey did begin to change, at the very least in terms of its tactical sophistication, as a result of contact between the NHL and European teams.[13]

Some aspects of that 1972 series also point to developments that were to change the face of international hockey over the 1980s. A starting point was the multi-layered negotiations that culminated in the 1972 Challenge Series, and the factors that led to this new development in hockey: an NHL all-star team playing the Soviet national team. In the aftermath of the Canadian withdrawal from international hockey in 1970, Hockey Canada officials had been trying to arrange challenge matches or tournaments involving professionals and European national teams; and Alan Eagleson was also trying independently to arrange a series between NHL players and the Soviets.[14] The new factor in this complicated equation was the NHL's willingness to co-operate much more than it had in the past, by making available its best players.

This new willingness was largely attributable to the appearance of the World Hockey Association. At first considered an impudent rival by NHL owners, the WHA demonstrated the seriousness of its challenge to the NHL's dominance over the hockey labour market by signing Bobby Hull away from the Chicago Black Hawks, with a contract subsidized by the entire league.[15] The spectre of an all-out bidding war made the NHL owners suddenly more willing to collaborate with the Players Association, in order to keep them "onside." Eagleson, for his part, skilfully exploited this new leverage to establish the NHLPA — and himself — as a necessary partner in negotiations for any games beyond players' normal contractual obligations. One of the difficulties this was to raise, though, was that Hockey Canada's agreements on player supply were with the NHL, which subsequently refused to have Hull or other WHA players on the Team Canada roster. This position was sustained against the wishes of Team Canada and Boston Bruin manager Harry Sinden, and in the face of a great public outcry, including an intervention by Prime Minister Trudeau. This served to illustrate the NHL's continued hold over Canadian hockey, as well as the unwillingness of its largely U.S.-based owners to make any sacrifice to a "national interest" that they perceived as counter to their own commercial interests.

At the same time, the Canadian government did take an active role in the negotiations that established the series. The Department of External Affairs wanted Canada back in international hockey, in keeping with the Trudeau government's foreign policy objectives. Trudeau and Soviet Premier Aleksei Kosygin had exchanged visits in 1971 and had agreed in a general way that a resumption of hockey competition would contribute to the opening up of relations between the two countries. Hockey Canada was advised that Canadian embassies in Moscow, Prague, and Stockholm were prepared to assist in negotiations aimed at establishing open play between Canadians and Europeans. In fact, the Soviets, who were used to a government presence in all important affairs, insisted that negotiations and arrangements for the series be handled through the two countries' foreign offices. The Canadian government role was therefore significant, even though the limits of its powers to impose its will on a multinational corporation (the NHL) were underlined by the Hull affair.

Nonetheless, the victory of Team Canada in 1972, important as it was in restoring the Canadian sense of pride in our hockey, did little to address the underlying tensions between perceived Canadian national interests and the NHL's financial interests that had produced the decline in the first place. Team Canada 1972 was an ad hoc team assembled a few weeks before the tournament. Although the team was made up of outstanding players, the agreements that set up the 1972 series did not address the longer-term challenge of establishing a national team that would play together throughout a season. The NHL agreed to continue to supply players for ad hoc teams to compete in world championships, but because these tournaments take place in the spring — during Stanley Cup playoff races or the playoffs themselves — subsequent Team Canadas would never receive a full complement of headline players, and they slipped back into embarrassing defeats. After a particularly weak performance in 1977, the government appointed a Parliamentary Committee on International Hockey, which held public hearings and took briefs from interested parties. Its findings mostly served to confirm what the 1969 Task Force had already indicated: the problems followed from the fact that something important to Canadians (our representation and our reputation in international hockey) depended upon players employed by an essentially U.S.-controlled corporation. Given the legacy of the CAHA's dominance by the NHL, hockey couldn't emerge — like alpine skiing did, for example — as a sport in which public investment and private capital acted as balanced partners in pursuit of international sporting successes. Certainly, the continued (albeit softened) presence of an older antipathy between spectator sport and "culture" made it unlikely that hockey could be promoted as a publicly supported "cultural institution" like the National Ballet.

Operating within these limits, the Parliamentary Committee on International Hockey recommended that Canada re-establish a national team structure. As a result, a Canadian team was entered for the 1980 Olympics, after an absence from the 1972 and 1976 Olympic competitions. Subsequently a national team-in-being was re-established under Dave King. The team operated like the Bauer team, with a core of players not under contract to NHL teams, but in world championships the permanent squad was usually reconstructed by taking on professionals on loan from NHL teams. The national team offered the same chance for players to represent their country and pursue an education that the Bauer concept did, and it is not the target of the same level of NHL hostility. Nonetheless, the national team still suffered from the fact that it had to compete for top young players with the NHL. This was made even more difficult by the trend towards a younger draft age, by the fact that successive expansions created many new jobs in professional hockey, and, most recently, by the dramatic rise in the salaries that even journeymen professional players can enjoy. The incentive for a player to choose the national team program has been even further undermined, moreover, by the fact that players might spend a year with the team only to be "bumped" at tournament time by players on loan from the NHL. Given these circumstances, the team has done remarkably well. There have been enough solid junior and college players who have not been offered lucrative professional deals for King to produce capable defensive teams; and the odd player, such as Joe Juneau, has been able to parlay success in international hockey into a good offer from an NHL team.

It is illuminating here to make a brief comparison with soccer, the only other major commercial team sport in which a professional league structure co-exists with another structure of international competition — the World Cup — that provides a focal point for nationalist prides and rivalries, as well as a source of enormous television revenues and publicity for the sport. The World Cup competition is scheduled in soccer's off-season, although qualifying matches take place over a two-year period and clubs are bound to release players selected for national team matches, even by another country. Most of the nationally based professional leagues accommodate this agreement by not scheduling matches on the dates of World Cup qualifiers. Another more important difference is that the World Cup is a much bigger event — both as a commercial event and an event in European (and Latin American) popular culture — than the world hockey championships. In many countries it is even bigger than the Olympic Games. The World Cup therefore produces media attention for the game of soccer in a way that benefits the game at every level, at least in those countries that do well in the tournament. Major-league commercial soccer — defined by high player salaries and a significant presence in popular culture — exists in most countries of Europe, which means that power is more diffused than it is in hockey, where one league is so much bigger and richer than the rest. Indeed, the better comparison may now be between the NHL and the NBA, which clearly saw the Barcelona Olympics as a timely opportunity to promote itself, its celebrity players, and the game of basketball before international audiences. Certainly the potential of this kind of marketing opportunity has not been lost on the new NHL commissioner, Gary Bettman, himself a former NBA executive.

Yet, in hockey, the increasingly global labour market appears for now to have decreased the Canadian interest in international hockey. Twenty years ago European players were a novelty. Today, Oiler fans have savoured the skills of players like Kurri and Tikkanen for years, while names like Stastny and Salming have become part of NHL lore. Another contributing factor has probably been the overexposure of Soviet and Russian club tours, in which exhibitions involving unknown players failed to generate public interest. There was also the relative failure of the older generation of Soviet stars in the NHL; so that names like Fetisov and Makarov no longer evoke the same awe they once did. Younger Russians like Pavel Bure and Alexander Mogilny began to set the NHL alight in 1992-93, but Soviet hockey has now been demystified. So, although a reassembled Russian national squad would still be a worthy opponent for a Team Canada with Gretzky and Lemieux, international games simply don't evoke the same interest they did twenty years ago. Undoubtedly, the end of the Cold War is an additional contributing factor to this circumstance.

Some commentators would also argue that many Canadian fans prefer our own "rougher" style of play to the international style, and that the now familiar rivalries between Canadiens and Bruins, and Oilers and Flames, mean more to us than international tournaments involving rivals that many fans still do not take seriously. Yet these claims echo the reasoning once used by English soccer officials to justify their own reluctance to get involved in competitions with "foreigners." It was said that English fans preferred their local rivalries and their own more "direct" style of play to the passing skills and tactical sophistication of the "sneaky" continentals. Today, however, games with famous continental teams, involving players who are household names in the global culture of "futbol," are big money-spinners. Revenue from European competitions makes the difference between profits and problems for ambitious, big-budget teams. Indeed, soccer represents another instance, even more striking than hockey, of the larger shift from the historical "representativeness" of sports teams towards the more consumer-oriented attachments of the modern fan.[16]

Canadian Hockey and the Changing Politics of Identities

This brings us back to the paradox raised in Alan Tomlinson's observation about international sport. There has always been a tension between the rhetoric of globalism that surrounds international sport at the official level and the nationalist passions and myths of national superiority that the popular media routinely fuel. Nonetheless, sports have provided highly compelling dramatizations of mythical national qualities and occasions for the public assertion of "us" against "them." At least part of the power of these dramatizations stems from the fact that sports ground these mythical national qualities in *real* conflicts where the struggles involved go beyond mere rhetoric and appearance.[17] In practical terms, Canadians really have struggled against Russians in hockey, including physical confrontations between individual Canadian and Russian players. And, by the same token, "our boys" have been engaged in similar dramatic struggles with Swedes, Czechs, Finns, and Americans — all from countries that have challenged Canadians' proprietorial attitude towards hockey and whose players have often represented a different way of playing the game.

In these international contests, hockey has acted as a medium not just for the expression of Canadian identity, but also for the reaffirmation of a preferred version of "national character": tough and hard, passionate yet determined, individualistic. This is why the losses to European teams become occasions for national self-examination. This is, finally, a central reason why it is still credible to call hockey "our national religion" or "common coin," despite the hyperbole of such phrases and despite the apparent decline in interest in international hockey.

Yet in recent years the mythic power of hockey in Canada has become increasingly difficult to sustain. This is partly due to the longstanding U.S. domination of the NHL at the corporate level, as well as the more recent internationalization of the hockey labour market, which has made both European and U.S. players familiar figures in Canadian popular culture. The 1990s could even see some form of NHL expansion to Europe; or hockey's presence in Canadian culture could be further undermined by other sports such as basketball or by the availability of other consumer choices. What seems clear in any event is that the internationalization of sports entertainment will bring hockey into fierce competition for audiences and revenues: in Canada, in the United States, and in Europe. In these competitions Europe may become a critical battleground; and it will be one where hockey enjoys an advantage given the sport's popularity in some European nations. Indeed, some observers suggest that Europe offers considerably more growth potential to hockey than does further expansion in the United States, where basketball appears to be steadily consolidating its pre-eminence as the primary winter sport in American popular culture. One effect of European expansion would almost certainly be to make hockey seem less distinctively Canadian.

In the future top-level international men's hockey will most likely be conducted under the auspices of the NHL, together with whatever European and U.S. interests will negotiate promotional arrangements with the league. When this occurs international hockey will join the pantheon of "world class" international commercial spectacles like the Olympics and soccer's World Cup — spectacles that will be the objects of competition between "entrepreneurial cities" and where national identifications will persist, but primarily in the service of marketing. In such circumstances there is little to support the kind of Canadian government involvement in hockey that has characterized the last two decades. Hockey Canada is arguably already redundant at the international level, and its domestic responsibilities could easily be taken over by the CAHA. This does not mean that there will be no role for public expenditures in hockey in the future, but only that those expenditures are likely to have a quite different character than in the period from the early 1970s to the 1990s.

The sheer scope of changes in Canada have made the equation between hockey and "Canadianness" increasingly problematic. Most importantly, Canada is a much more polyglot country than it was in the first two decades after the war. We've always been a country peopled by immigrants; but in earlier times the popular culture of the anglo-phone and francophone majorities easily sustained pride of place. For children and adolescents who identified with these majority cultures, learning to play hockey, or even learning to watch it knowledgeably, was an actively pursued marker of becoming Canadian. Today hockey competes with many other activities for children's allegiances; and while millions of children still play and watch the game, it no longer provides the common experience of Canadian childhood that it did when Canada was still primarily the site of an anglophone and fran-cophone culture.

It is also important to remember that girls have usually had differ-ent childhood memories of hockey. Today, the continued movement of women into the public sphere means that there is a large and increas-ingly influential group of Canadians in public life who are less inclined to consider hockey symbolic of their Canadian identities. Moreover, in recent years other advocacy groups who are challenging the rights of Canada's postwar elites have made a significant mark in Canadian pub-lic policy debates. Most notably they've begun to challenge how white middle-class males from our so-called two "founding nations" have monopolized the definition of the public interest and much of the every-day common sense of Canadian life. There is a significant degree of resistance to these challenges, but the successes of new social move-ments and new advocacy groups point to how much Canada has changed politically and culturally in the years since the whole coun-try joined in celebrating Team Canada's triumph over the Soviets in 1972, let alone the victories of senior teams from Penticton and Whitby in the 1950s.

It is likely that the growing "politics of difference" in Canadian life will create new pressures to reorient federal government sport policy as a whole away from its twenty-year preoccupation with high-perfor-mance international competition. There is also the possibility that as more and more people who have been on the margins of Canadian pol-itics and culture make themselves heard, sports of any kind will not be seen as favourable places to spend public money. A plausible sce-nario might see some modest expenditures directed to supporting increased recreational choices in different communities: including, in the case of hockey, teams for young children, girls and women, old-timers, First Nations Canadians, and special populations. What is more likely, though, is a continuing reduction of government funding for sport, as successive national and regional governments struggle with deficit reduction. Already many national sports organizations have been forced to seek larger and larger parts of their budgets from the private sector. It is probable that in the future any public money available to sport will become even more closely tied to broader economic "development" strategies — including stadium subsidies or the provision of funds designed to attract and to stage "world class" events — rather than locally based recreational programs. Still, none of this has been fully determined, and a great many political battles remain to be fought. As these battles take shape the only thing that can be said with any certainty in the case of hockey is that the automatic equation of hockey and "Canadianness" that has existed for much of the postwar era will be far less significant in the future than it has been in the past.

Chapter Twelve

Conclusion: Hockey and Canadian Culture in the Age of Globalization

The word "globalization" is used a lot these days, often in highly misleading ways. For example, much of what is referred to as "global culture" really isn't global at all in origin — it originates in Western nations, and especially in the United States. Furthermore, globalization should not be taken to suggest any necessary movement to a harmonious, freely trading, "global village." On the contrary, there appears to be as much ethnic and racial hatred, national chauvinism, and trade protectionism in the world as there has ever been. In this sense, persistent cultural and economic nationalisms, localisms, and "the politics of place" can be seen to be fighting it out with new internationalist tendencies, often in the most contradictory of ways.[1]

Still, there are two distinct and significant tendencies that are aptly referenced by the concept of globalization. First, there has been a notable reworking of political economic practices and processes on an international scale since the early 1970s. The tendencies towards centralized industrial mass production, mass consumption, and welfare-state investment that supported the postwar boom in Western societies have been reworked in conjunction with new international communications networks and technologies, the push for more "flexible" labour processes and markets, and the erosion of Keynesian economic strategies. Second, the term globalization forcibly reminds us of the transnational character of modern marketing and of the continuing internationalization of Western commercially produced popular culture. Companies, products, and celebrities such as Disney, CNN, Coca Cola, Benetton, Reebok, and Madonna *really are* part of an increasingly global culture — a media-dominated popular culture that is variously enjoyed and hated, willingly incorporated into local and national popular cultures and strenuously resisted around the world.

This emergent global popular culture continues to be unambiguously modern, if the word *modern* can be taken to mean the degree to which constant innovation, uncertainty, and agitation are the norms that define more and more areas of contemporary human experience. The idea of modernity has also been linked to the push towards scientific reason, universal rationality, and cultural unity that emerged in Western cultures during the eighteenth and nineteenth centuries. Because the degree of innovation, uncertainty, and agitation has become so great over the last two decades — including the fragmentation of markets, the plurality of identities, unprecedented cultural mixing and matching, and a heavy dependence upon media imagery — some commentators argue that Western societies have now entered a distinctively "postmodern" condition.[2] We're more inclined to see contemporary popular culture as a manifestation of desires, limits, and pressures that have arisen within modernity rather than beyond it. But whatever the perspective, it is important to recognize that national and global popular cultures today continue to be significantly shaped by contemporary capitalism; and they're still riddled with the contradictions and tensions — between choice and constraint, pleasure and duty, resistance and containment — that have always existed between the field of "the popular" and the pressures and limits associated with wage work, commodity production, and capital accumulation.

The tensions and contradictions surrounding popular cultures also continue to be manifest through the issue of identities. Racial, ethnic, gender, and occupational identities as well as popular identifications with certain cultural products and practices, local communities, and the nation-state have all been part of the complex mix that has gone into the making of various national popular cultures and, indeed, of the emerging global popular culture. In the face of these diverse identifications the experience of modern life has been a continuing push and pull between different forms of attachment, and between various attempts by specialists in symbolic production (intellectuals, artists, academics, journalists, political leaders) to define cultural hierarchies that privilege some identities — and some vested interests — over others. In Canada we've felt this push and pull in a particularly dramatic way. Indeed, for much of the last century Canadians have agonized about the possibility of recognizing diversity without creating separation. There has also been endless discussion about the kind of common culture and Canadian identity that best defines the "national interest" and the nature of our imagined "national community."

Nonetheless, it has proved to be immensely difficult to achieve much consensus on the precise meaning of the Canadian national interest or the exact ordering of people's allegiances and identities within the national community. The invented traditions, civic rituals, and visions of national culture promoted over the last century have rarely inspired anything that approximates the imagined ideal of universal communality. The distinctiveness of Quebec society alone has always lent itself to suspicions about the possibility of a homogeneous Canadian common culture and a singular national identity. Moreover, there have always been subordinated groups — aboriginal Canadians, people from ethno-cultural groups other than English and French, working-class people, and most women — who have been historically excluded from the process of imagining Canada as a national community. Over the last century the promoters of a distinctive Canadian national culture have generally been male, middle class, moral entrepreneurs and intellectuals who have attempted to construct their visions of a common culture "from above."

At several points in our discussion we've noted how intellectual elites have understood popular tastes and many popular recreations to be of questionable value. Popular culture has been seen as shallow, vulgar, undiscriminating, overly hedonistic, excessively violent, and intellectually undemanding. For the most part, Canadian intellectuals have not displayed a lot of enthusiasm for the idea of viewing sport as a valuable part of the national culture. Spectator sports, in particular, have been denigrated as activities too closely tied to popular tastes, too centred on the body rather than the mind, too rooted in local passions, and too closely connected to the sensuous worlds of drink and gambling.[3]

This understanding of sport has often been subtly mediated by the idea that carefully regulated and respectable amateur sport is an effective vehicle for promoting health, hygiene, masculinity, and qualities of leadership. In this form — as "rational recreation" and amateur athletics — sport gained greater support as a socially useful activity in the late nineteenth and early twentieth centuries. Its perceived social usefulness lay largely in its capacity to reorganize popular culture in a way consonant with the values and economic interests of the dominant segment of the anglo professional and business classes. Not only did amateur sport promise to spread middle-class visions of the world among the working classes, it also tacitly reinforced status distinctions ("gentlemen" versus "professionals") while simultaneously preaching the democratic idea that everyone was equal on the playing field.

This class-based vision of sport was always compromised, contested, and contradictory. The amateur tradition in sport achieved a notable level of prominence in Canadian popular culture; but amateur sport never fully lived up to the hopes of those moral entrepreneurs who promoted it primarily for its ideological utility. Virtually from the outset, many Canadians simply absorbed what they wanted from the middle-class sporting associations responsible for popularizing and regulating amateur sport; and they rejected what they felt was alien to their own local cultures and experiences. In this sense, amateurism was frequently drawn into an inescapable relationship with older popular sporting traditions that were far less hostile to intense and emotional partisanship, commercialism, and spectacle. With these strongly felt community attachments and the pressures and limits of Canada's changing political economy, the line between amateur and commercial sports became increasingly blurred between the 1890s and the 1920s.

Given Canada's strong tradition of Victorian moral entrepreneurship, there is great irony in the fact that a commercialized, violent, and significantly Americanized sporting product — NHL hockey — eventually emerged as one of the most distinctive markers of Canadian commonality. There was a remarkable explosion of organized hockey teams in Canada from the end of the nineteenth century to the First World War. But hockey didn't really begin to leave an indelible mark on Canadian culture until the means of symbolic production — telegraphy, magazines, radio, and, finally, television — had become fully national in their technical reach, thereby creating the possibility of national audiences. This nationalization of symbolic production occurred against a background of developments that were beginning to make Canada an extension of the American domestic market for cultural goods and entertainments.

In the 1920s the NHL emerged as hockey's equivalent to other nationally branded products that were making their mark in an emerging continental consumer culture. The NHL was able to trade on pro hockey's Canadian roots and the game's community and working-class traditions even as it expanded into the United States and appealed to the growing Canadian interest in the big-money worlds of major-league commerce and entertainment. With the advent of national radio broadcasts Canadians began to follow NHL hockey with an almost religious fervour, and from the 1930s through the 1960s there was simply nothing in Canadian life that regularly brought so many Canadians from different parts of the country together to share the same cultural experience. By the 1950s the link between hockey and Canadian identity became taken for granted, a simple matter of common sense.

The strength of that perceived attachment to the game, the organizational power of the NHL, and the apparent naturalness of the league's subcultural traditions largely explain why hockey was both swept up in the developing nationalism of the postwar era and remained stubbornly resistant to it. At the very moment in the early 1950s that the Massey Commission articulated a highbrow response to Canada's apparent absorption into American culture, the Canadian enthusiasm for hockey demonstrated the strengths of a *popular* nationalism rooted in collective memories and attachments to "home" — to neighbours and workmates — and to familiar national symbols and personalities.[4] Canadians followed and cared about teams in Boston, Chicago, Detroit, and New York; yet the very act of watching hockey seemed to reinforce a set of identities that was distinctively Canadian. The Canadian losses to European and Soviet teams in the 1950s and 1960s emerged as the primary threat to the pride taken in those identities, which were still rooted in memories of a fraternal sense of camaraderie and community.

But there were also other threats in hockey to perceived Canadian identities. Some people saw the NHL itself as a symbol of the Americanization of Canadian culture, and they raised serious questions about the NHL's dominance of the game. At the same time there were calls for a stronger Canadian presence in international amateur play. Both views implied a reworking of the well-established tradition according to which the NHL was both the pinnacle of the hockey world and its source of authority — to the extent that most hockey fans saw the interests of the game to be synonymous with the interests of the league. Not only did the critics' stances fly in the face of the NHL's vested interests, but they also unsettled many traditionalists in the hockey subculture. The fact that the national team concept was embraced enthusiastically by many people outside the game — physical educators, advocates of recreational sport, and bureaucrats — only added to a sense of suspicion among hockey traditionalists.

Debate grew in the late 1960s and early 1970s about whether the NHL's pursuit of increased profitability through continued expansion into the United States was "good for Canadian hockey." Many coaches, parents, and public officials also expressed growing concern that the NHL's complete control over minor hockey and its unwillingness to take the lead in eliminating fighting from the game were no longer in the national interest. Died-in-the-wool Canadian hockey fans were not averse to the threat of government intervention when it led to the establishment of a franchise in Vancouver, but they balked at the prospect of intervention by governments or the courts in other areas of the game. Indeed, the passionate defences mounted by hockey tradition- alists of the NHL's inherent right to regulate its own affairs or of the right of minor-hockey officials to exclude girls from playing on boys' teams sometimes left the impression that to criticize the status quo was to be "un-Canadian."

All of these threats and problems in the 1970s — and competing conceptions of hockey's relationship to the perceived national inter- est — contributed to an increased involvement of the Canadian state in the hockey subculture. However, other than the ill-fated national team experiment of the 1960s there was never a significant policy ini- tiative that offered any workable alternative to the monopolistic and highly commercialized structure of Canadian hockey. On the contrary, federal government policies always accepted the commercial founda- tions of the game. Moreover, from the early 1980s into the 1990s the federal government has actively supported a view linking the devel- opment of national sport policy with broader movements for deregu- lation, accumulation, and regional development — goals to be pursued through the creation of venues and opportunities for "world class" sporting events. To put it another way, when the federal government began to recognize hockey's importance in the national popular cul- ture in the 1960s and 1970s, debates over the game's place in the national community were generally resolved in ways consistent with dominant political and economic interests. The national team exper- iment, the Task Force report, and the founding of Hockey Canada were all manifestations of popular nationalist and "progressive" ideas that were ultimately drawn into and came to express the corporatist state orientation of the era. Since the late 1970s, government involvement in hockey has followed the Canadian state's broader shift towards dereg- ulation and the use of public money in the areas of culture and sport to promote the new politics of accumulation.

This new politics of accumulation is connected closely to the inter- national reworking of capitalist production and to the concomitant

expansion of global consumer identities. In the current phase of capitalist modernity — with its continuing dissolution of older ways of
experiencing time and space — the drive for constant innovation and
the sheer plurality of meanings and possible points of identification
continually fight it out with older popular traditions that offer stability amidst the chaos of modern life. With the possibility of new spaces
for identity formation — and new groups wanting increased political,
social, and economic entitlements — Canadians are witnessing new
challenges to the "common sense" that has underwritten dominant
economic and political interests in Canada since the 1960s. But we
are also witnessing widespread accommodation to the new politics of
accumulation, a splintering of political agendas, and a resurgence of
interest in local issues and affairs that seems to reflect increased pes-
simism about the possibility of creating a national community with
any effective control over its own culture, politics, or economy.

In this chaotic cultural, political, and economic environment, the
idea of a single Canadian identity and an all-embracing Canadian nationalism has become more problematic than ever. This has given hockey
even greater symbolic currency in recent years, as one of the few "institutions," along with our system of national government, our public
health-care system, and the CBC, that we still imagine to be "truly
Canadian." As a result we are now seeing celebrations of the Canadian
hockey "tradition" in a wider range of places than ever before — in
art galleries, television movies, commercial and government advertising, and even commemorative stamps. There is little doubt that these
reminders of hockey's significant presence in Canadians' collective
memories help to keep alive the idea of a national common culture.
Yet we have to ask whether the sense of national identification associated with hockey still holds any real evocative power. Is it reasonable to expect the national pastime to provide a stable anchor of meaning
in a country that seems to be coming apart on so many other levels?
Does Canadian hockey today really represent any degree of significant
continuity with earlier traditions in the game? If it does, which of these
traditions do we still want to follow and which do we want to leave
behind? For example, do we still want to identify ourselves with the
tradition of aggressive masculinity that many people in the hockey
subculture continue to see as the epitome of Canadianness?

In pondering these questions we should not underestimate the continuing power of sport to mobilize national sentiments. The Toronto
Blue Jays' World Series victory in 1992 was a powerful reminder of
that. But despite the large numbers of Canadians across the country
who found themselves rooting for what temporarily became "Canada's

team," the Blue Jays' win will never have a mythic stature comparable to the 1972 victory in the Canada-Soviet hockey series. It is not
just that baseball has a different register in Canadian popular culture
than hockey, it is also that the meanings and practices that attach to
nationalism in an era of increasingly global communications and popular culture have changed so profoundly.

The understanding of this transition is complicated by the fact that
the precise content of national identities in modern Western nations
has often been contested and viewed differently in popular and elite
cultures. Moreover, national identity has always been just one of many
simultaneously held identities. Yet throughout the twentieth century,
national identities have been immensely significant anchors of meaning, often occupying a high level on people's socially constructed hierarchies of cultural identification. Now, however, it seems that national
identities — or at least those dominant forms of identification that
have congealed around modern nation-states — have begun to frac-
ture and to lose some of their formerly commanding presence. Indeed,
the actual ways in which people identify with nations today are influenced by experiences drawn from a far more complex field of materials and ideas than was the case in times when identity itself was much
less a matter of choice.

At a time when language and customs were very specific to place,
and when transnational communications of any sort were readily limited and controlled, it was comparatively easy for intellectuals, artists,
academics, journalists, and political leaders to popularize almost mys-
tical discourses of attachment to place and to preferred visions of culture. It was also easier than it is today to construct and sustain popular
stereotypes of "the other." Now, in the nations of the affluent world at
least, old relationships between national culture and political sovereignty are being widely challenged by an increasingly postnational capitalism and a more standardized global popular culture that offers an
"increasingly placeless geography of image and simulation" in which
the entertainment centres of major cities around the world come to
look very much the same and share more than ever in a common circuit of "world class" entertainments.[5]

The identifications that consumers develop around international
entertainments, including sport, are often ones that an earlier generation of nationalists would have resented, especially — as in the case
of the Blue Jays, for example — when national symbols are simply
pressed into the service of marketing. However, far too often the struggle to reassert national identity in Canada has been arbitrary and exclusionary, an attempt to imagine and to forge a false unity based on

invented traditions and older relations of power. At its worst, this has simply degenerated into the attempt to polarize and purify how we see ourselves in relation to others. Anglo-Canadian nationalists have always been good at this with respect to categorizing Canada's relationship to the United States; Quebec nationalists have played the same game in their categorizations of English Canada. But surely, beyond these puri- fied self-imaginings we always need to ask whether older national and nationalist identities can be transcended in favour of less exclusion- ary ones, or "whether these nationalisms will simply transform in regres- sive and alienating ways."[6]

The problem is that beyond the rather vague promise of an emerg- ing international cosmopolitanism there is little in the content of "global culture" to counterpose to the exclusionary dimensions of older nation- alisms. Nor is there much in the vacuous cosmopolitanism that is pop- ularized in the marketing of global products — whether they are "world class" sports or Mondetta sportswear — that would challenge in any way the hidden face of power in imagined national communities. The major force that has emerged to challenge older exclusionary tenden- cies — and it is an extremely important one — has been the clamour for social entitlements and for different visions of nation raised by new social movements in conjunction with the breakup of an older com- mon sense, an older hegemony. Since the 1960s a significant fractur- ing of older hierarchies of identity and the proliferation of new points of cultural attachment have opened up spaces for re-imagining the role that hockey might play in Canadian life — for example, in respect to relations between men and women or in the education of children. By extension this could lead to a re-imagining of our own Canadian self- understanding.

Gradually, over the last two decades, more and more Canadians have actually begun to act like the country "belongs to them," rather than to the businessmen, politicians, professionals, and bureaucrats who have constituted the power bloc in this country in the postwar era. This populism doesn't necessarily lead to progressive visions of the national community — we have Preston Manning to remind us of that — but at least it creates new spaces for negotiation, new open- ings for a struggle to connect the national popular culture to progres- sive groups wanting to create a more inclusive, more democratic Canada. It should not be surprising, then, that hockey has been caught up in similar struggles over the last two decades, though on a smaller scale. As more and more Canadians have begun to act like hockey really "belongs to them" rather than to the NHL or the CAHA, many of the traditions that have long defined the Canadian hockey subculture have been contested and have begun to erode. This erosion of hockey tradition has been exacerbated by a much broader set of social and economic pressures and limits that have been changing the game — things like the ongoing suburbanization of minor hockey, continued NHL expansion, the large-scale infusion of European players into the NHL, and the growth of women's hockey.

In evaluating these changes it is especially notable how the NHL's current pursuit of new markets is leading it to move away, albeit haltingly, from the "Canadian" traditions of toughness and aggressive masculinity that have long occupied a privileged place at the core of the hockey subculture. Even more notable is the extent to which the language and objectives of our market-centred promotional culture now seem to have become so completely naturalized in the game. Children today typically see their hockey cards as investments rather than as things to flip or throw in school yards. People now talk routinely about hockey "markets" more than "communities." The boards around many rinks are covered with sponsors' logos, and *Hockey Night in Canada* has quietly been transformed into *Molson Hockey Night in Canada*. In the big-money game of the 1990s, custody of hockey's traditions seems to have been awarded to modern marketing.

Expressions of concern about how hockey has changed can now be heard from many quarters. At one level, "think pieces" considering these changes have recently become a staple of the sports pages in major Canadian newspapers. At another level, many of these concerns have been discussed in several elegiac books, in which men such as Ken Dryden and Peter Gzowski have warmly remembered the place of hockey in their boyhoods and tried to articulate the changing place of the game in Canadian life. The popularity of such books points to a large constituency of intelligent, middle-aged male fans for whom hockey is indeed very much a part of boyhood memories and their formative images of Canada. They are fans who still love the game, but who can't help feeling uneasy about the idea of hockey in Dallas, Miami, and San Jose. While these fans are often uneasy about the current obsession with money in the game, NHL expansion, or the apparent erosion of hockey's Canadian heritage, many of them are not necessarily unhappy about how the game's traditions of paternalism and aggressive masculinity are losing some of their force. These are the fans who admire Wayne Gretzky for speaking out against fighting in the NHL — fans whose visions of Canadianness do not include the celebration of chippiness, macho posturing, or thuggery.

There is, of course, another kind of popular critical response to the changes in contemporary hockey, a response whose most visible spokesman is Don Cherry. Its main elements include Cherry's now-familiar diatribes against Europeans taking Canadians' jobs, against a lack of toughness he attributes to the European finesse players, and against the NHL's recent and limited efforts to cut down on fighting. Although Cherry has become a caricature, he still speaks to, and in essence for, a wide constituency of hockey fans. These fans are usually "ordinary Canadians," mostly male, and often with an active connection to the Canadian hockey subculture. They simply don't like many of the changes in "their" game. They don't like the moves to curtail fighting, and most of them don't like the campaigns waged by reformers to change the character of minor hockey. Underneath these specific charges, they also resent the fact that Canadian hockey seems to be transforming to conform to standards and agendas that come from "somewhere else." This offends their sense of proprietorship of the game; they *feel* their hockey deeply, and they feel "it's not our game anymore."

The sense of loss felt by many of these men derives precisely from their depth of absorption in the game. They played it and often still do. They sometimes work in a volunteer capacity in minor hockey. They attend NHL games when they can afford to, and junior games when they can't. They watch as much hockey as they can on television and listen to more on the radio. They know NHL statistics and they treasure their knowledge of hockey lore and trivia. A few of them phone sports-talk radio programs to express their frustration at what seems like a takeover of the game that has been so much a part of their lives and their identities. The targets of their resentment vary: a short list might include new NHL rules, Peter Pocklington, Gil Stein, European players, European playing styles, high player salaries, the Mighty Ducks, and women who have moved into public life and don't automatically support the allocation of community expenditures for rinks or indirect subsidies to pro teams.

It is especially aggravating to these die-hard male fans when so many of their concerns seem the product of broader tendencies and social movements over which individuals seem to have little influence. This is especially true with respect to the powerful economic pressures on the NHL. Today many teams are playing to near capacity crowds and the regional and cable television revenues in current team markets don't promise to increase substantially in the near future. At the same time even long-established NHL owners are feeling their (traditionally large) profit margins eroded by high player salaries, and they are searching to find new ways of generating revenue beyond the live gate. Newer owners have had even greater problems. They have had to overcome debts incurred because of the high cost of entry to the league while having to pay salaries high enough to make their teams competitive.

Under these circumstances NHL owners have become mindful of the need to cultivate new markets and to generate more money from existing ones. Their strategy is not that dissimilar from the one taken by NHL owners in the late 1920s; that is, the NHL is once again trying to move the game upmarket. Pro hockey's very status as major-league entertainment, not just continentally or internationally but in Canada itself, may well depend on its ability to attract affluent audiences that can support multimillion-dollar salaries *and* comfortable profits. This necessarily means repositioning the game to appeal to people who may be less inclined to applaud fighting or rough play outside the rules. The patrons who will pay $16,000 for a pair of season's "club" tickets in the new Vancouver arena are not likely to be avid junior hockey fans.

Smoothing out the roughest edges of hockey in the pursuit of new markets is certainly not without precedent in the game's own history, and it has parallels in the marketing of reggae or salsa music, television sit-coms about British working-class life, and, indeed, soccer as a workingman's game, to wider and more affluent audiences. When the target audience is international, it is often the distinctively national as well as class or racial associations that tend to be either de-emphasized or transformed into something that other audiences will relate to and identify with. And so it may be with the "Canadianness" of hockey. At its top levels hockey will most likely become a much less Canadian game. As this occurs, we will simply have to get used to the "loss," if we want to enjoy the game's presence in global popular culture. Still, the example of soccer, today the most global game of all, suggests that the globalization of major-league hockey need not diminish either our passion for hockey or its place in the everyday life of Canadian communities. Years of following the Bruins and the Blackhawks have not made fans any less Canadian, any more than years of following the fortunes of their favourite stars in the German and Spanish football leagues have weakened the cultural independence of the Danes or the Irish.

What is also worth noting here is the extent to which the transformations of hockey at the top levels, in some sense away from its mythic attachment to Canadian life, have also been accompanied by a resurgence of interest at the recreational and community levels. The decrease in the number of boys playing organized minor hockey has been more than offset by growth in other areas. Old-timers hockey and industrial hockey are booming, as are hockey programs for girls, women, and

special populations. There has also been a remarkable growth in organized ball hockey, complete with league play and national championships, and more and more children are playing an even newer version
of ball hockey wearing "in-line" skates. At the spectator level, teams
like the NHL Old-timers and the Flying Fathers continue to play to
large crowds in smaller cities across the country. As the price of NHL
hockey goes up in Edmonton and Vancouver there is increasing talk
of bringing back junior hockey. Moreover, with the addition of
Charlottetown the American Hockey League has six teams in Maritime
cities, thereby providing plenty of good quality hockey for a substantial regional Canadian audience.

While hockey is flourishing both as a form of recreation and community entertainment, the game simply does not have the same claim
on the time of Canadian children that it had for the generations of
boys who grew up between the 1940s and 1980s. Today's generation
of young people faces more recreational choices and more potential
points of identification through commercially produced popular culture than any other generation in Canadian history, and there is nothing to guarantee that they will identify with hockey any more than
with basketball or dance music. Even children who do choose to identify with hockey are likely to grow up idolizing players who come from
places like Stockholm or Moscow as much as from Ste. Foy or
Scarborough.

Moreover, the men who can remember the period between the end
of the war and the early 1980s — the men most likely to have internalized the Canadian hockey mystique — are aging. Indeed, it is these
men who are now playing old-timers hockey in such large numbers.
They are taking their wives and children to junior games and fuelling
the boom in hockey pools and playing cards. As this demographically
significant generation continues to age, much of the taken-for-grant-
edness associated with hockey in Canada is likely to fade, and the mystique of Canadian hockey threatens to be reduced — like so much of
the heritage industry today — to the marketing of nostalgia.

Notes

1. Hockey and the Politics of Culture

1 Douglas Fisher, "A Hockey Series that Challenged Canadians' View of Themselves," in Morris Mott, ed., *Sports in Canada: Historical Readings* (Toronto: Copp Clark Pitman, 1989), p.290.
2 George Woodcock, *Strange Bedfellows: The State and the Arts in Canada* (Vancouver: Douglas and McIntyre), pp.12-15.
3 Johan Huizinga, *Homo Ludens: A Study of the Play Element in Culture* (Boston: Beacon Press, 1955[1938]).
4 Michael Novak, *The Joy of Sports* (New York: Basic Books, 1976).
5 For example, see Christopher Lasch, "The Corruption of Sports," in *The Culture of Narcissism* (New York: Norton, 1979).
6 See Raymond Williams, *Culture and Society* (London: Chatto and Windus, 1958), and *The Long Revolution* (Harmondsworth, Midd.: Penguin, 1961).
7 See Matthew Arnold, *Culture and Anarchy* (Cambridge: Cambridge University Press, 1932[1869]); and T.S. Eliot, *Notes Toward the Definition of Culture* (London: Faber, 1948).

8 Allan Bloom, *The Closing of the American Mind* (New York: Simon and Schuster, 1987).

9 See Patrick Brantlinger, *Bread and Circuses: Theories of Mass Culture as Social Decay* (Ithaca, N.Y.: Cornell University Press, 1983).

10 See, for example, Alan Swingewood, *The Myth of Mass Culture* (London: Macmillan, 1977); and Mike Featherstone, "Common Culture or Uncommon Cultures?" in *Consumer Culture and Postmodernism* (London: Sage, 1991).

11 See, for example, Theodor Adorno and Max Horkheimer, *Dialectic of Enlightenment* (New York: Seabury Press, 1972[1944]); and Herbert Marcuse, *One Dimensional Man* (London: Routledge and Kegan Paul, 1964).

12 Cited in Paul Rutherford, *When Television Was Young: Primetime Canada, 1952-1967* (Toronto: University of Toronto Press, 1990), p.21.

13 Rutherford, *When Television Was Young*, p.16.

14 See George Grant, *Lament For a Nation: The Defeat of Canadian Nationalism* (Toronto: McClelland and Stewart, 1965); and Harold Innis, "The Strategy of Culture" (1952), in Eli Mandel, ed., *Contexts of Canadian Criticism* (Toronto: University of Toronto Press, 1971).

15 Bruce Kidd and John Macfarlane, *The Death of Hockey* (Toronto: New Press, 1972).

16 Doug Beardsley, *Country on Ice* (Winlaw, B.C.: Polestar Press, 1987), p.184.

17 Peter Gzowski, *The Game of Our Lives* (Markham, Ont.: Paperjacks, 1983), p.85.

18 Kidd and Macfarlane, *Death of Hockey*, pp.18-19.

19 Beardsley, *Country on Ice*, p.185.

20 Kidd and Macfarlane, *Death of Hockey*, pp.106, 132.

21 Our discussion here is influenced by Pierre Bourdieu, *Distinction: A Social Critique of the Judgement of Taste* (Cambridge, Mass.:Harvard University Press, 1984).

22 See John Hoberman, *Sport and Political Ideology* (Austin: University of Texas Press, 1984), pp.72-108.

2. Origins of the Modern Game

1 J.W. Fitsell, *Hockey's Captains, Colonels and Kings* (Erin, Ont.: The Boston Mills Press, 1987), p.16.

2 Syd Wise and Douglas Fisher, *Canada's Sporting Heroes* (Don Mills, Ont.: General Publishing, 1974), p.44.

3 Wayne Simpson, "Hockey," in Don Morrow, Mary Keyes, Wayne Simpson, Frank Cosentino, Ron Lappage, eds., *A Concise History of Sport in Canada* (Toronto: Oxford University Press, 1987), p.170.

4 Wise and Fisher, *Canada's Sporting Heroes*, p.44.

5 See John Betts, *America's Sporting Heritage: 1850-1950* (Reading, Mass.: Addison Wesley, 1974); Ian Jobling, "Urbanization and Sport in Canada, 1867-1900," in R. Gruneau and J. Albinson, eds., *Canadian Sport: Sociological Perspectives* (Don Mills, Ont.: Addison Wesley, 1976); and Alan Metcalfe, *Canada Learns to Play: The Emergence of Organized Sport, 1807-1904* (Toronto: McClelland and Stewart, 1987).
6 Allen Guttmann, *From Ritual to Record: The Nature of Modern Sports* (New York: Columbia University Press, 1978), ch.2.
7 Anthony Giddens, *Sociology: A Brief but Critical Introduction* (New York: Harcourt, Brace, and Jovanovich, 1982), p.10.
8 Alan Ingham and John Loy, "The Social System of Sport: A Humanistic Perspective," *Quest*, 19 (1973).
9 Melvin Adelman, *A Sporting Time: New York City and the Rise of Modern Athletics, 1820-1880* (Urbana: University of Illinois Press, 1986).
10 Fitsell, *Hockey's Captains, Colonels and Kings*, pp.27-29.
11 This newspaper report is cited in Fitsell, *Hockey's Captains, Colonels and Kings*, p.29.
12 We are indebted to Bill Fitsell, who noted this point during an interview.
13 Cited in Donald Guay, *L'histoire du Hockey au Québec* (Chicoutimi: les éditions JCL, 1990), pp.35-36.
14 See Guay, *L'histoire du Hockey au Québec*, p.73; and Metcalfe, *Canada Learns to Play*, p.63.
15 Guay, *L'histoire du Hockey au Québec*, p.75.
16 Guay, *L'histoire du Hockey au Québec*, p.53; and Fitsell, *Hockey's Captains, Colonels and Kings*, pp.50-51.
17 Metcalfe, *Canada Learns to Play*, p.63.
18 Ibid., p.24.
19 Ibid., p.22.
20 See Alan Metcalfe, "Organized Sport and Social Stratification in Montreal: 1840-1901," in Gruneau and Albinson, *Canadian Sport*.
21 Metcalfe, *Canada Learns to Play*, p.24.
22 Ibid., p.31.
23 Our interpretation and language here have been influenced by Benedict Anderson, *Imagined Communities: Reflections on the Origin and Spread of Nationalism* (London: Verso, 1983).
24 See Maria Tipett, *Making Culture: English-Canadian Institutions and the Arts Before the Massey Commission* (Toronto: University of Toronto Press, 1990), ch.1.
25 See Richard Gruneau, *Class, Sports and Social Development* (Amherst: University of Massachusetts Press, 1983), pp.95-108.
26 Adelman, *A Sporting Time*, p.9.
27 Metcalfe, *Canada Learns to Play*, p.63.
28 Ibid., p.64.
29 Ibid.
30 Fitsell, *Hockey's Captains, Colonels and Kings*, pp.66-69.

31 For a more fully developed discussion of the differences between "technical" and "moral" rules, see Gruneau, *Class, Sports and Social Development*, pp.60-65.

32 Cited in Don Morrow, "A Case Study of Amateur Conflict: The Athletic War in Canada, 1906-08," in Mott, *Sports in Canada*, p.203.

33 Morrow, "A Case Study of Amateur Conflict," p.203; Metcalfe, *Canada Learns to Play*, pp.122-123.

34 See Bryan Palmer, *Working-Class Experience: The Rise and Reconstitution of Canadian Labour, 1800-1980* (Toronto: Butterworth, 1983).

35 See Metcalfe, *Canada Learns to Play*, p.121; and Gruneau, *Class, Sports and Social Development*, pp.108-110.

36 Cited in Metcalfe, *Canada Learns to Play*, p.123.

37 Metcalfe, *Canada Learns to Play*, pp.109-110.

38 Patricia Vertinsky, "The Effect of Changing Attitudes Towards Sexual Morality Upon the Promotion of Physical Education for Women in Nineteenth-Century America," *Canadian Journal of History of Sport and Physical Education*, 7,2 (1976), cited in Helen Lenskyj, "Femininity First: Sport and Physical Education for Ontario Girls, 1890-1930," in Mott, *Sports in Canada*.

39 Fitsell, *Hockey's Captains, Colonels and Kings*, p.72.

40 See, for example, Metcalfe, *Canada Learns to Play*, p.11.

41 Giddens, *Sociology*, pp.31-42.

42 Our discussion here is indebted to Marshall Berman, *All That Is Solid Melts into Air: The Experience of Modernity* (London: Verso, 1983).

43 Simon Frith, *Sound Effects: Youth, Leisure and the Politics of Rock 'n Roll* (London: Constable, 1983), p.250.

44 See Peter DeLottinville, "Joe Beef of Montreal: Working Class Culture and the Tavern, 1869-1889," *Labour/Le Travailleur*, 8,9 (1981/82); and Metcalfe, *Canada Learns to Play*, pp.140-141.

45 Stuart Hall, "Notes on Deconstructing 'The Popular,'" in Raphael Samuel, ed., *People's History and Socialist Theory* (London: Routledge and Kegan Paul, 1981), pp.227-228.

3. The Making of Early Professional Hockey

1 Metcalfe, *Canada Learns to Play*, pp.64-65.

2 Ibid., p.134.

3 Paul Rutherford, *The Making of the Canadian Media* (Toronto: McGraw Hill-Ryerson, 1978), p.61.

4 Our discussion here draws on Hugh Cunningham, *Leisure in the Industrial Revolution* (New York: St. Martin's Press, 1980); and Frith, *Sound Effects*, ch.11.

5 Our discussion here is influenced by David Harvey, *The Condition of Postmodernity* (Cambridge: Basil Blackwell, 1989), p.102.

6 Chandra Mukerji, *From Graven Images: Patterns of Modern Materialism* (New York: Columbia University Press, 1983).

7 William Leiss, Stephen Kline, and Sut Jhally, *Social Communication in Advertising*, 2nd ed. (Scarborough, Ont.: Nelson, 1990), p.65.

8 Stephen Hardy, "'Adopted by All the Leading Clubs': Sporting Goods and the Shaping of Leisure, 1800-1900," in Richard Butsch, ed., *For Fun and Profit: The Transformation of Leisure into Consumption* (Philadelphia: Temple University Press, 1990).

9 Ibid., p.90.

10 See Metcalfe, *Canada Learns to Play*, p.68.

11 Quoted in Hardy, "'Adopted by All the Leading Clubs,'" p.88.

12 See Jackson Lears, "American Advertising and the Reconstruction of the Body, 1880-1930," in Kathryn Grover, ed., *Fitness in American Culture* (Amherst: University of Massachusetts Press, 1989).

13 Metcalfe, *Canada Learns to Play*, p.159.

14 Ibid., p.137.

15 Ibid.

16 Guay, *L'histoire du Hockey au Québec*, pp.73-74.

17 Metcalfe, *Canada Learns to Play*, p.138.

18 Rutherford, *Making of the Canadian Media*, p.3.

19 Metcalfe, *Canada Learns to Play*, p.31.

20 Ibid., p.164.

21 Ibid., pp.164-165.

22 See Bryan Palmer's discussion of baseball and working-class life in his *A Culture in Conflict: Skilled Workers and Industrial Capitalism in Hamilton Ontario, 1860-1914* (Montreal: McGill-Queen's University Press, 1979).

23 Metcalfe, *Canada Learns to Play*, p.93.

24 See, for example, Thorstein Veblen, *The Theory of the Leisure Class* (New York: Mentor Books, 1953 [1899]) for a classic statement; for a more recent discussion see Anthony Mangan, *Athleticism in the Victorian and Edwardian Public School* (Cambridge: Cambridge University Press, 1981).

25 See R.F. Harney, "Homo Ludens and Ethnicity," *Polyphony*, 7,1 (1985).

26 Morris Mott, "The Problems of Professionalism: The Manitoba Amateur Athletic Association and the Fight Against Pro Hockey, 1904-1911," in E.A. Corbet and A.W. Rasporich, eds., *Winter Sports in the West* (Calgary: Historical Society of Alberta, 1990).

27 See Guay, *L'histoire du Hockey au Québec*, pp.177-179.

28 Chas Critcher has documented a similar shift in the history of English soccer clubs; see his "Football Since the War," in Bernard Waites et al., eds., *Popular Culture: Past and Present* (London: Croom Helm, 1982).

29 See Gruneau, *Class, Sports and Social Development*, pp.115-116.

30 Mott, "The Problems of Professionalism," p.139.

31 Fitsell, *Hockey's Captains, Colonels and Kings*, p.82.

32 Ibid., p.84.

33 Ibid., p.87.
34 Guay, *L'histoire du Hockey au Québec*, p.178.
35 Fitsell, *Hockey's Captains, Colonels and Kings*, p.117.
36 Metcalfe, *Canada Learns to Play*, p.169.
37 Fitsell, *Hockey's Captains, Colonels and Kings*, p.117.
38 Ibid., pp.117-118.
39 Ibid., p.118.
40 Metcalfe, *Canada Learns to Play*, p.170.
41 Wise and Fisher, *Canada's Sporting Heroes*, pp.48-49.
42 See Guay, *L'histoire du Hockey au Québec*, pp.209-212.
43 Metcalfe, *Canada Learns to Play*, pp.69-70.
44 Ibid., p.72.
45 See Don Morrow, "A Case Study in Amateur Conflict: The Athletic War in Canada, 1906-1908," in Mott, *Sports in Canada*, pp.204-205; and Metcalfe, *Canada Learns to Play*, pp.110-113.
46 Metcalfe, *Canada Learns to Play*, p.72.

4. Media, Audiences, and the NHL Monopoly

1 Rutherford, *Making of the Canadian Media*, p.65.
2 See Wilfred Kesterton, "The Growth of the Newspaper in Canada," in Benjamin D. Singer, ed., *Communications in Canadian Society* (Don Mills, Ont.: Addison-Wesley, 1983), pp.6-10; and Rutherford, *Making of the Canadian Media*, pp.38-65.
3 Leiss, Kline and Jhally, *Social Communication in Advertising*, p.102.
4 Rutherford, *Making of the Canadian Media*, pp.60-61.
5 See Metcalfe, *Canada Learns to Play*, pp.178-179.
6 Tippett, *Making Culture*, p.10.
7 Scott Young, *One Hundred Years of Dropping the Puck: The History of the OHA* (Toronto: McClelland and Stewart, 1989), p.19.
8 D'Arcy Jenish, *The Stanley Cup: One Hundred Years of Hockey at its Best* (Toronto: McClelland and Stewart, 1992), p.17.
9 Ibid., p.55.
10 See Guay, *L'histoire du Hockey au Québec*, pp.100-103.
11 See Eric Whitehead, *Cyclone Taylor: A Hockey Legend* (Toronto: Doubleday, 1977), p.106; and Jenish, *The Stanley Cup*, pp.63-65.
12 On salaries, see Kidd and Macfarlane, *Death of Hockey*, p.108; on profits, see Guay, *L'histoire du Hockey au Québec*, p.124.
13 See Foster Hewitt, *Hockey Night in Canada: The Maple Leafs' Story* (Toronto: Ryerson Press, 1953), p.57; and Donald Guay, *L'histoire du Hockey au Québec*, pp.215-218.
14 On Tommy Gorman's purchase of the Senators see Chrys Goyens and Allan Turowetz, *Lions in Winter* (Markham, Ont.: Penguin Books, 1987), p.54; on the selling of the Quebec players see Hewitt, *Hockey Night in Canada*, p.58.

15 Hewitt, *Hockey Night in Canada*, pp.72-73.
16 Goyens and Turowetz, *Lions in Winter*, pp.58-59 and Kidd and Macfarlane, *Death of Hockey*, pp.110-113.
17 Hewitt, *Hockey Night in Canada*, p.76; and Kidd and Macfarlane, *Death of Hockey*, p.110.
18 David Cruise and Alison Griffiths, *Net Worth: Exploding the Myths of Pro Hockey* (Toronto: Viking, 1991), pp.30-31.
19 See Palmer, *Working-Class Experience*, pp.185-195.
20 See Leiss, Kline, and Jhally, *Social Communication in Advertising*, p.101; and Rutherford, *Making of the Canadian Media*, pp.43-48.
21 Our discussion in this section is indebted to Sut Jhally, "The Spectacle of Accumulation: Material and Cultural Factors in the Evolution of the Sports/Media Complex," *Insurgent Sociologist*, 12,3 (1984); and Douglas Kellner, *Television and the Crisis of Democracy* (Boulder, Col.: Westview Press, 1990), pp.28-35.
22 Robert McChesney, "Media Made Sport: A History of Sports Coverage in the United States," in Lawrence Wenner, ed., *Media, Sports, and Society* (Newbury Park, Cal.: Sage, 1989), p.57.
23 Scott Young, *The Boys of Saturday Night: Inside Hockey Night in Canada* (Toronto: Macmillan, 1990), p.38.
24 On the NHL "pool" see Charles Coleman, *The Trail of the Stanley Cup*, Vol.2 (Sherbrooke: The National Hockey League, 1969), p.9. The Patricks' stipend is variously described in hockey histories as falling between $258,000 and $272,000; for example, see Kidd and Macfarlane, *Death of Hockey*, p.111; and Brian Macfarlane, *The Lively World of Hockey: An Intimate History of the National Hockey League, 1917-1968* (Toronto: Signet Books, 1968), p.40.
25 Coleman, *Trail of the Stanley Cup*, Vol. 2, p.170.
26 Our discussion here is indebted to Colin Jones, "The Economics of the National Hockey League," in Gruneau and Albinson, *Canadian Sport*, pp.225-258.
27 Cruise and Griffiths, *Net Worth*, p.38.
28 Quoted in Jenish, *Stanley Cup*, p.120.
29 Scott Young, *Hello Canada! The Life and Times of Foster Hewitt* (Toronto: Seal Books, 1985), pp.31-61.
30 Young, *Boys of Saturday Night*, p.61.
31 Quoted in Palmer, *Working-Class Experience*, p.194.
32 Quoted in David Mills, "The Blue Line and the Bottom Line: Entrepreneurs and the Business of Hockey in Canada, 1927-90," in Paul Staudohar and James A. Mangan, eds., *The Business of Professional Sports* (Urbana: University of Illinois Press, 1991); and William Houston, *Inside Maple Leaf Gardens: The Rise and Fall of the Toronto Maple Leafs* (Toronto: McGraw Hill-Ryerson, 1989), p.14.
33 Young, *One Hundred Years of Dropping the Puck*, pp.198-199.
34 Rutherford, *When Television Was Young*, p.242.
35 Young, *Boys of Saturday Night*, p.78.

36 Rutherford, *When Television Was Young*, p.245.

5. The Work World of Pro Hockey

1 Eric Nesterenko, "Hockey Player," in Studs Terkel, ed., *Working* (New York: Avon Books, 1972), p.319.

2 Rick Heinz, *Many Are Called ... Few Are Signed: The Hard Realities of Professional Hockey* (Toronto: Heinz Publishing, 1988), p.7.

3 "Steroids a Staple for Some Juniors, Charges Laforge," *The Toronto Star*, August 16, 1992.

4 Ken Dryden, *The Game* (Toronto: Macmillan, 1983), p.39.

5 See Mark Lavoie, "Stacking, Performance Differentials, and Salary Discrimination in Professional Ice Hockey," *Sociology of Sport Journal*, 6 (1989).

6 Dryden, *The Game*, p.19.

7 Quoted in Dryden, *The Game*, p.92.

8 See, for examples, Heinz, *Many Are Called*, p.11; and M. A. Smith, *Life After Hockey* (St. Paul, Minn.: Codner Books, 1987), p.8.

9 Nesterenko, "Hockey Player," p.319.

10 Dryden, *The Game*, p.19.

11 Ibid., p.93.

12 Quoted in Dryden, *The Game*, p.85, emphasis in original.

13 Quoted in Smith, *Life After Hockey*, p.132.

14 Nesterenko, "Hockey Player," pp.318-319.

15 See Don Sabo, "Sport, Patriarchy, and Male Identity: New Questions about Men and Sport," *Arena Review*, 9 (1985).

16 See, for example, Peter Gzowski's revealing discussion of Bobby Hull in *Game of Our Lives*, pp.202-206.

17 See Rob Beamish, "The Impact of Corporate Ownership on Labor-Management Relations in Hockey," in Staudohar and Mangan, *Business of Professional Sports*.

18 See, for example, the discussion in Cruise and Griffiths, *Net Worth*, pp.52-192.

19 Quoted in Heinz, *Many Are Called*, p.130.

20 Even the most flamboyant NHL owners such as Peter Pocklington or Harold Ballard have operated within larger corporate entities with diverse economic portfolios. Thus, Rob Beamish notes that NHL "owners" are technically not "individuals at all." Nonetheless, NHL teams feature a pattern of corporate ownership where effective control frequently lies in the hands of a single individual or family. See Beamish, "Impact of Corporate Ownership," p.216.

21 Al Strachan, "Wirtz Just Widens Rift with Foolish Bravado," *The Globe and Mail*, April 1, 1992, and "Power Play Shaping Up Among NHL Governors," *The Globe and Mail*, April 4, 1992.

22 Cruise and Griffiths, *Net Worth*, p.287.

23 We owe this observation to Stephen Brunt, "Credibility a Problem for NHL Owners," *The Globe and Mail*, April 6, 1992.

24 See, for example, Cruise and Griffiths, *Net Worth*.

25 Rappoport, "Owners Buy Time But Price is Steep," *The Globe and Mail*, April 13, 1992.

6. Careers, Myths, and Dreams

1 Roland Barthes, *Mythologies* (London: Paladin Books, 1973 [1957]).

2 There is a vast literature on the meaning of "ideology." Our use of the term is influenced by John Thompson, *Ideology and Modern Culture: Critical Social Theory in the Era of Mass Communication* (Stanford, Cal.: Stanford University Press, 1990).

3 Quoted in *The Globe and Mail*, May 31, 1993.

4 See Gary Loewen, "In Business, No. 99's Just a Grinder," *The Globe and Mail*, April 14, 1992.

5 A similar point is made in John Berger's novel, *A Painter of Our Time* (Harmondsworth, Middx.: Penguin, 1965), about a radical painter whose life ambition was to paint the 1948 Olympic Games. At one point Berger's hero notes, "In sport ... liberation is collective. I have seen games of football in which I have glimpsed all I ever believed the productive relations among men might be." This notion is discussed critically in Gruneau, *Class, Sports and Social Development*, pp.30-32,147-152.

6 Kidd and Macfarlane, *Death of Hockey*, p.56.

7 See Ken Dryden and Roy MacGregor, *Home Game* (Toronto: McClelland and Stewart, 1989), p.101.

8 Andrew Wernick, *Promotional Culture* (London: Sage, 1991).

9 Michael D. Smith and Frederic Diamond, "Career Mobility in Professional Hockey," in Gruneau and Albinson, *Canadian Sport*.

10 Smith and Diamond, "Career Mobility in Professional Hockey," p.283.

11 Ibid., p.287.

12 See Gzowski, *Game of Our Lives*, p.206.

13 See Cruise and Griffiths, *Net Worth*, p.10.

14 Information on salary levels in the NHL from the 1940s through the 1980s can be found at various points in Cruise and Griffiths, *Net Worth*; a useful discussion of salary levels in the 1980s can also be found in Heinz, *Many Are Called*, pp.84-86.

15 See Cruise and Griffiths, *Net Worth*, pp.1-25.

16 See Heinz, *Many Are Called*, p.117.

17 Gzowski, *Game of Our Lives*, p.206.

18 See Joshua Meyrowitz, *No Sense of Place: The Impact of Electronic Media on Social Behaviour* (New York: Oxford University Press, 1985).

19 Roy MacGregor, *The Last Season* (Markham, Ont.: Penguin, 1985).

20 See Nesterenko, "Hockey Player," and the interviews published in Smith, *Life After Hockey*.
21 Dryden, *The Game*, p.79.
22 Smith, *Life After Hockey*, p.50.
23 Ibid., p.142.
24 On this point see the remarks of sport psychologist David Tucker in Heinz, *Many Are Called*, p.219.
25 Richard Sennett and Jonathan Cobb, *The Hidden Injuries of Class* (New York, Knopf, 1972).
26 Michael Ignatieff, *The Needs of Strangers* (Harmondsworth, Middx.: Penguin, 1984), p.138.

7. The Game Beyond the Pros

1 Information provided by the national office of the Canadian Amateur Hockey Association, June 1993.
2 There is considerable variation in the names and skill levels of these divisions and tiers in different parts of the country. For example, midget teams in one community might be competitive with junior B or C teams in another. In areas with limited numbers of teams, players from different divisions and tiers might be mixed, thereby introducing added confusion to the divisional ranking system.
3 Dryden, *The Game*, p.136.
4 John Shotter, "The Development of Personal Powers," in M.P. Richards, ed., *The Integration of a Child into a Social World* (London: Cambridge University Press, 1974).
5 Noted by Neil Campbell, *The Globe and Mail*, Feb. 3, 1990, p.A10.
6 Submission to the Therien Committee on Minor Hockey, Quebec Assembly; see also Dryden and MacGregor, *Home Game*, p.63.
7 Noted in *The Edmonton Journal*, Jan. 12, 1990.
8 *The Edmonton Journal*, Jan. 12, 1989.
9 Quoted in James Christie, *The Globe and Mail*, Jan. 12, 1989.
10 Smith, *The Globe and Mail*, Dec. 29, 1990.
11 See E. Vaz, *The Professionalization of Young Hockey Players* (Lincoln: University of Nebraska Press, 1982); and Harry Webb, "The Professionalization of Attitudes Toward Play Among Adolescents," in G. Kenyon, ed., *Aspects of Contemporary Sport Sociology* (Chicago: The Athletic Institute, 1969).
12 For a particularly hard-hitting examination of these big-league pressures, see Cruise and Griffiths, *Net Worth*, pp.344-357.
13 Quoted in Robert Olver, *The Making of Champions: Life in Canada's Junior A Leagues* (Markham, Ont.: Penguin, 1990), p. 92.
14 On this point see Douglas Thom and Donald Ward, *The Total Hockey Player: Brawn Is Not Enough* (Calgary: Detselig Enterprises, 1981).
15 Quoted in James Christie, *The Globe and Mail*, Feb. 13, 1989, p.A13.

16 See Heinz, *Many Are Called*; and James Christie, *The Globe and Mail*, Feb. 13, 1989, p.A13.
17 See Guay, *L'histoire du Hockey au Québec*, pp.151-157.
18 For an overview of these cases see Ann Hall and Dorothy Richardson, *Fair Ball: Toward Sex Equality in Canadian Sport* (Ottawa: Canadian Advisory Council on the Status of Women, 1982).

8. Violence, Fighting, and Masculinity

1 *The Hockey News*, Feb. 27, 1989, p.9.
2 See Michael D. Smith, *Violence and Sport* (Toronto: Butterworths, 1983), pp.124-125.
3 Norbert Elias, *The Civilizing Process, Vol.I: The History of Manners* (Oxford: Basil Blackwell, 1978); and *The Civilizing Process, Vol.II: State Formation and Civilization* (Oxford: Basil Blackwell, 1982).
4 Quoted in Anthony Giddens, *The Constitution of Society* (Berkeley: University of California Press, 1984), p.241.
5 Giddens, *Constitution of Society*, p.241.
6 Eric Dunning, "Sport as a Male Preserve: Notes on the Social Sources of Masculine Identity and Its Transformations," *Theory, Culture, and Society*, 3,1 (1986).
7 *The Hockey News*, Feb. 24, 1989, p.8.
8 *The Edmonton Journal*, Oct. 6, 1990, p.E1.
9 Robert Faulkner, "Violence, Camaraderie and Occupational Character in Hockey," in D. Landers, ed., *Social Problems in Athletics* (Urbana: University of Illinois Press, 1976), p.97.
10 Quoted in Beardsley, *Country on Ice*, p.133.
11 Olver, *Making of Champions*, p.87.
12 See, for example, Vaz, *Professionalization of Young Hockey Players*; and Smith, *Violence in Sport*.
13 Quoted in Beardsley, *Country on Ice*, p.149.
14 *The Hockey News*, Feb. 24, 1989.
15 Ibid.
16 Quoted in Dryden and MacGregor, *Home Game*, pp.181-182.
17 *The Hockey News*, Feb. 24, 1989.
18 *The Hockey News*, Feb. 17, 1989, p.9.
19 Al Strachan, "Geography Influences Views of Cherry, Gretzky on Hockey Fights," *The Globe and Mail*, Feb. 13, 1990.
20 Richard Holt, *Sport and the British* (London: Oxford University Press, 1990), pp.171-173.
21 Robert Connell, *Gender and Power* (Cambridge: Polity Press, 1987), pp.98-99.

22 See Rosemary Deem, "The Politics of Women's Leisure," in J. Horne, D. Jary, and A. Tomlinson, eds., *Sport, Leisure, and Social Relations* (London: Routledge and Kegan Paul, 1987); and David Whitson and Donald Macintosh, "Gender and Power: Explanations of Gender Inequality in Canadian National Sport Organizations," *International Review of Sport Sociology*, 24 (1989).

23 Bruce Kidd, "The Men's Cultural Centre: Sports and Dynamics of Women's Oppression/Men's Oppression," in M. Messner and D. Sabo, eds., *Sport, Men, and the Gender Order* (Urbana, Ill.: Human Kinetics Press, 1990). See also Dryden and MacGregor's description in *Home Game* of the "male ambience" of the old Saskatoon Arena.

24 See Jean Barman, "Sports and the Development of Character," in Mott, *Sports in Canada*, pp.234-246.

25 See Eugen Weber, "Pierre de Coubertin and the Introduction of Organized Sport in France," *Journal of Contemporary History*, 5, 2 (1970).

26 This point is explored in another context in Gary Alan Fine, *With the Boys: Little League Baseball and Preadolescent Culture* (University of Chicago Press, 1987).

27 Our discussion here draws on Robert Connell et al., *Making the Difference* (Sydney: George Allen and Unwin, 1982); and "Men's Bodies," in Robert Connell, *Which Way Is Up: Essays on Class, Sex and Culture* (Sydney: George Allen and Unwin, 1983).

9. Communities, Civic Boosterism, and Fans

1 Our discussion here is indebted to Harvey, *Condition of Postmodernity*, pp.121-173.

2 Robert Nisbet, *The Sociological Tradition* (New York: Basic Books, 1966).

3 For some Canadian examples see Palmer, *A Culture in Conflict*; and Thomas Dunk, *It's a Working Man's Town* (Montreal: McGill-Queen's University Press, 1991).

4 See, for example, Rex Lucas, *Minetown, Milltown, Railtown* (Toronto: University of Toronto Press, 1971); and Donald Wetherell and Irene Kmet, *Useful Pleasures: The Shaping of Leisure in Alberta, 1896-1945* (Regina: Canadian Plains Research Centre, 1990).

5 For examples of ethnicity in small-town life see Angela Djao and Roxanne Ng, "Structured Isolation: Immigrant Women in Saskatchewan," in K. Storrie, ed., *Women: Isolation and Bonding* (Toronto: Methuen, 1987); on the "closed" nature of small-town life see David Rayside, "Small-Town Life and the Politics of Community," *Journal of Canadian Studies*, 24,1 (1989).

6 For example, see Mark Abley, *Beyond Forget* (Vancouver: Douglas and McIntyre, 1986).

7 Dryden and MacGregor, *Home Game*, p.35.

8 Ibid., p.23.
9 Philip Hansen and Alicja Muszynski, "Crisis in Rural Life and Crisis in Thinking: Directions for Critical Research," *Canadian Review of Sociology and Anthropology*, 27,1 (1990).
10 Hansen and Muszynski, "Crisis in Rural Life," p.17.
11 Ibid., p.19, note 8.
12 Paul Voisey, *Vulcan: The Making of a Prairie Community* (Toronto: University of Toronto Press, 1988), p.165.
13 Susan Heald and Margot Blight, "Susanna Moodie Revisited: 'Roughing It' in 1986," in Storrie, *Women: Isolation and Bonding*; see also Patricia Hunter and David Whitson, "Women, Leisure, and Familism: Relationships and Isolation in Small-town Canada," *Leisure Studies*, 10,3 (1991).
14 Tanis Talbot, "Hockey as a Symbol of Patriarchy: A Review of *Welcome Home*," *Women's Law Forum Newsletter*, University of Alberta, January 1993.
15 Carl Betke, "Sports Promotion in the Western Canadian City: The Example of Early Edmonton," *Urban History Review*, 12,2 (1983).
16 Ibid., p.53.
17 See H. Konrad, "Barren Bulls and Charging Cows: Cowboy Celebrations in Copal and Calgary," in Frank Manning, ed., *The Celebration of Society: Perspectives on Contemporary Cultural Performance* (Bowling Green, Ohio: Bowling Green University Press, 1983); and Colin Campbell, "The Stampede: Cowtown's Sacred Cow," in Chuck Reasons, ed., *Stampede City: Power and Politics in the West* (Toronto: Between the Lines, 1984).
18 For a useful discussion of this point see Chuck Reasons, "It's Just a Game? The 1988 Winter Olympics," in Reasons, *Stampede City*.
19 Our discussion here is indebted to Voisey, *Vulcan*, p.240; and Alan Artibise, *Winnipeg: A Social History of Urban Growth, 1874-1914* (Montreal: McGill-Queen's University Press, 1975).
20 Elliot Gorn, "Dodgers of Dreams," *Tikkun*, 5,5 (1990), p.79.
21 George Lipsitz, *Time Passages: Collective Memory and American Popular Culture* (Minneapolis: University of Minnesota Press, 1990), p.177.
22 Bourdieu, *Distinction*, pp.32-41.
23 John Fiske, *Understanding Popular Culture* (Boston: Unwin Hyman, 1989), p.141.
24 Holt, *Sport and the British*, p.162.
25 Raymond Williams, *Towards 2000* (London: Pelican Books, 1985), pp.187-190. For a useful Canadian discussion along similar lines see Stan Persky, "City Without Citizens," in Max Wyman, ed., *Vancouver Forum: Old Powers, New Forces* (Vancouver: Douglas and McIntyre, 1992).

10. Hockey and the New Politics Of Accumulation

1 See Mott, "Problems of Professionalism."

2 Carl Betke, "Winter Sports in the Early Urban Environment of Prairie Canada," in Corbet and Rasporich, *Winter Sports in the West.*

3 Coleman, *Trail of the Stanley Cup*, p.135.

4 Ibid., p.110.

5 See Colin Jones, "The Economics of the National Hockey League," and "The Economics of the NHL Revisited," in Gruneau and Albinson, *Canadian Sport.*

6 Harvey, *Condition of Postmodernity.*

7 See Dryden and MacGregor, *Home Game*, ch.1.

8 The Campbell quote appears in Dan Diamond and Lew Stubbs, *Hockey, Twenty Years: The NHL Since 1967* (Toronto: Doubleday, 1987), p.1.

9 For a more detailed discussion of this point see Jones, "Economics of the National Hockey League."

10 See, for example, R. Baade and R. Dye, "Sports Stadiums and Area Development: A Critical Review," *Economic Development Quarterly*, 2,3 (1988).

11 Our discussion here is influenced by J. Logan and H. Molotch, *Urban Fortunes: The Political Economy of Place* (Berkeley: University of California Press, 1987); and A. Ingham, J. Howell, and T. Schilperoort, "Professional Sports and Community: A Review and Exegesis," *Exercise and Sports Science Reviews* (1988), pp.427-465.

12 This discussion draws on David Harvey, "Flexible Accumulation Through Urbanization: Reflections on 'Post-Modernism' in the American City," *Antipode*, 19,3 (1987).

13 Harvey, "Flexible Accumulation Through Urbanization"; and B. Frieden and F. Sagalyn, *Downtown Inc.: How America Rebuilds its Cities* (Cambridge, Mass.: MIT Press, 1989).

14 Ingham, Howell, and Schilperoort, "Professional Sports and Community," p.454.

15 Ibid., p.460.

16 William Thorsell, *The Globe and Mail*, Nov. 17, 1990.

17 Our discussion here is influenced by Brian Fawcett, "The Trouble With Globalism," in Max Wyman, ed., *Vancouver Forum* (Vancouver: Douglas and MacIntyre, 1992) and selected columns during 1990-91 from Fawcett's *Globe and Mail* "Fifth Column."

18 Originally cited in John Schmeltzer, *Chicago Tribune*, and reprinted in *The Edmonton Journal*, July 16, 1991.

19 See Theodore Levitt, *The Marketing Imagination* (London: Collier Macmillan, 1983). Our discussion of Levitt is indebted to Kevin Robbins, "Tradition and Translation: National Culture in its Global Context," in John Corner and Sylvia Harvey, eds., *Enterprise and Heritage: Crosscurrents of National Culture* (London:Routledge, 1991).

20 Our discussion here draws on Ulf Hannerz, "Cosmopolitans and Locals in World Culture," *Theory, Culture and Society*, 7 (1990); Robbins, "Tradition and Translation"; and Brian Stoddart, "Wide World of Golf: A Research Note on the Interdependence of Sport, Culture and Economy," *Sociology of Sport Journal*, 7,4 (1990).
21 John Corner and Sylvia Harvey, "Introduction: Great Britain Limited," in Corner and Harvey, *Enterprise and Heritage*.
22 Harvey, "Flexible Accumulation Through Urbanization," p.278, and *Condition of Postmodernity*, pp.265, 273, and 289-295.

11. International Hockey: Patriotism, Profits, and Shifting Identities

1 E. Hobsbawm and T. Ranger, eds., *The Invention of Tradition* (Cambridge: Cambridge University Press, 1983); and Anderson, *Imagined Communities*.
2 John Clarke and Chas Critcher, "1966 and All That: England's World Cup Victory," and John Humphrey, "No Holding Brazil: Football, Nationalism and Politics," both in Alan Tomlinson and Gary Whannel, eds., *Off the Ball: The Football World Cup* (London: Pluto Press, 1986).
3 Alan Tomlinson, "Going Global: The FIFA Story," in Tomlinson and Whannel, *Off the Ball*, p.97.
4 John Wilson, *Politics and Leisure* (Boston: Unwin Hyman, 1988), p.149.
5 On Britain see Richard Holt, *Sport and the British* (London: Oxford University Press, 1990). On Canada see Mott, *Sports in Canada*; Metcalfe, *Canada Learns to Play*; and Ann Hall et al., *Sport in Canadian Society* (Toronto: McClelland and Stewart, 1991).
6 Tomlinson, "Going Global," p.83.
7 See Donald Macintosh and David Whitson, *The Game Planners: Transforming the Canadian Sport System* (Montreal: McGill-Queen's University Press, 1991).
8 See Donald Macintosh et al., *Sport and Politics in Canada* (Montreal: McGill-Queen's University Press, 1987).
9 Our discussion here draws on Young, *One Hundred Years of Dropping the Puck*, pp.217-221.
10 A useful summary of the national team's overall performance can be found in Brian Conacher, *Hockey in Canada: The Way It Is* (Toronto: Gateway Press, 1970).
11 Macintosh, *Sport and Politics in Canada*, p.57.
12 See Fisher, "A Hockey Series," pp.285-286; and Kidd and Macfarlane, *Death of Hockey*, pp.87-90.
13 Perhaps the most eloquent and sophisticated discussion of such changes can be found in Dryden, *The Game*.
14 Fisher, "A Hockey Series," p.287.

15 See Gary Davidson (with Bill Libby), *Breaking the Game Wide Open* (New York: Atheneum, 1974), pp.141-191.
16 See Critcher, "Football Since the War"; and Tomlinson and Whannel, *Off the Ball*.
17 See Gruneau, *Class, Sports and Social Development*, p.75.

12. Conclusion: Hockey and Canadian Culture in the Age of Globalization

1 Harvey, *Condition of Postmodernity*, p.358.
2 The concept of "postmodernism" is extremely complex, with meanings and interpretations that variously include debates in aesthetics, history, philosophy, and literary studies. We've used the term here in a very specific way. For more detailed discussions of postmodernism, see Featherstone, *Consumer Culture and Postmodernism*; and Harvey, *Condition of Postmodernity*.
3 Some of the language used in our discussion here draws on Featherstone, *Consumer Culture and Postmodernism*, pp.133-143.
4 For another discussion of the Massey Commission's failure to understand the significance of commercial popular culture, see J.M. Bumstead, "Canadian and American Culture in the 1950s," in J. M. Bumstead, ed., *Interpreting Canada's Past*, Vol.2. (Toronto: Oxford University Press, 1986).
5 Some of the language used in our discussion here draws on Ien Ang and David Morley, "Mayonnaise Culture and Other European Follies," *Cultural Studies*, 3,2 (1989); also see Robbins, "Tradition and Translation."
6 Kevin Robbins, "Reimagined Communities? European Image Spaces Beyond Fordism," *Cultural Studies*, 3,2 (1989).

Index